STAR WARS®
· L E G A C Y ·

LEGACY

(Forty years after the Battle of Yavin and beyond)

As this era began, Luke Skywalker had unified the Jedi Order into a cohesive group of powerful Jedi Knights. It was a time of relative peace, yet darkness approached on the horizon. Now, Skywalker's descendants face new and resurgent threats to the galaxy, and to the balance of the Force.

The events in this story begin approximately 137 years after the Battle of Yavin.

STAR WARS® LEGACY

VOLUME FOUR

↣ ALLIANCE ↢

STORY
**John Ostrander and
Jan Duursema**

SCRIPT
John Ostrander

ART
**Omar Francia and
Alan Robinson**

COLORS
Brad Anderson

LETTERS
Michael Heisler

COVER ART
Dan Scott

DARK HORSE BOOKS®

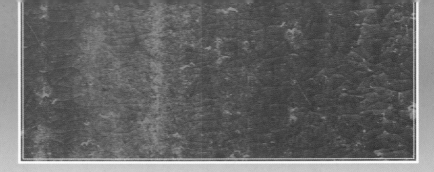

PUBLISHER
Mike Richardson

COLLECTION DESIGNER
Scott Cook

ART DIRECTOR
Lia Ribacchi

ASSOCIATE EDITOR
Dave Marshall

ASSISTANT EDITOR
Freddye Lins

EDITOR
Randy Stradley

Special thanks to Elaine Mederer, Jann Moorhead, David Anderman, Leland Chee, Sue Rostoni, and Carol Roeder at Lucas Licensing.

STAR WARS: LEGACY VOLUME FOUR—ALLIANCE
Star Wars © 2008 Lucasfilm Ltd. & ™. All rights reserved. Used under authorization. Text and illustrations for Star Wars are © 2008 Lucasfilm Ltd. Dark Horse Books® and the Dark Horse logo are registered trademarks of Dark Horse Comics, Inc. All rights reserved. No portion of this publication may be reproduced or transmitted, in any form or by any means, without the express written permission of Dark Horse Comics, Inc. Names, characters, places, and incidents featured in this publication either are the product of the author's imagination or are used fictitiously. Any resemblance to actual persons (living or dead), events, institutions, or locales, without satiric intent, is coincidental.

This volume collects issues twenty through twenty-two and twenty-seven of the Dark Horse comic-book series *Star Wars: Legacy*.

Published by
Dark Horse Books
A division of Dark Horse Comics, Inc.
10956 SE Main Street
Milwaukie, OR 97222

darkhorse.com
starwars.com

To find a comics shop in your area, call the Comic Shop Locator Service toll-free at 1-888-266-4226

First printing: December 2008
ISBN 978-1-59582-223-9

1 3 5 7 9 10 8 6 4 2
Printed in China

One hundred thirty years after its defeat at Endor, the resurgent Empire—goaded by the Sith—reclaimed control of the galaxy, crushing the Galactic Alliance and scattering the Jedi Order.

Since then, Galactic Alliance Admiral Gar Stazi and his small fleet of surviving renegades have carried out hit-and-run attacks on the galaxy's Imperial oppressors. Yet as their resources dwindle, so does their effectiveness, and unless Stazi can bolster his forces, they will soon be fighting for little more than survival.

A new mission undertaken by the Admiral will not only test the temper and the stamina of the ruling Emperor Darth Krayt, but it will interrupt the Dark Lord's current concern with finding and using the last living Skywalker to obtain final domination . . .

STAR WARS

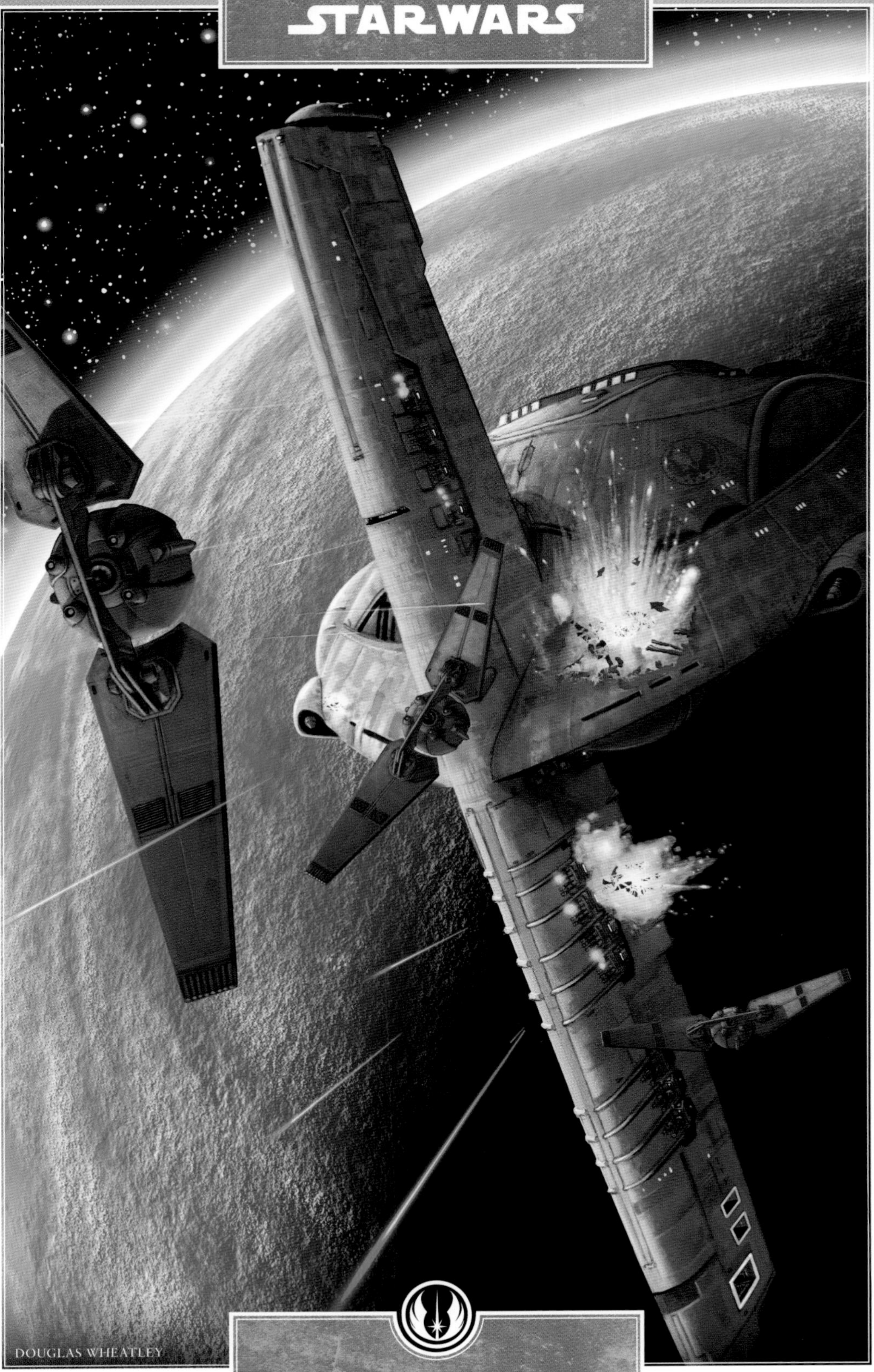
DOUGLAS WHEATLEY

INDOMITABLE

INDOMITABLE

SCRIPT
John Ostrander

ART
Omar Francia

COLORS
Brad Anderson

LETTERS
Michael Heisler

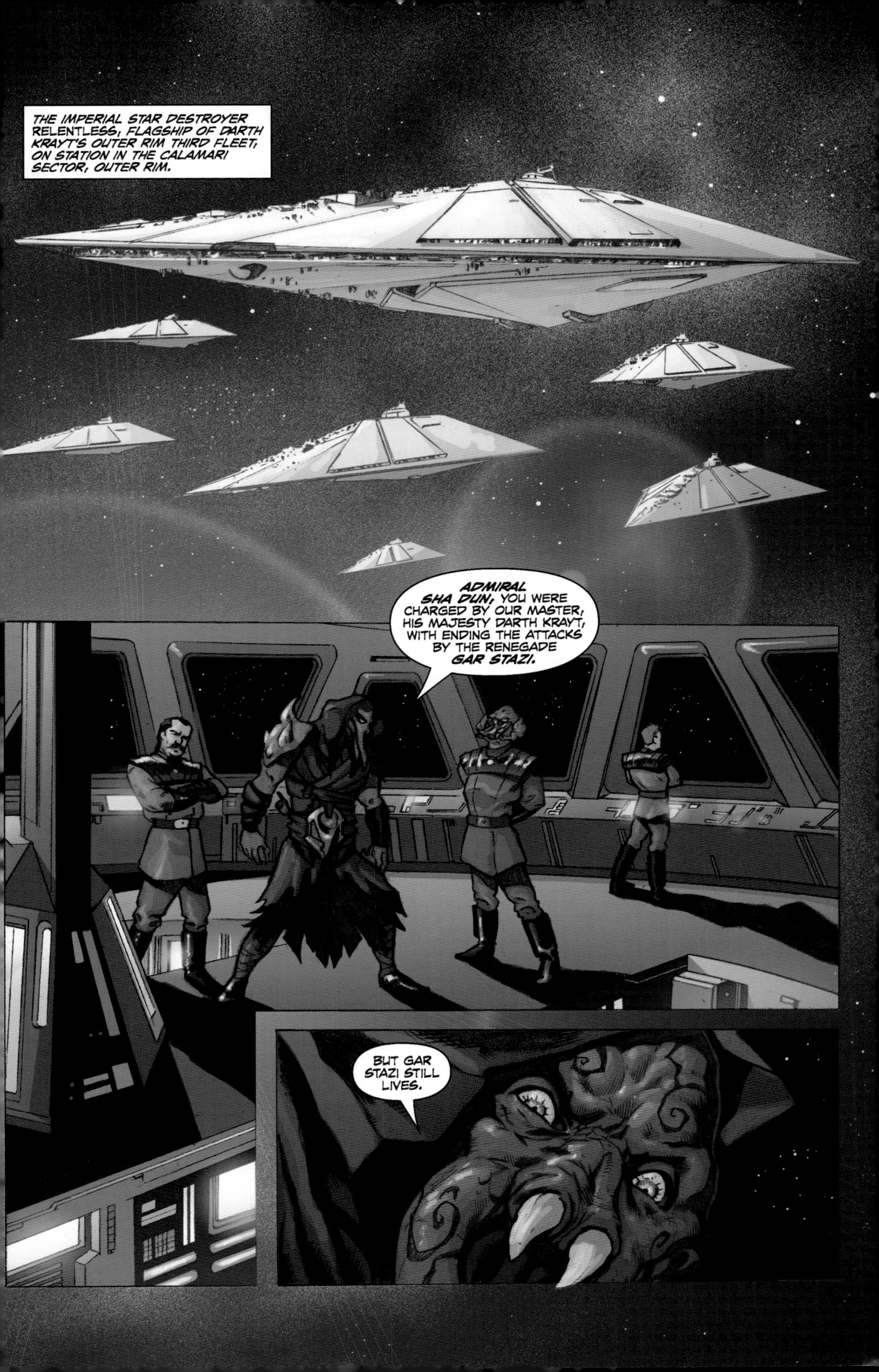
THE IMPERIAL STAR DESTROYER RELENTLESS, FLAGSHIP OF DARTH KRAYT'S OUTER RIM THIRD FLEET; ON STATION IN THE CALAMARI SECTOR, OUTER RIM.
ADMIRAL SHA DUN, YOU WERE CHARGED BY OUR MASTER, HIS MAJESTY DARTH KRAYT, WITH ENDING THE ATTACKS BY THE RENEGADE GAR STAZI.
BUT GAR STAZI STILL LIVES.

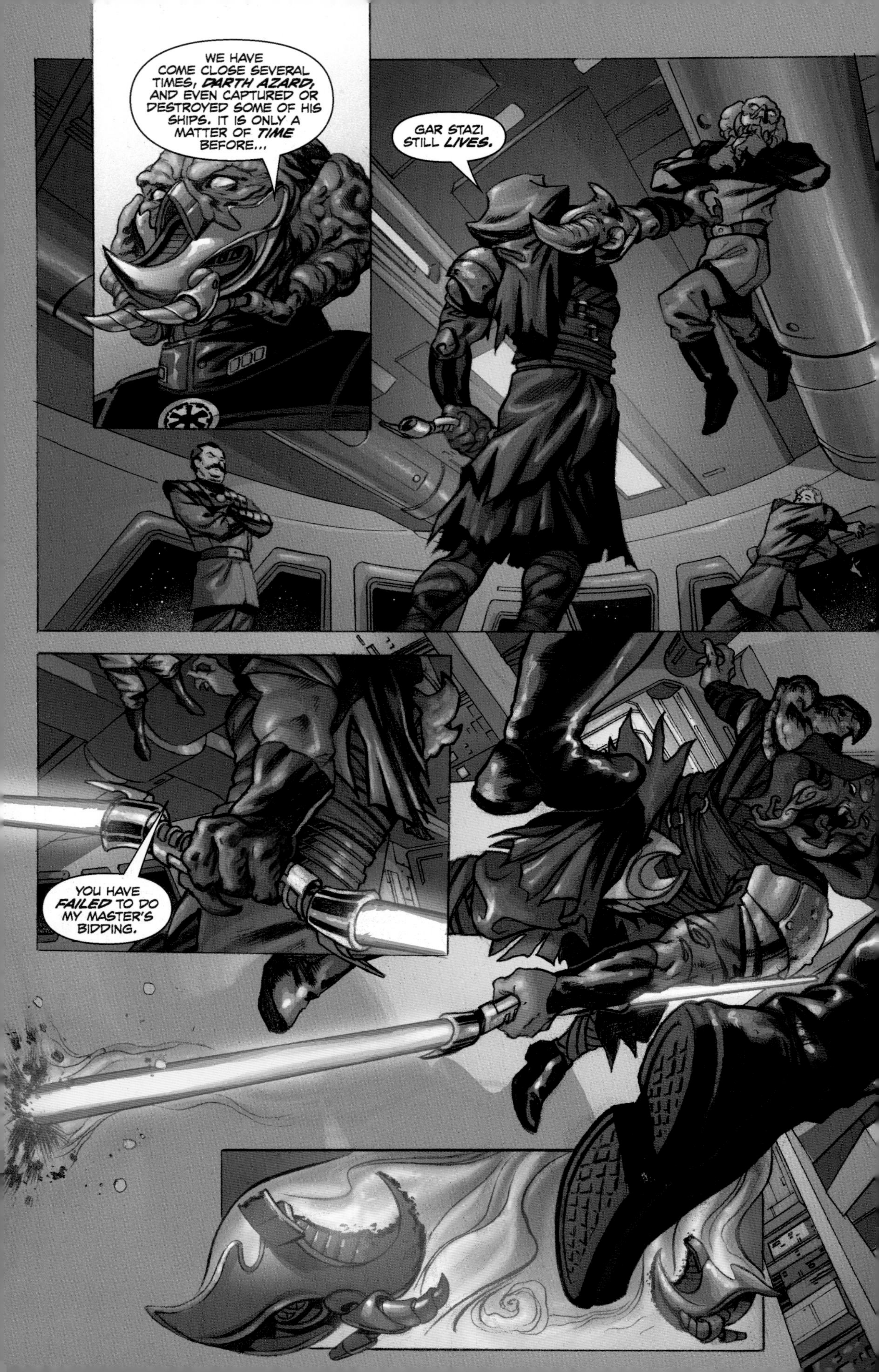
WE HAVE COME CLOSE SEVERAL TIMES, DARTH AZARD, AND EVEN CAPTURED OR DESTROYED SOME OF HIS SHIPS. IT IS ONLY A MATTER OF TIME BEFORE...
GAR STAZI STILL LIVES.
YOU HAVE FAILED TO DO MY MASTER'S BIDDING.

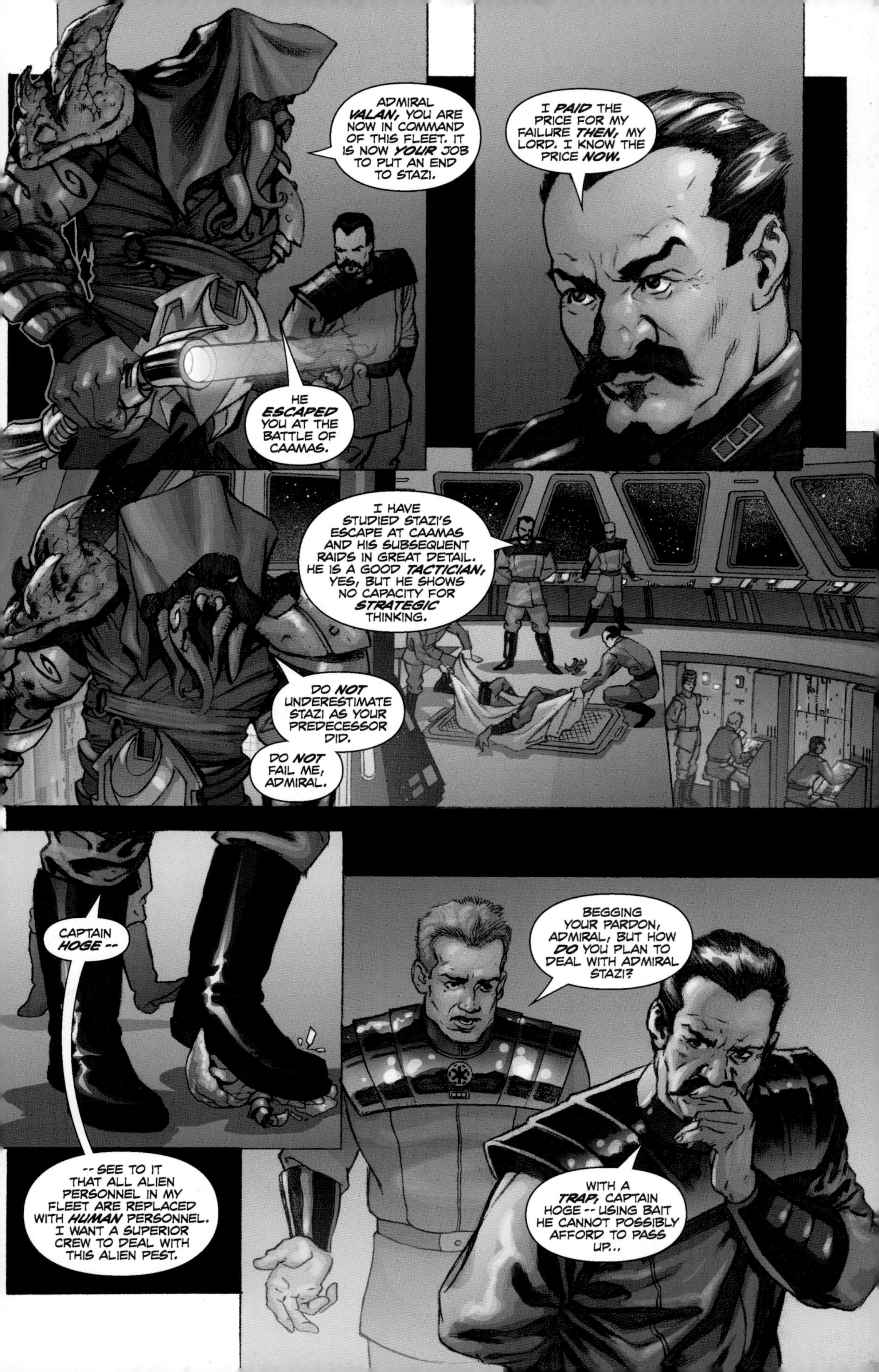
ADMIRAL VALAN, YOU ARE NOW IN COMMAND OF THIS FLEET. IT IS NOW YOUR JOB TO PUT AN END TO STAZI.
HE ESCAPED YOU AT THE BATTLE OF CAAMAS.
I PAID THE PRICE FOR MY FAILURE THEN, MY LORD. I KNOW THE PRICE NOW.
I HAVE STUDIED STAZI'S ESCAPE AT CAAMAS AND HIS SUBSEQUENT RAIDS IN GREAT DETAIL. HE IS A GOOD TACTICIAN, YES, BUT HE SHOWS NO CAPACITY FOR STRATEGIC THINKING.
DO NOT UNDERESTIMATE STAZI AS YOUR PREDECESSOR DID.
DO NOT FAIL ME, ADMIRAL.
CAPTAIN HOGE --
-- SEE TO IT THAT ALL ALIEN PERSONNEL IN MY FLEET ARE REPLACED WITH HUMAN PERSONNEL. I WANT A SUPERIOR CREW TO DEAL WITH THIS ALIEN PEST.
BEGGING YOUR PARDON, ADMIRAL, BUT HOW DO YOU PLAN TO DEAL WITH ADMIRAL STAZI?
WITH A TRAP, CAPTAIN HOGE -- USING BAIT HE CANNOT POSSIBLY AFFORD TO PASS UP...

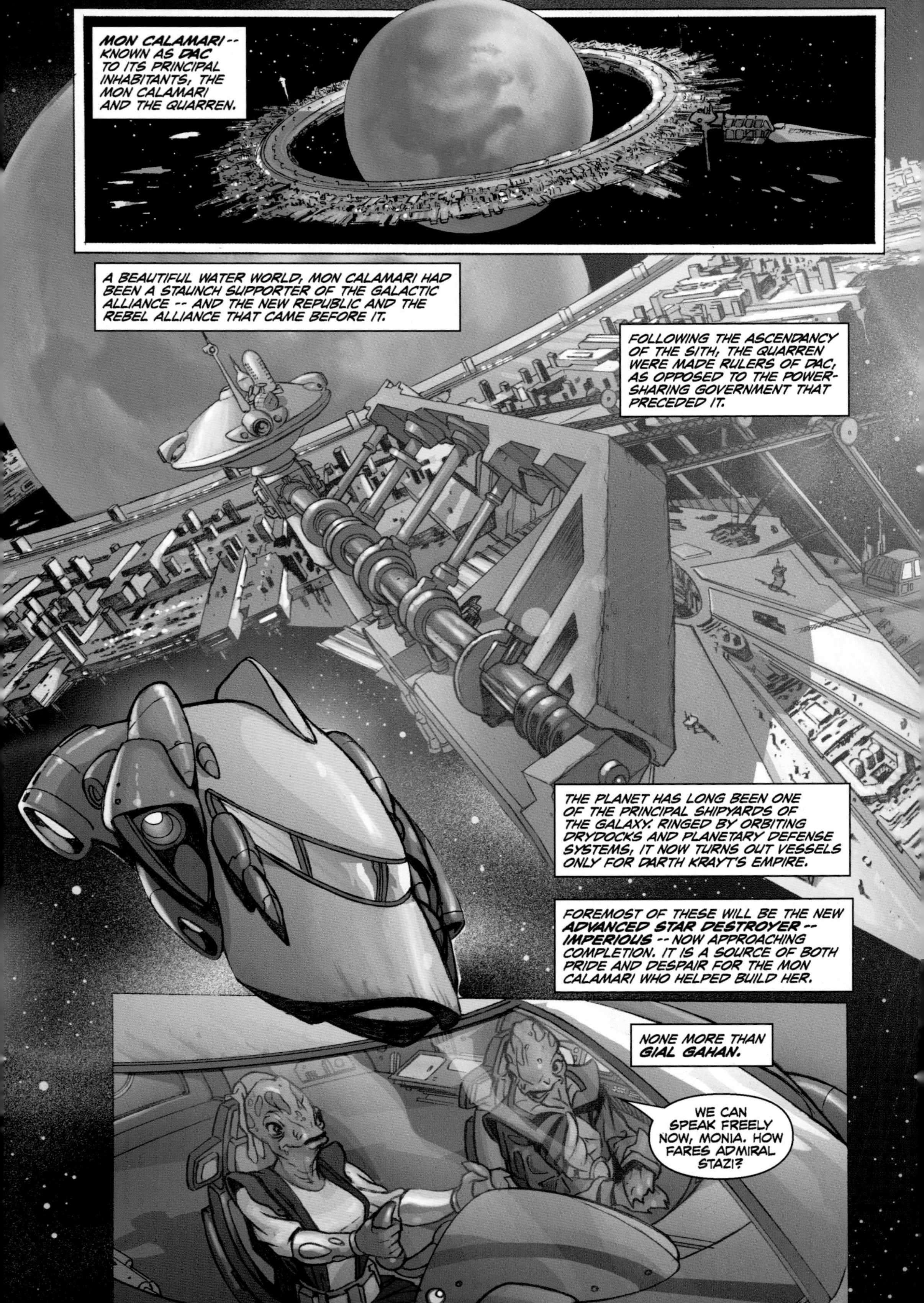
MON CALAMARI -- KNOWN AS DAC TO ITS PRINCIPAL INHABITANTS, THE MON CALAMARI AND THE QUARREN.
A BEAUTIFUL WATER WORLD, MON CALAMARI HAD BEEN A STAUNCH SUPPORTER OF THE GALACTIC ALLIANCE -- AND THE NEW REPUBLIC AND THE REBEL ALLIANCE THAT CAME BEFORE IT.
FOLLOWING THE ASCENDANCY OF THE SITH, THE QUARREN WERE MADE RULERS OF DAC, AS OPPOSED TO THE POWER-SHARING GOVERNMENT THAT PRECEDED IT.
THE PLANET HAS LONG BEEN ONE OF THE PRINCIPAL SHIPYARDS OF THE GALAXY. RINGED BY ORBITING DRYDOCKS AND PLANETARY DEFENSE SYSTEMS, IT NOW TURNS OUT VESSELS ONLY FOR DARTH KRAYT'S EMPIRE.
FOREMOST OF THESE WILL BE THE NEW ADVANCED STAR DESTROYER -- IMPERIOUS -- NOW APPROACHING COMPLETION. IT IS A SOURCE OF BOTH PRIDE AND DESPAIR FOR THE MON CALAMARI WHO HELPED BUILD HER.
NONE MORE THAN GIAL GAHAN.
WE CAN SPEAK FREELY NOW, MONIA. HOW FARES ADMIRAL STAZI?

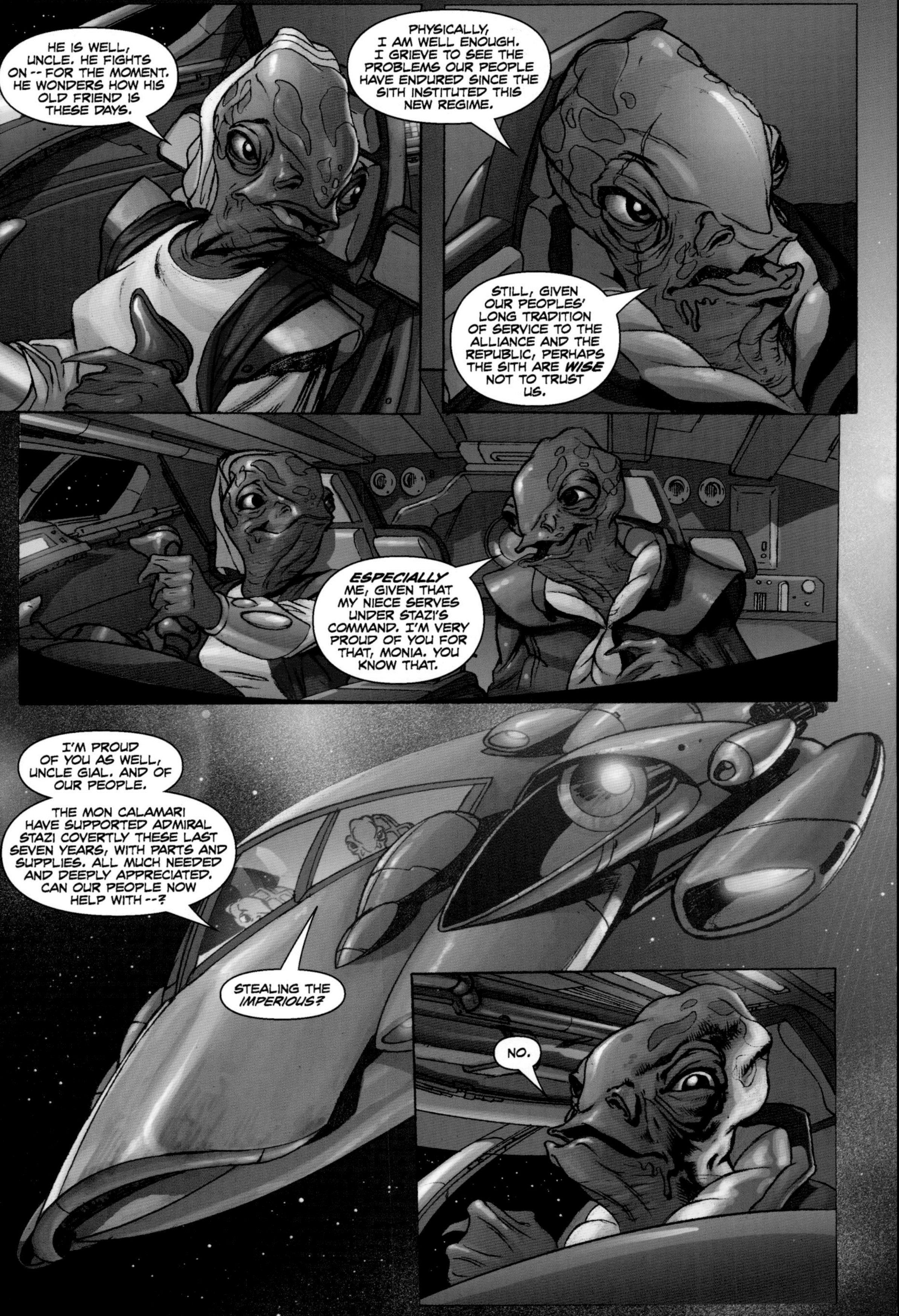
HE IS WELL, UNCLE. HE FIGHTS ON -- FOR THE MOMENT. HE WONDERS HOW HIS OLD FRIEND IS THESE DAYS.
PHYSICALLY, I AM WELL ENOUGH. I GRIEVE TO SEE THE PROBLEMS OUR PEOPLE HAVE ENDURED SINCE THE SITH INSTITUTED THIS NEW REGIME.
STILL, GIVEN OUR PEOPLES' LONG TRADITION OF SERVICE TO THE ALLIANCE AND THE REPUBLIC, PERHAPS THE SITH ARE *WISE* NOT TO TRUST US.
ESPECIALLY ME, GIVEN THAT MY NIECE SERVES UNDER STAZI'S COMMAND. I'M VERY PROUD OF YOU FOR THAT, MONIA. YOU KNOW THAT.
I'M PROUD OF YOU AS WELL, UNCLE GIAL. AND OF OUR PEOPLE.
THE MON CALAMARI HAVE SUPPORTED ADMIRAL STAZI COVERTLY THESE LAST SEVEN YEARS, WITH PARTS AND SUPPLIES. ALL MUCH NEEDED AND DEEPLY APPRECIATED. CAN OUR PEOPLE NOW HELP WITH --?
STEALING THE *IMPERIOUS?*
NO.

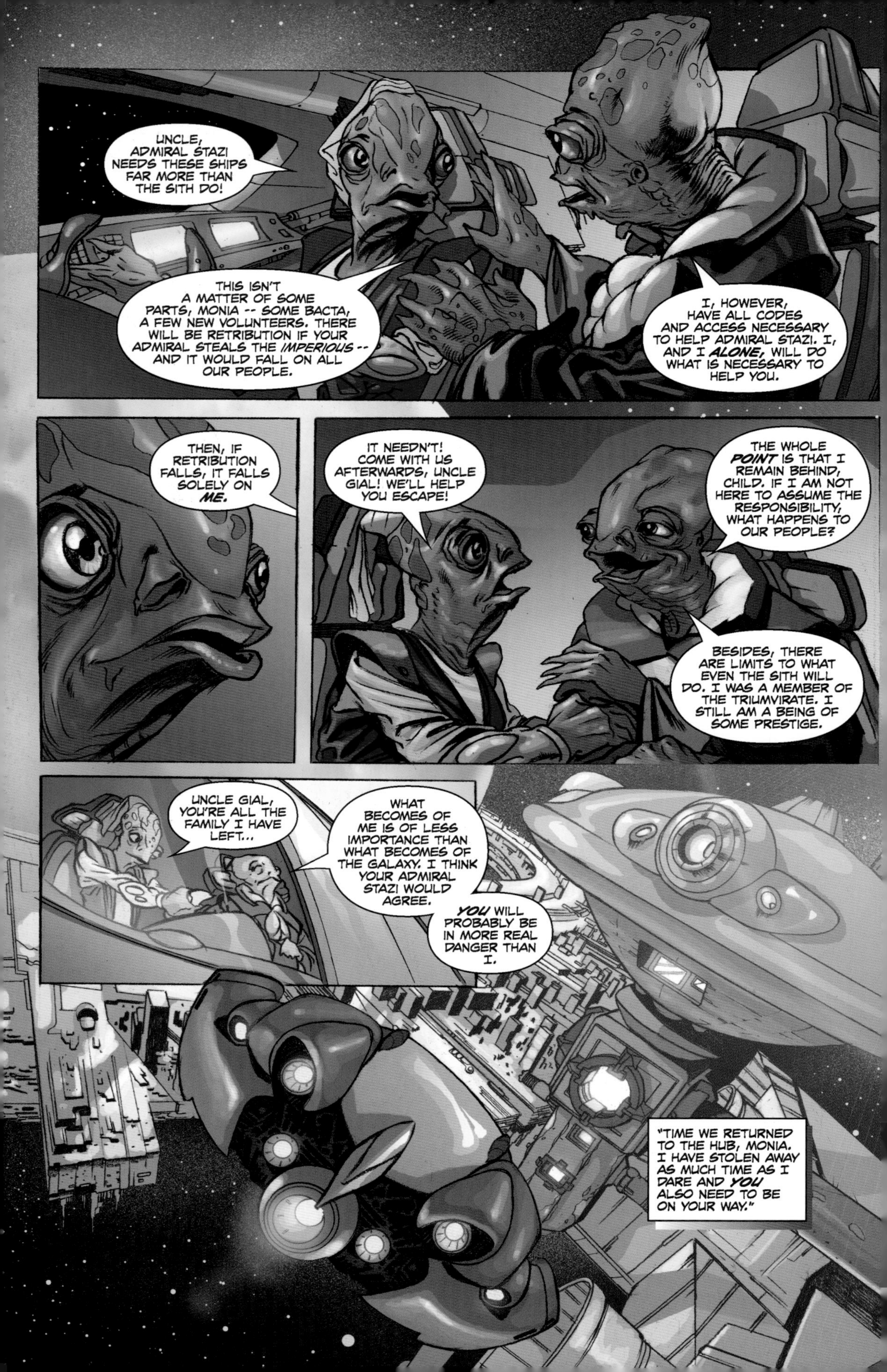
UNCLE, ADMIRAL STAZI NEEDS THESE SHIPS FAR MORE THAN THE SITH DO!
THIS ISN'T A MATTER OF SOME PARTS, MONIA -- SOME BACTA, A FEW NEW VOLUNTEERS. THERE WILL BE RETRIBUTION IF YOUR ADMIRAL STEALS THE *IMPERIOUS* -- AND IT WOULD FALL ON ALL OUR PEOPLE.
I, HOWEVER, HAVE ALL CODES AND ACCESS NECESSARY TO HELP ADMIRAL STAZI. I, AND I *ALONE,* WILL DO WHAT IS NECESSARY TO HELP YOU.
THEN, IF RETRIBUTION FALLS, IT FALLS SOLELY ON *ME.*
IT NEEDN'T! COME WITH US AFTERWARDS, UNCLE GIAL! WE'LL HELP YOU ESCAPE!
THE WHOLE *POINT* IS THAT I REMAIN BEHIND, CHILD. IF I AM NOT HERE TO ASSUME THE RESPONSIBILITY, WHAT HAPPENS TO OUR PEOPLE?
BESIDES, THERE ARE LIMITS TO WHAT EVEN THE SITH WILL DO. I WAS A MEMBER OF THE TRIUMVIRATE. I STILL AM A BEING OF SOME PRESTIGE.
UNCLE GIAL, YOU'RE ALL THE FAMILY I HAVE LEFT...
WHAT BECOMES OF ME IS OF LESS IMPORTANCE THAN WHAT BECOMES OF THE GALAXY. I THINK YOUR ADMIRAL STAZI WOULD AGREE.
YOU WILL PROBABLY BE IN MORE REAL DANGER THAN I.
"TIME WE RETURNED TO THE HUB, MONIA. I HAVE STOLEN AWAY AS MUCH TIME AS I DARE AND *YOU* ALSO NEED TO BE ON YOUR WAY."

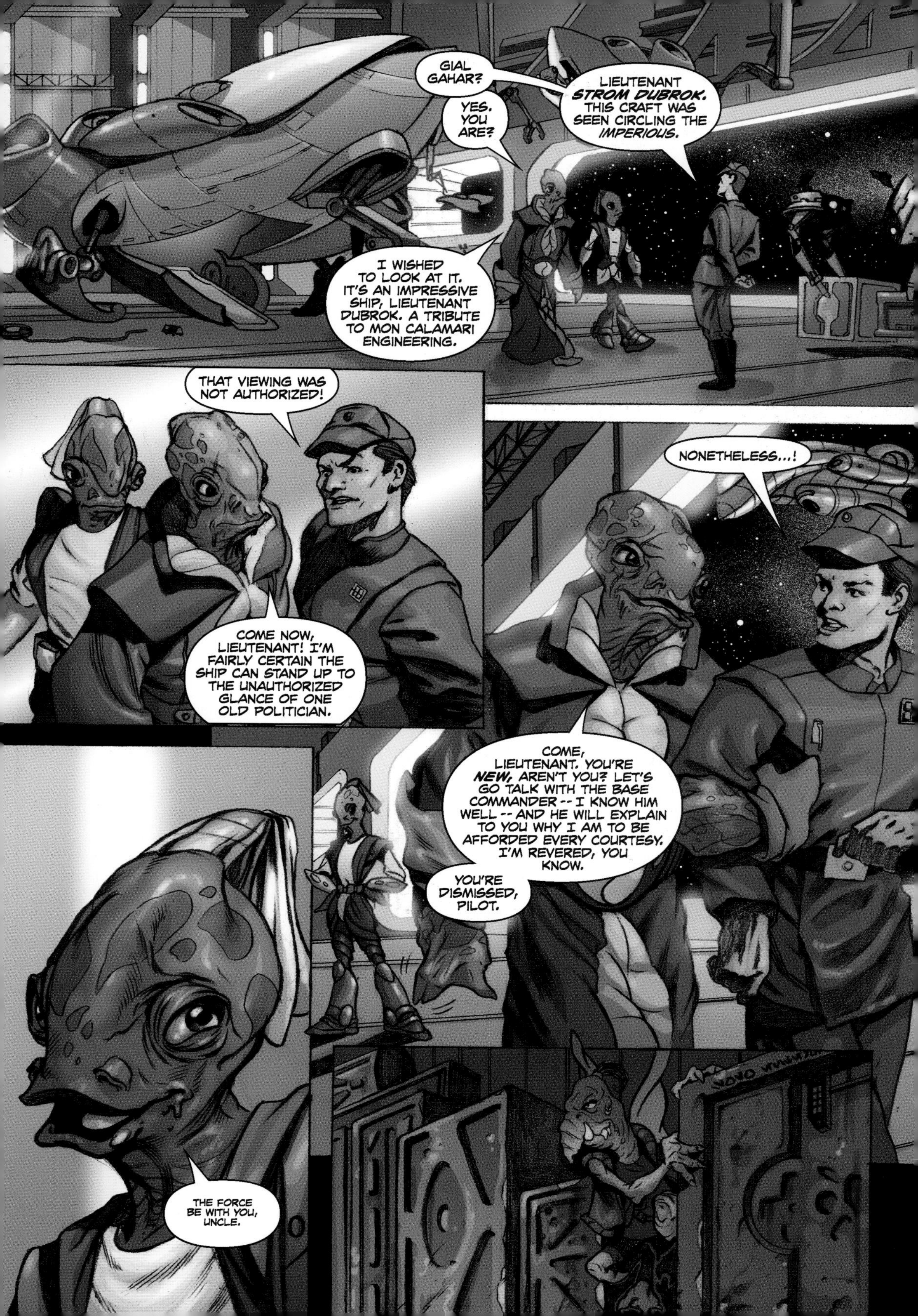
GIAL GAHAR?
YES. YOU ARE?
LIEUTENANT STROM DUBROK. THIS CRAFT WAS SEEN CIRCLING THE IMPERIOUS.
I WISHED TO LOOK AT IT. IT'S AN IMPRESSIVE SHIP, LIEUTENANT DUBROK. A TRIBUTE TO MON CALAMARI ENGINEERING.
THAT VIEWING WAS NOT AUTHORIZED!
COME NOW, LIEUTENANT! I'M FAIRLY CERTAIN THE SHIP CAN STAND UP TO THE UNAUTHORIZED GLANCE OF ONE OLD POLITICIAN.
NONETHELESS...!
COME, LIEUTENANT. YOU'RE NEW, AREN'T YOU? LET'S GO TALK WITH THE BASE COMMANDER -- I KNOW HIM WELL -- AND HE WILL EXPLAIN TO YOU WHY I AM TO BE AFFORDED EVERY COURTESY. I'M REVERED, YOU KNOW.
YOU'RE DISMISSED, PILOT.
THE FORCE BE WITH YOU, UNCLE.

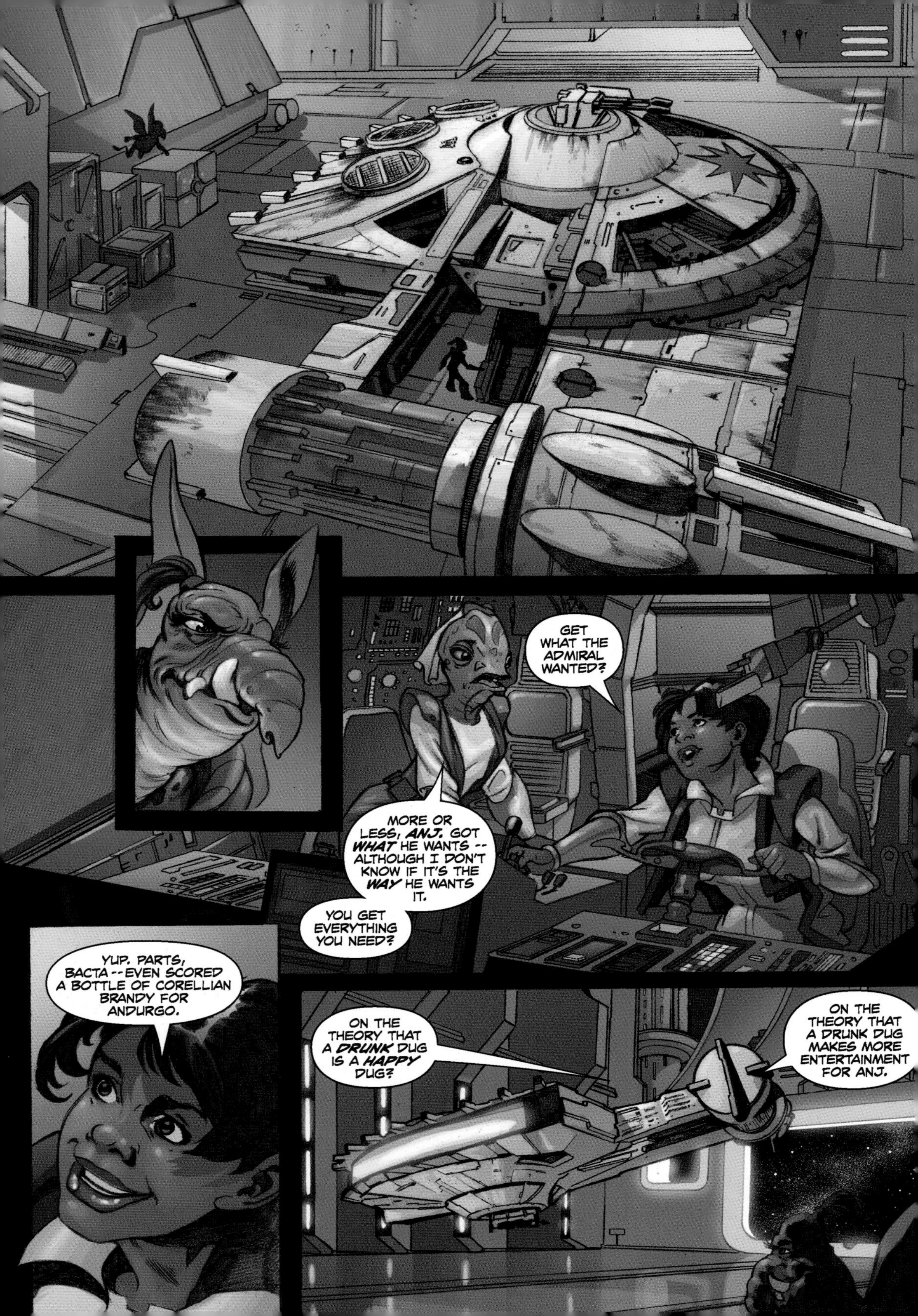
GET WHAT THE ADMIRAL WANTED?
MORE OR LESS, ANJ. GOT WHAT HE WANTS -- ALTHOUGH I DON'T KNOW IF IT'S THE WAY HE WANTS IT.
YOU GET EVERYTHING YOU NEED?
YUP. PARTS, BACTA -- EVEN SCORED A BOTTLE OF CORELLIAN BRANDY FOR ANDURGO.
ON THE THEORY THAT A DRUNK DUG IS A HAPPY DUG?
ON THE THEORY THAT A DRUNK DUG MAKES MORE ENTERTAINMENT FOR ANJ.

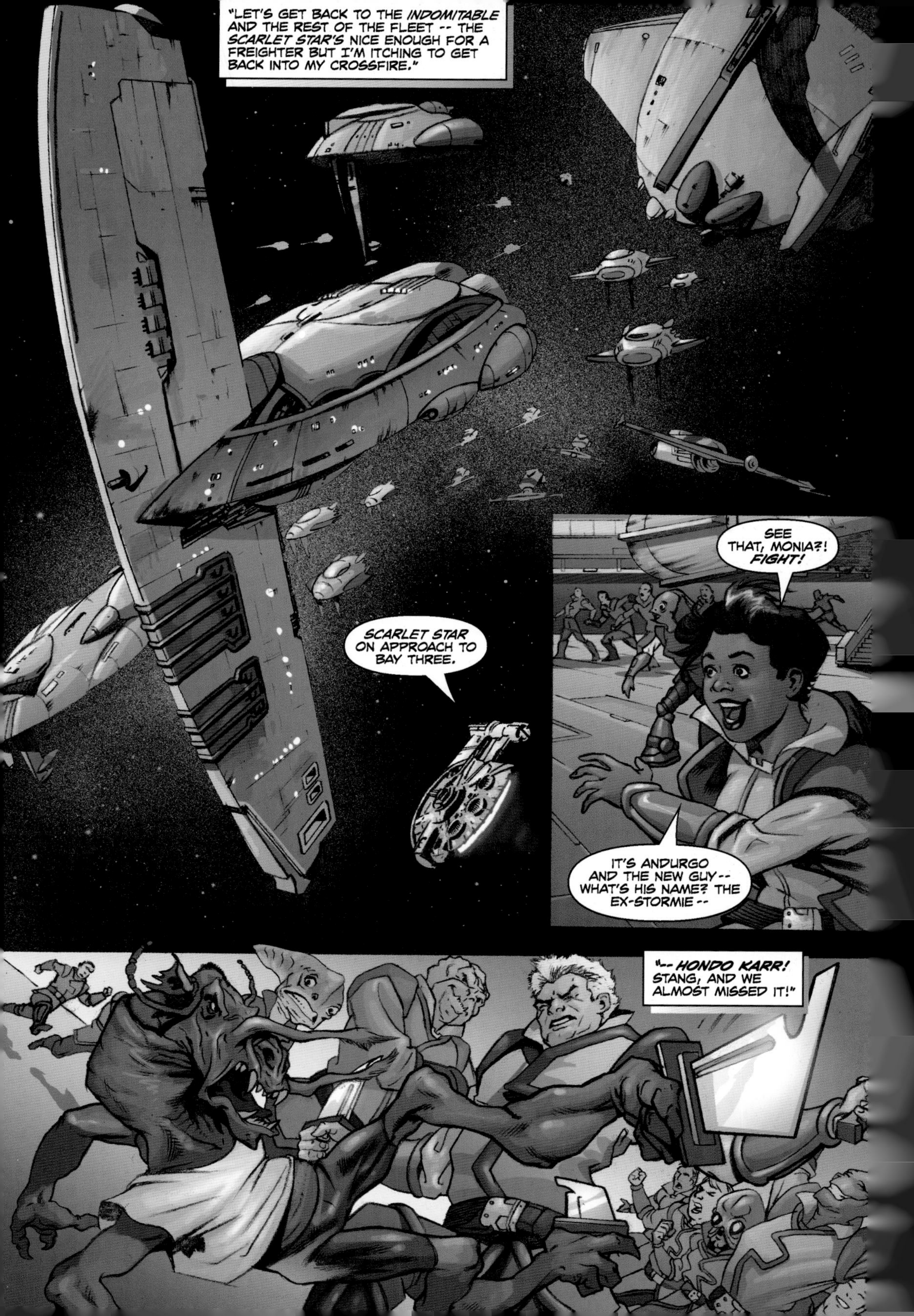
"LET'S GET BACK TO THE *INDOMITABLE* AND THE REST OF THE FLEET -- THE *SCARLET STAR'S* NICE ENOUGH FOR A FREIGHTER BUT I'M ITCHING TO GET BACK INTO MY CROSSFIRE."
SCARLET STAR ON APPROACH TO BAY THREE.
SEE THAT, MONIA?! *FIGHT!*
IT'S ANDURGO AND THE NEW GUY-- WHAT'S HIS NAME? THE EX-STORMIE --
"-- *HONDO KARR!* STANG, AND WE ALMOST MISSED IT!"

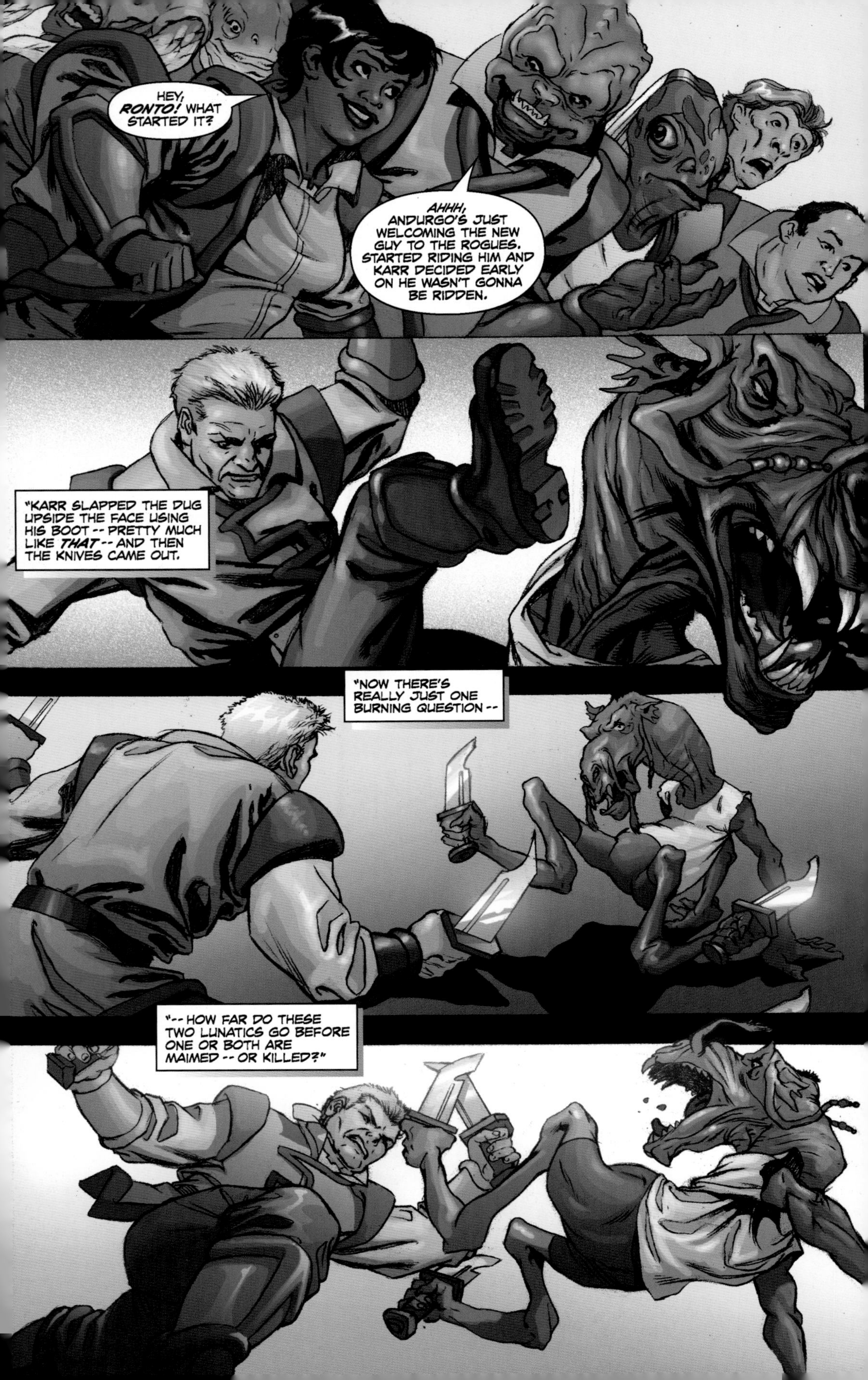
HEY, RONTO! WHAT STARTED IT?
AHHH, ANDURGO'S JUST WELCOMING THE NEW GUY TO THE ROGUES. STARTED RIDING HIM AND KARR DECIDED EARLY ON HE WASN'T GONNA BE RIDDEN.
"KARR SLAPPED THE DUG UPSIDE THE FACE USING HIS BOOT -- PRETTY MUCH LIKE THAT -- AND THEN THE KNIVES CAME OUT.
"NOW THERE'S REALLY JUST ONE BURNING QUESTION --
"-- HOW FAR DO THESE TWO LUNATICS GO BEFORE ONE OR BOTH ARE MAIMED -- OR KILLED?"

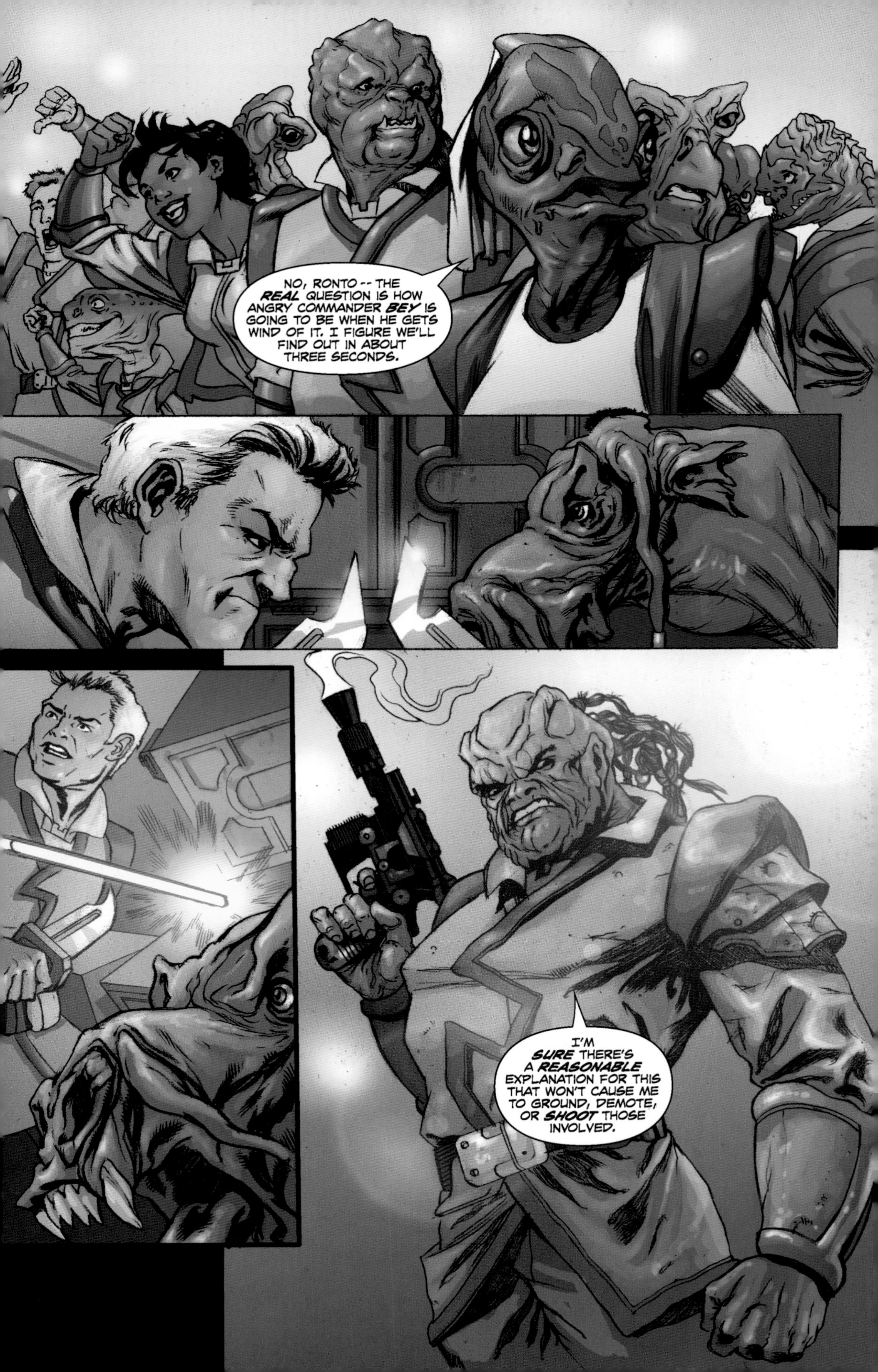
NO, RONTO -- THE **REAL** QUESTION IS HOW ANGRY COMMANDER **BEY** IS GOING TO BE WHEN HE GETS WIND OF IT. I FIGURE WE'LL FIND OUT IN ABOUT THREE SECONDS.
I'M **SURE** THERE'S A **REASONABLE** EXPLANATION FOR THIS THAT WON'T CAUSE ME TO GROUND, DEMOTE, OR **SHOOT** THOSE INVOLVED.

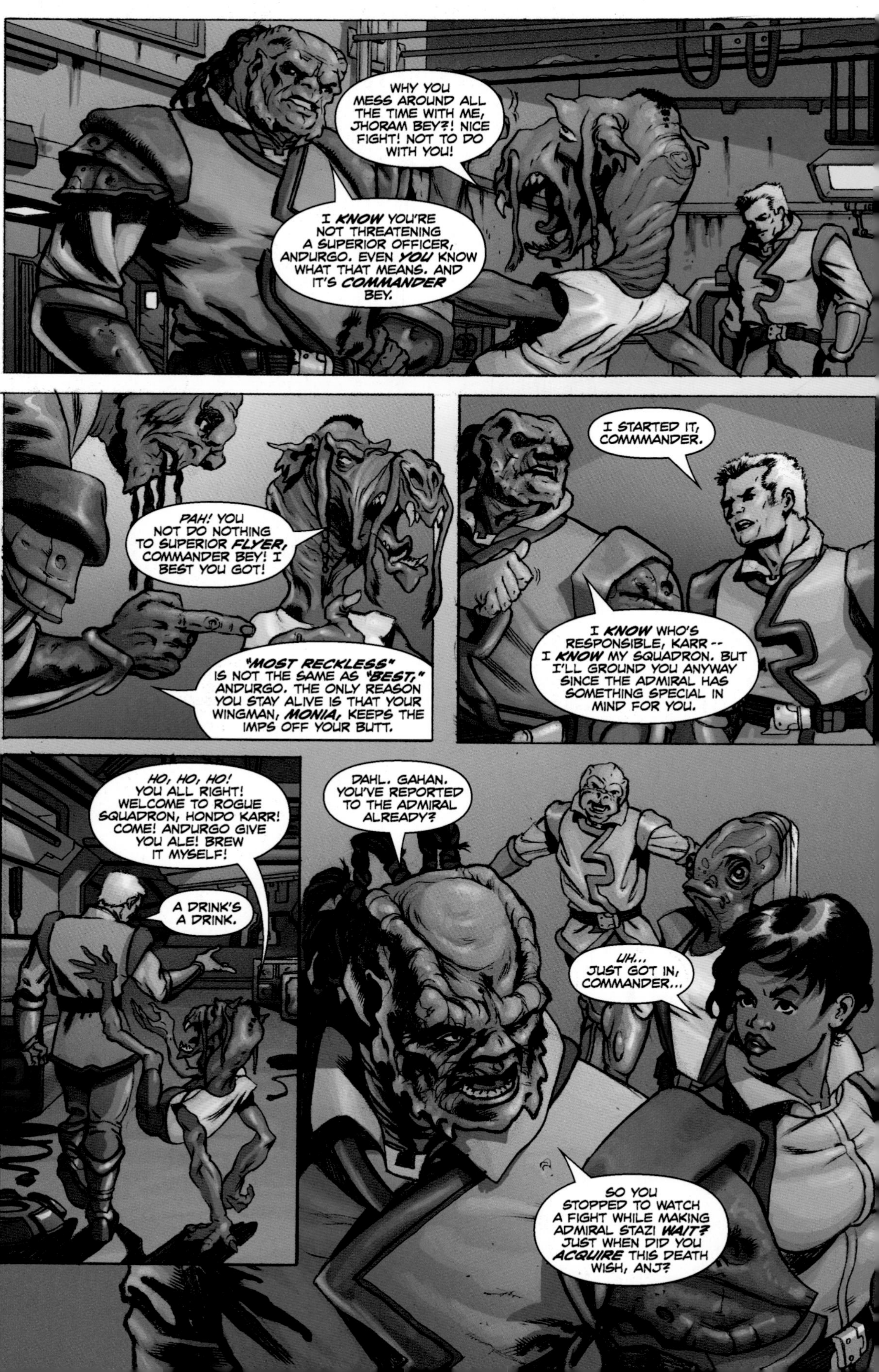
WHY YOU MESS AROUND ALL THE TIME WITH ME, JHORAM BEY?! NICE FIGHT! NOT TO DO WITH YOU!
I KNOW YOU'RE NOT THREATENING A SUPERIOR OFFICER, ANDURGO. EVEN YOU KNOW WHAT THAT MEANS. AND IT'S COMMANDER BEY.
PAH! YOU NOT DO NOTHING TO SUPERIOR FLYER, COMMANDER BEY! I BEST YOU GOT!
"MOST RECKLESS" IS NOT THE SAME AS "BEST," ANDURGO. THE ONLY REASON YOU STAY ALIVE IS THAT YOUR WINGMAN, MONIA, KEEPS THE IMPS OFF YOUR BUTT.
I STARTED IT, COMMMANDER.
I KNOW WHO'S RESPONSIBLE, KARR -- I KNOW MY SQUADRON. BUT I'LL GROUND YOU ANYWAY SINCE THE ADMIRAL HAS SOMETHING SPECIAL IN MIND FOR YOU.
HO, HO, HO! YOU ALL RIGHT! WELCOME TO ROGUE SQUADRON, HONDO KARR! COME! ANDURGO GIVE YOU ALE! BREW IT MYSELF!
A DRINK'S A DRINK.
DAHL. GAHAN. YOU'VE REPORTED TO THE ADMIRAL ALREADY?
UH... JUST GOT IN, COMMANDER...
SO YOU STOPPED TO WATCH A FIGHT WHILE MAKING ADMIRAL STAZI WAIT? JUST WHEN DID YOU ACQUIRE THIS DEATH WISH, ANJ?

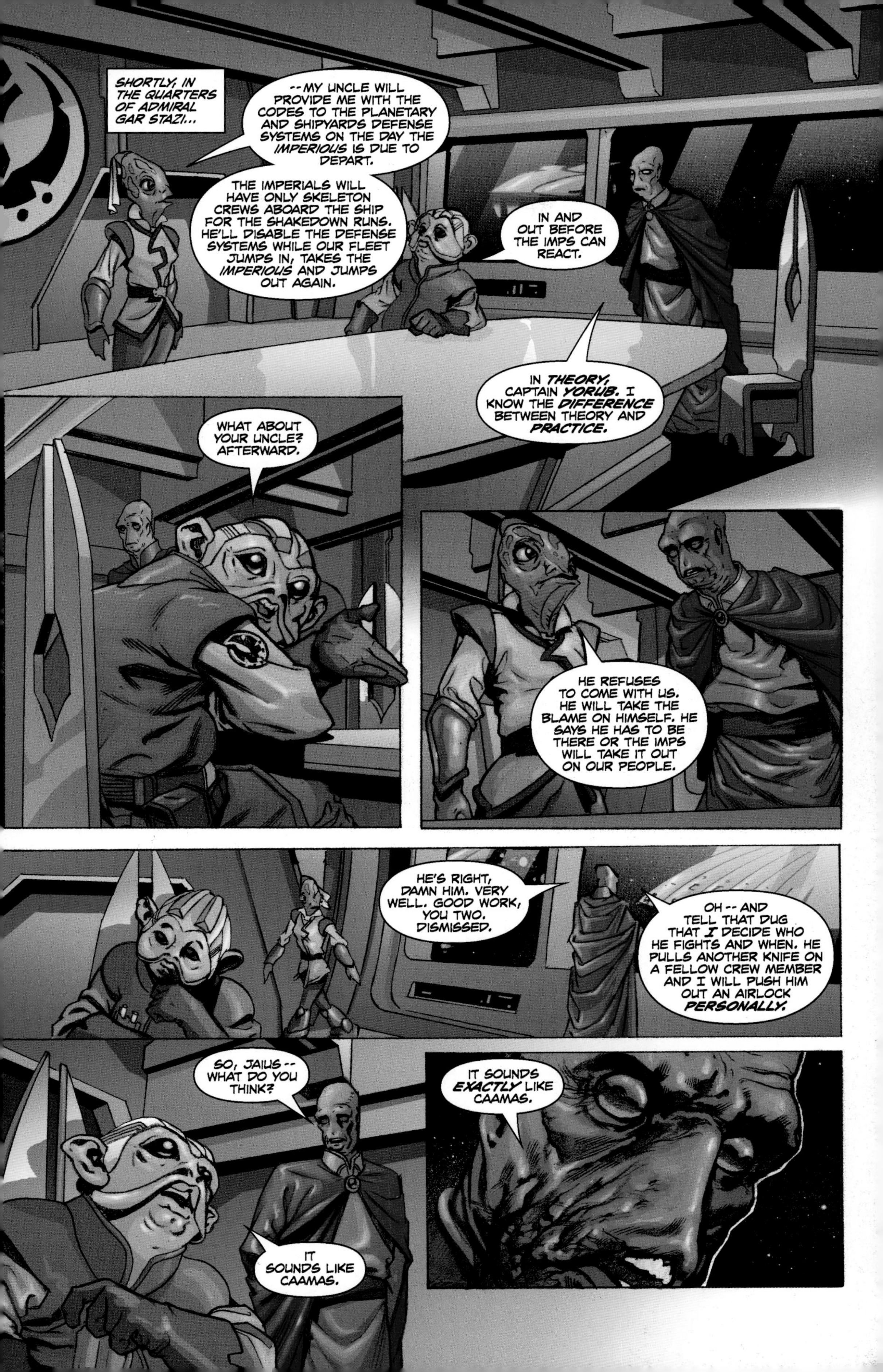
SHORTLY, IN THE QUARTERS OF ADMIRAL GAR STAZI...
--MY UNCLE WILL PROVIDE ME WITH THE CODES TO THE PLANETARY AND SHIPYARDS DEFENSE SYSTEMS ON THE DAY THE IMPERIOUS IS DUE TO DEPART.
THE IMPERIALS WILL HAVE ONLY SKELETON CREWS ABOARD THE SHIP FOR THE SHAKEDOWN RUNS. HE'LL DISABLE THE DEFENSE SYSTEMS WHILE OUR FLEET JUMPS IN, TAKES THE IMPERIOUS AND JUMPS OUT AGAIN.
IN AND OUT BEFORE THE IMPS CAN REACT.
IN THEORY, CAPTAIN YORUB. I KNOW THE DIFFERENCE BETWEEN THEORY AND PRACTICE.
WHAT ABOUT YOUR UNCLE? AFTERWARD.
HE REFUSES TO COME WITH US. HE WILL TAKE THE BLAME ON HIMSELF. HE SAYS HE HAS TO BE THERE OR THE IMPS WILL TAKE IT OUT ON OUR PEOPLE.
HE'S RIGHT, DAMN HIM. VERY WELL. GOOD WORK, YOU TWO. DISMISSED.
OH -- AND TELL THAT DUG THAT I DECIDE WHO HE FIGHTS AND WHEN. HE PULLS ANOTHER KNIFE ON A FELLOW CREW MEMBER AND I WILL PUSH HIM OUT AN AIRLOCK PERSONALLY.
SO, JAIUS -- WHAT DO YOU THINK?
IT SOUNDS LIKE CAAMAS.
IT SOUNDS EXACTLY LIKE CAAMAS.

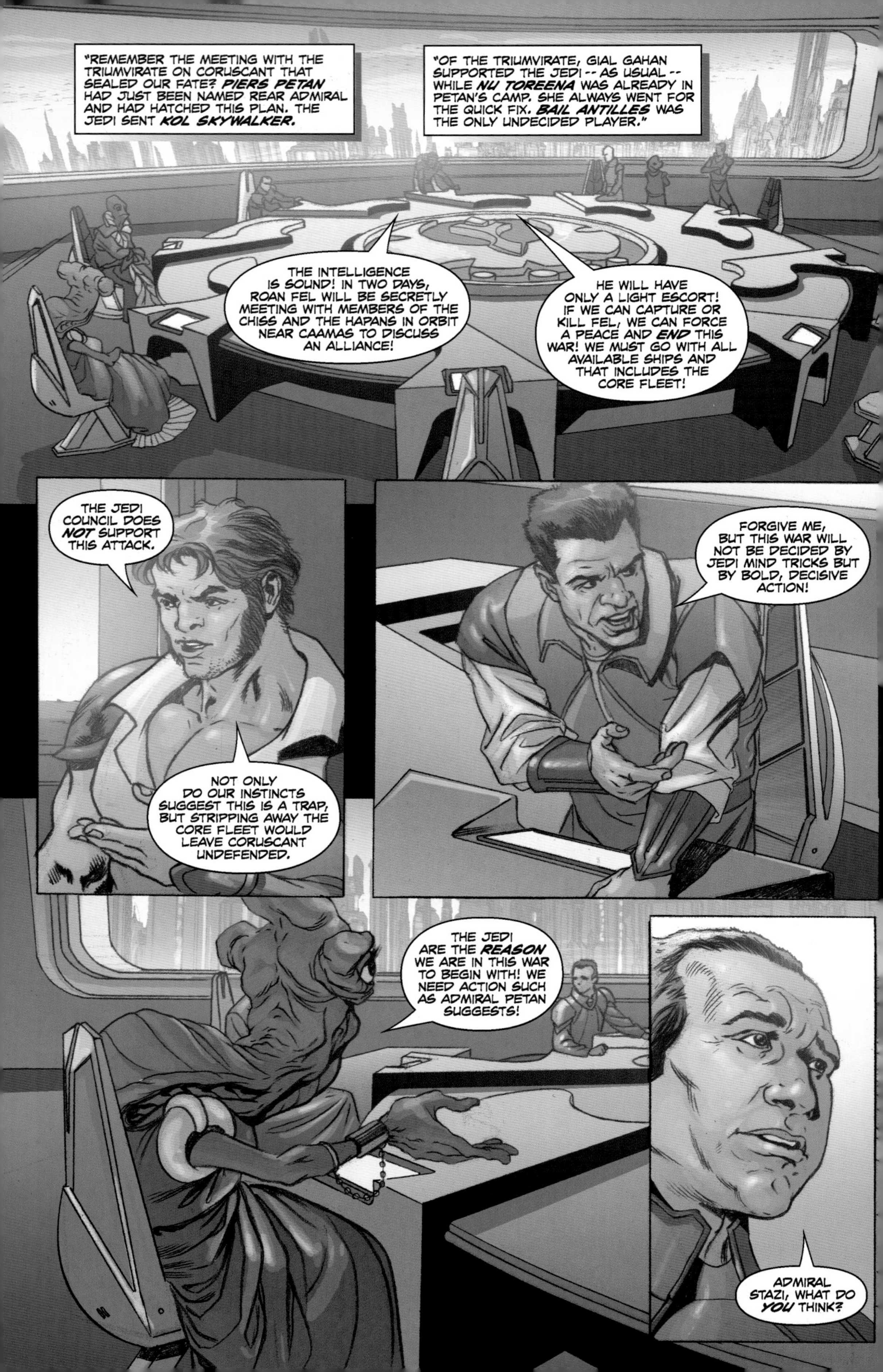
"REMEMBER THE MEETING WITH THE TRIUMVIRATE ON CORUSCANT THAT SEALED OUR FATE? PIERS PETAN HAD JUST BEEN NAMED REAR ADMIRAL AND HAD HATCHED THIS PLAN. THE JEDI SENT KOL SKYWALKER.
"OF THE TRIUMVIRATE, GIAL GAHAN SUPPORTED THE JEDI -- AS USUAL -- WHILE NU TOREENA WAS ALREADY IN PETAN'S CAMP. SHE ALWAYS WENT FOR THE QUICK FIX. BAIL ANTILLES WAS THE ONLY UNDECIDED PLAYER."
THE INTELLIGENCE IS SOUND! IN TWO DAYS, ROAN FEL WILL BE SECRETLY MEETING WITH MEMBERS OF THE CHISS AND THE HAPANS IN ORBIT NEAR CAAMAS TO DISCUSS AN ALLIANCE!
HE WILL HAVE ONLY A LIGHT ESCORT! IF WE CAN CAPTURE OR KILL FEL, WE CAN FORCE A PEACE AND END THIS WAR! WE MUST GO WITH ALL AVAILABLE SHIPS AND THAT INCLUDES THE CORE FLEET!
THE JEDI COUNCIL DOES NOT SUPPORT THIS ATTACK.
NOT ONLY DO OUR INSTINCTS SUGGEST THIS IS A TRAP, BUT STRIPPING AWAY THE CORE FLEET WOULD LEAVE CORUSCANT UNDEFENDED.
FORGIVE ME, BUT THIS WAR WILL NOT BE DECIDED BY JEDI MIND TRICKS BUT BY BOLD, DECISIVE ACTION!
THE JEDI ARE THE REASON WE ARE IN THIS WAR TO BEGIN WITH! WE NEED ACTION SUCH AS ADMIRAL PETAN SUGGESTS!
ADMIRAL STAZI, WHAT DO YOU THINK?

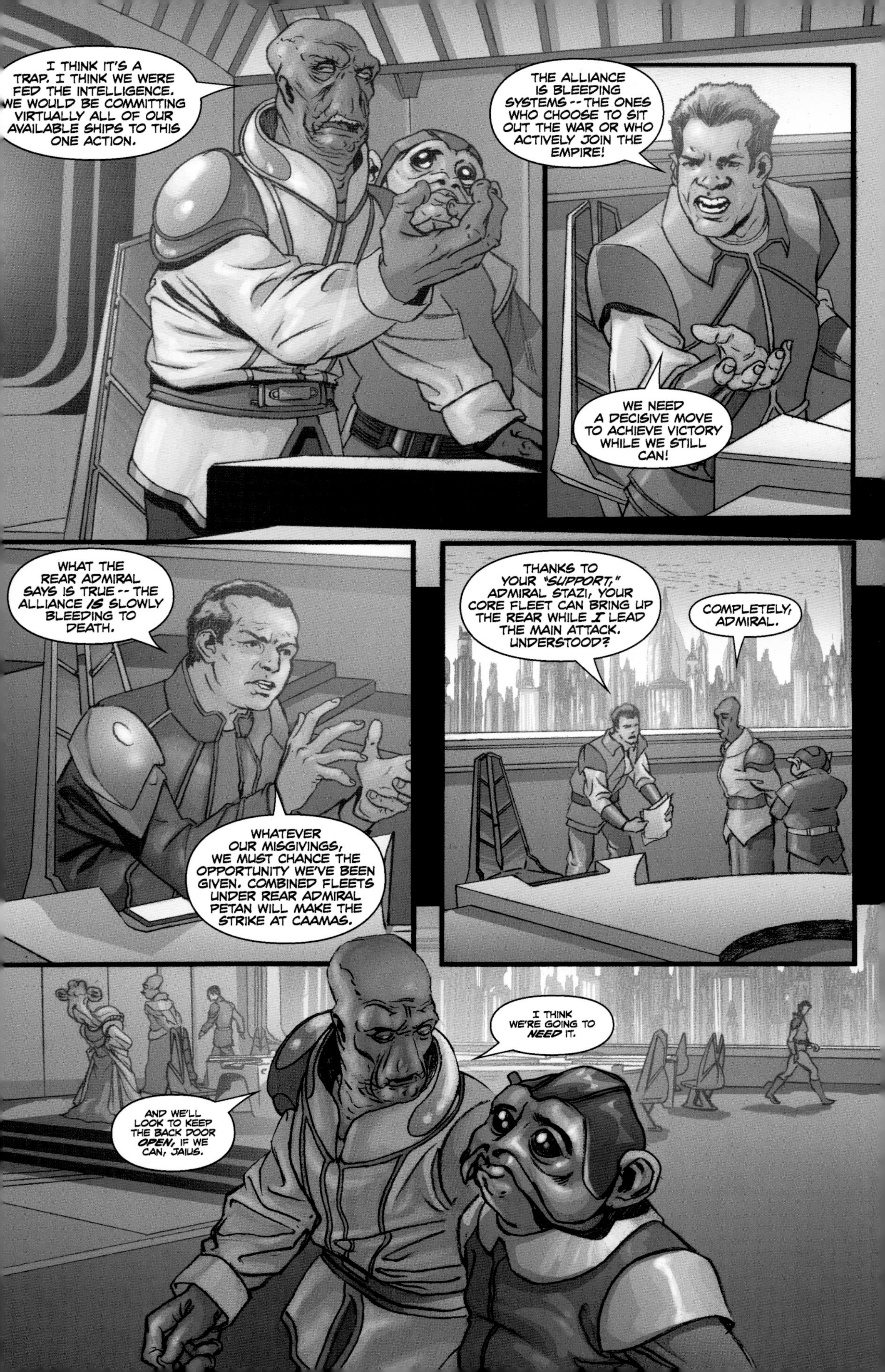
I THINK IT'S A TRAP. I THINK WE WERE FED THE INTELLIGENCE. WE WOULD BE COMMITTING VIRTUALLY ALL OF OUR AVAILABLE SHIPS TO THIS ONE ACTION.
THE ALLIANCE IS BLEEDING SYSTEMS -- THE ONES WHO CHOOSE TO SIT OUT THE WAR OR WHO ACTIVELY JOIN THE EMPIRE!
WE NEED A DECISIVE MOVE TO ACHIEVE VICTORY WHILE WE STILL CAN!
WHAT THE REAR ADMIRAL SAYS IS TRUE -- THE ALLIANCE *IS* SLOWLY BLEEDING TO DEATH.
WHATEVER OUR MISGIVINGS, WE MUST CHANCE THE OPPORTUNITY WE'VE BEEN GIVEN. COMBINED FLEETS UNDER REAR ADMIRAL PETAN WILL MAKE THE STRIKE AT CAAMAS.
THANKS TO YOUR *"SUPPORT,"* ADMIRAL STAZI, YOUR CORE FLEET CAN BRING UP THE REAR WHILE *I* LEAD THE MAIN ATTACK. UNDERSTOOD?
COMPLETELY, ADMIRAL.
AND WE'LL LOOK TO KEEP THE BACK DOOR *OPEN*, IF WE CAN, JAIUS.
I THINK WE'RE GOING TO *NEED* IT.

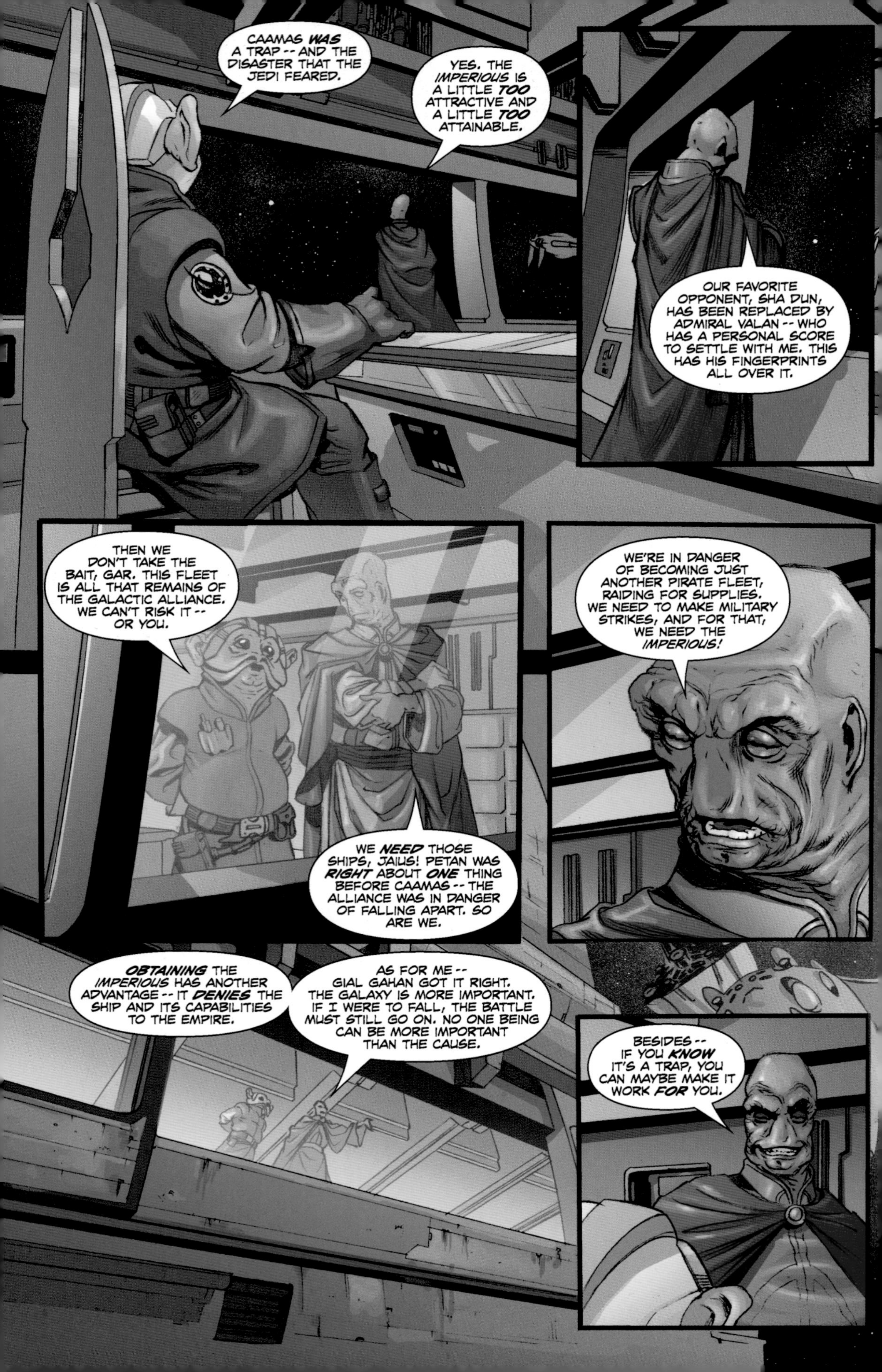
CAAMAS WAS A TRAP -- AND THE DISASTER THAT THE JEDI FEARED.
YES. THE IMPERIOUS IS A LITTLE TOO ATTRACTIVE AND A LITTLE TOO ATTAINABLE.
OUR FAVORITE OPPONENT, SHA DUN, HAS BEEN REPLACED BY ADMIRAL VALAN -- WHO HAS A PERSONAL SCORE TO SETTLE WITH ME. THIS HAS HIS FINGERPRINTS ALL OVER IT.
THEN WE DON'T TAKE THE BAIT, GAR. THIS FLEET IS ALL THAT REMAINS OF THE GALACTIC ALLIANCE. WE CAN'T RISK IT -- OR YOU.
WE NEED THOSE SHIPS, JAIUS! PETAN WAS RIGHT ABOUT ONE THING BEFORE CAAMAS -- THE ALLIANCE WAS IN DANGER OF FALLING APART. SO ARE WE.
WE'RE IN DANGER OF BECOMING JUST ANOTHER PIRATE FLEET, RAIDING FOR SUPPLIES. WE NEED TO MAKE MILITARY STRIKES, AND FOR THAT, WE NEED THE IMPERIOUS!
OBTAINING THE IMPERIOUS HAS ANOTHER ADVANTAGE -- IT DENIES THE SHIP AND ITS CAPABILITIES TO THE EMPIRE.
AS FOR ME -- GIAL GAHAN GOT IT RIGHT. THE GALAXY IS MORE IMPORTANT. IF I WERE TO FALL, THE BATTLE MUST STILL GO ON. NO ONE BEING CAN BE MORE IMPORTANT THAN THE CAUSE.
BESIDES -- IF YOU KNOW IT'S A TRAP, YOU CAN MAYBE MAKE IT WORK FOR YOU.

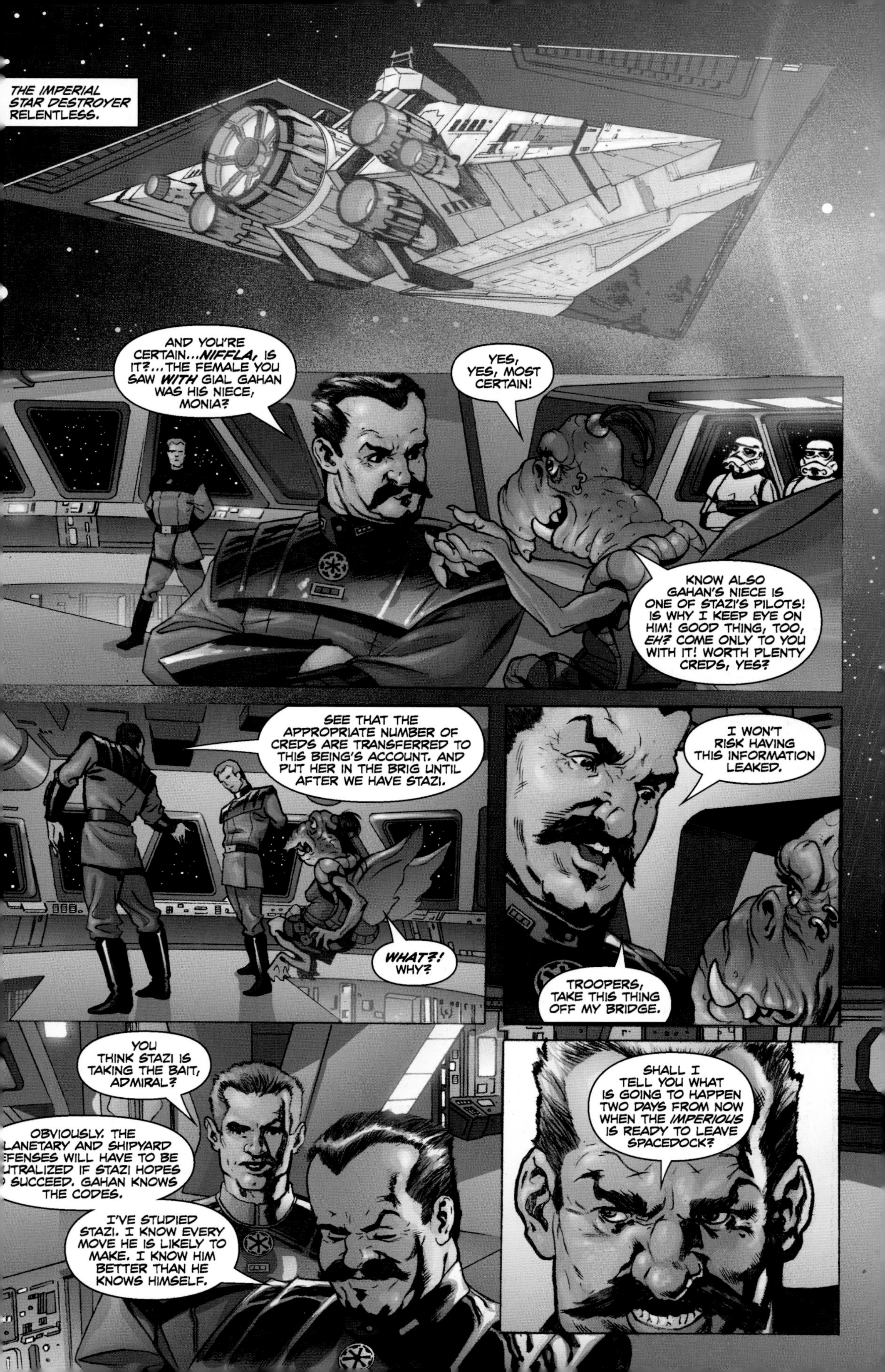

THE IMPERIAL STAR DESTROYER RELENTLESS.
AND YOU'RE CERTAIN... NIFFLA, IS IT?... THE FEMALE YOU SAW WITH GIAL GAHAN WAS HIS NIECE, MONIA?
YES, YES, MOST CERTAIN!
KNOW ALSO GAHAN'S NIECE IS ONE OF STAZI'S PILOTS! IS WHY I KEEP EYE ON HIM! GOOD THING, TOO, EH? COME ONLY TO YOU WITH IT! WORTH PLENTY CREDS, YES?
SEE THAT THE APPROPRIATE NUMBER OF CREDS ARE TRANSFERRED TO THIS BEING'S ACCOUNT. AND PUT HER IN THE BRIG UNTIL AFTER WE HAVE STAZI.
WHAT?! WHY?
I WON'T RISK HAVING THIS INFORMATION LEAKED.
TROOPERS, TAKE THIS THING OFF MY BRIDGE.
YOU THINK STAZI IS TAKING THE BAIT, ADMIRAL?
OBVIOUSLY. THE LANETARY AND SHIPYARD EFENSES WILL HAVE TO BE UTRALIZED IF STAZI HOPES O SUCCEED. GAHAN KNOWS THE CODES.
I'VE STUDIED STAZI. I KNOW EVERY MOVE HE IS LIKELY TO MAKE. I KNOW HIM BETTER THAN HE KNOWS HIMSELF.
SHALL I TELL YOU WHAT IS GOING TO HAPPEN TWO DAYS FROM NOW WHEN THE IMPERIOUS IS READY TO LEAVE SPACEDOCK?

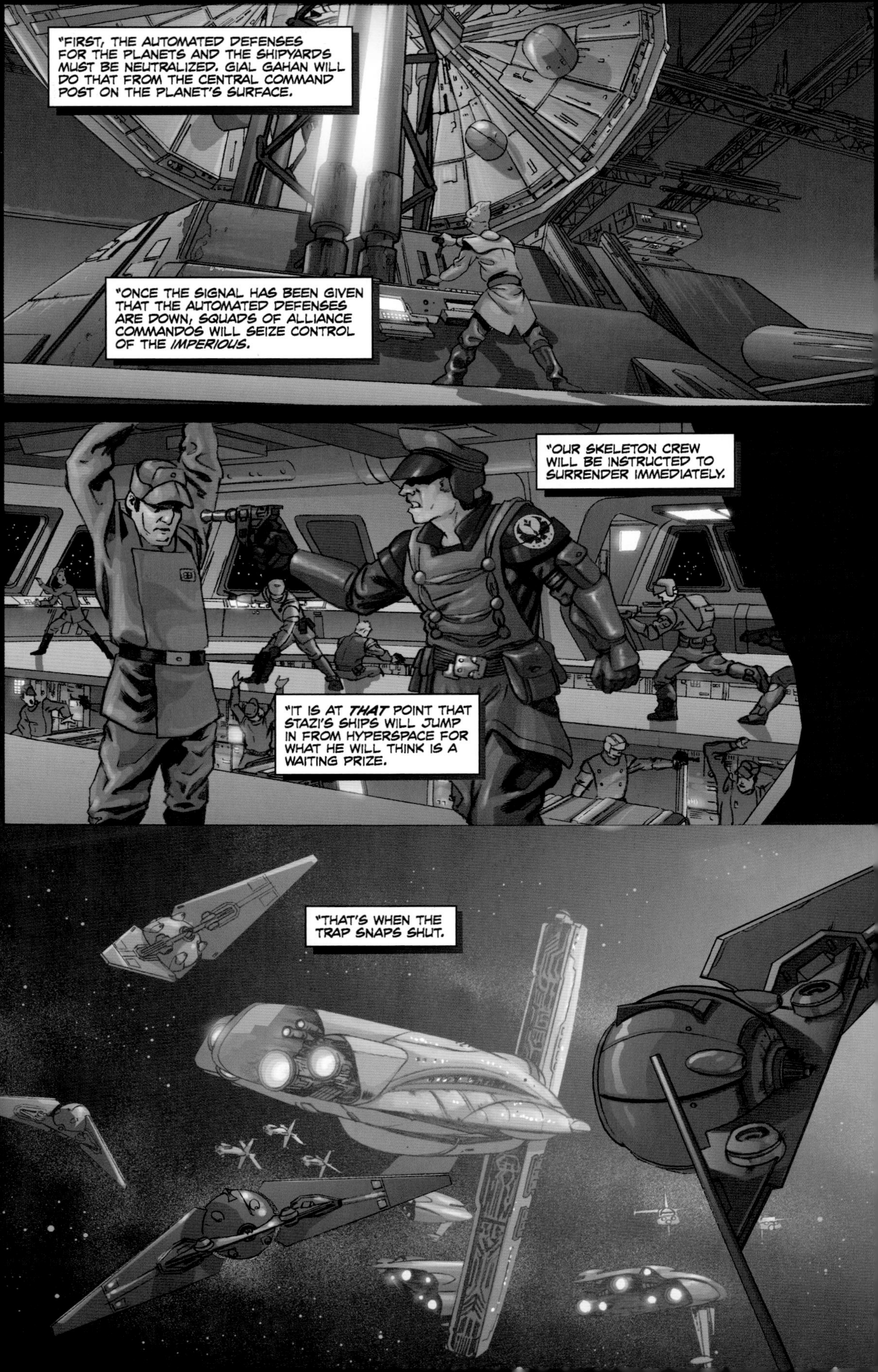
"FIRST, THE AUTOMATED DEFENSES FOR THE PLANETS AND THE SHIPYARDS MUST BE NEUTRALIZED. GIAL GAHAN WILL DO THAT FROM THE CENTRAL COMMAND POST ON THE PLANET'S SURFACE.
"ONCE THE SIGNAL HAS BEEN GIVEN THAT THE AUTOMATED DEFENSES ARE DOWN, SQUADS OF ALLIANCE COMMANDOS WILL SEIZE CONTROL OF THE *IMPERIOUS*.
"OUR SKELETON CREW WILL BE INSTRUCTED TO SURRENDER IMMEDIATELY.
"IT IS AT ***THAT*** POINT THAT STAZI'S SHIPS WILL JUMP IN FROM HYPERSPACE FOR WHAT HE WILL THINK IS A WAITING PRIZE.
"THAT'S WHEN THE TRAP SNAPS SHUT.

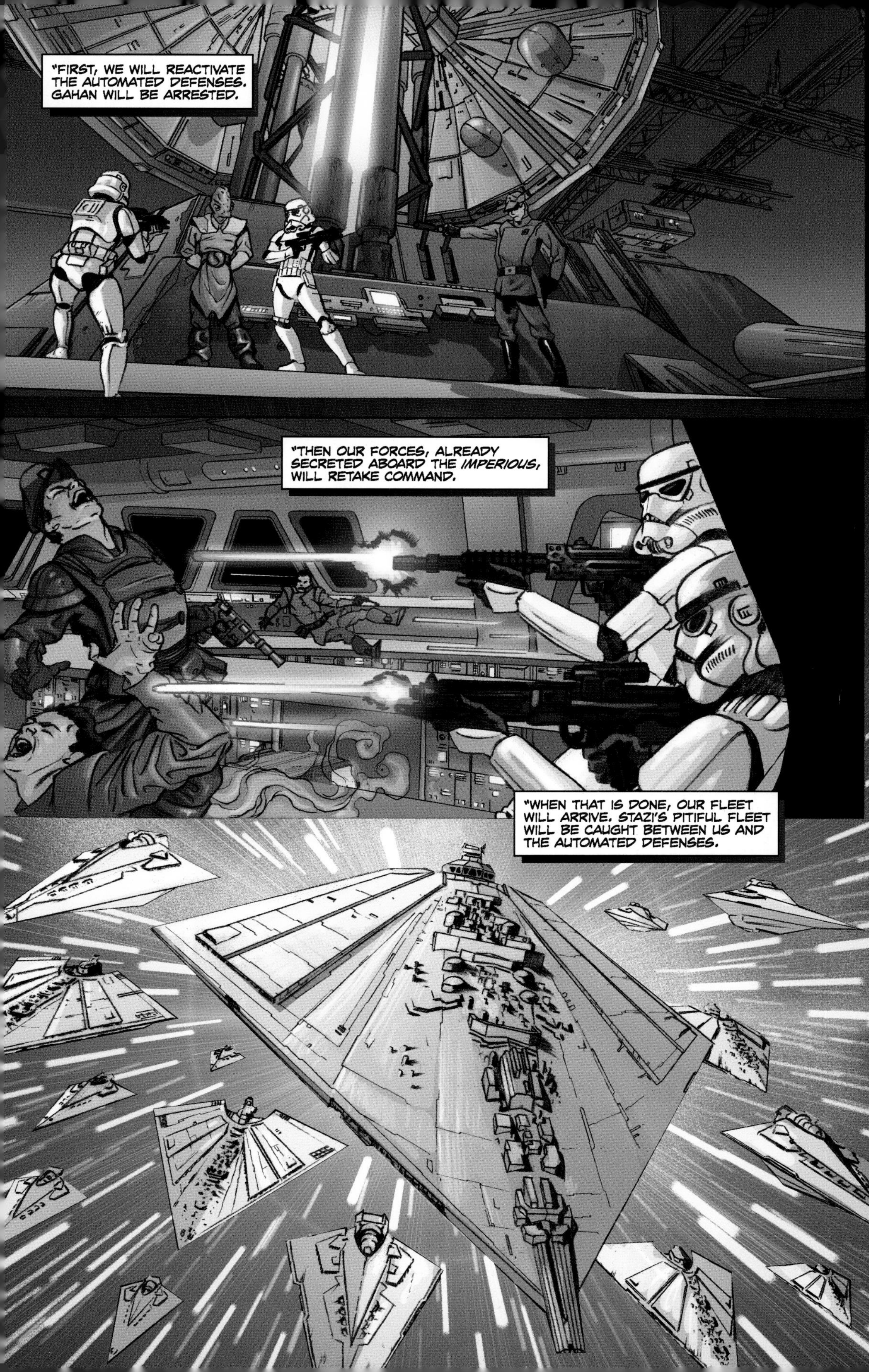
"FIRST, WE WILL REACTIVATE THE AUTOMATED DEFENSES. GAHAN WILL BE ARRESTED.
"THEN OUR FORCES, ALREADY SECRETED ABOARD THE *IMPERIOUS*, WILL RETAKE COMMAND.
"WHEN THAT IS DONE, OUR FLEET WILL ARRIVE. STAZI'S PITIFUL FLEET WILL BE CAUGHT BETWEEN US AND THE AUTOMATED DEFENSES.

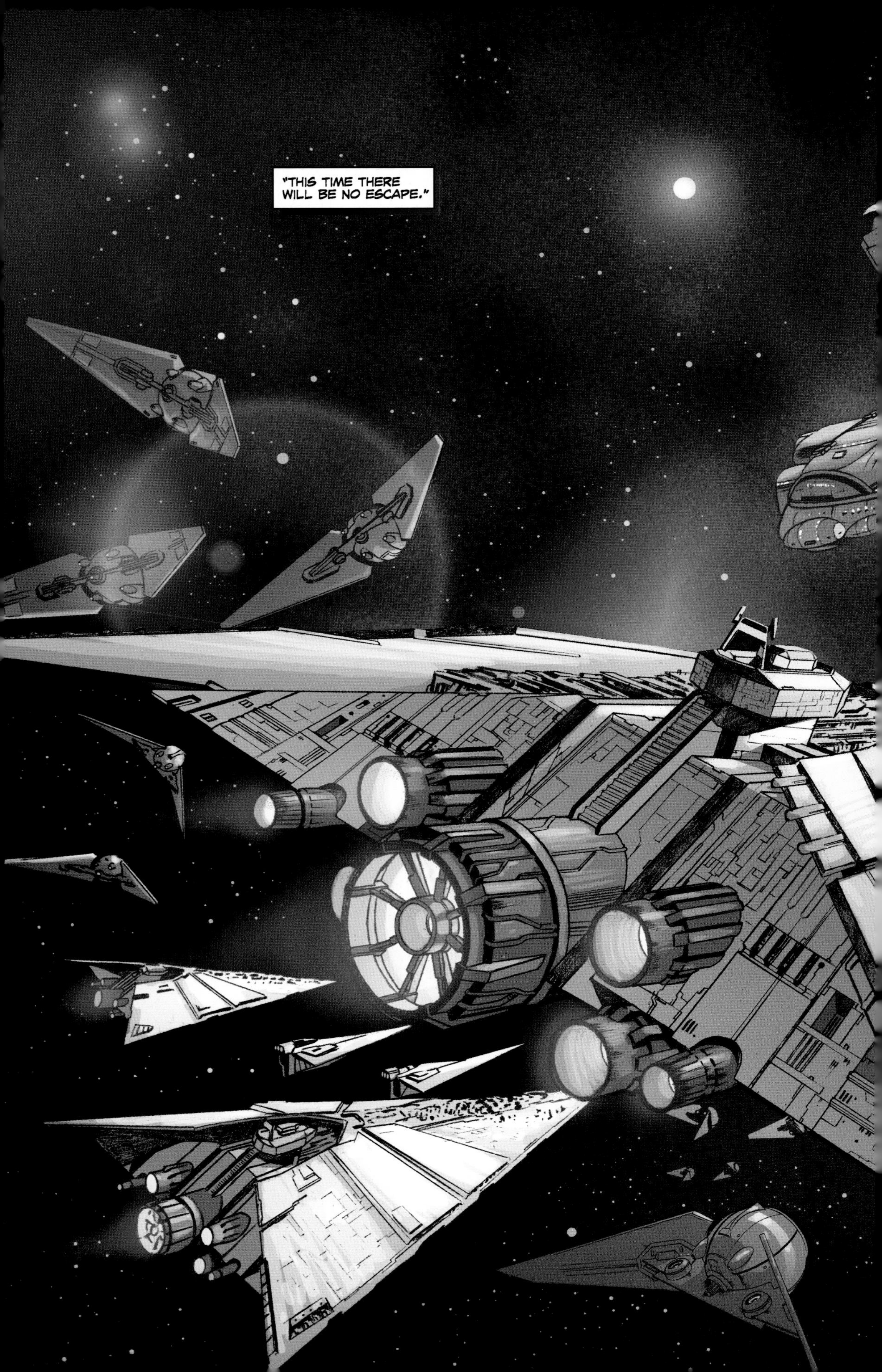
"THIS TIME THERE
WILL BE NO ESCAPE."

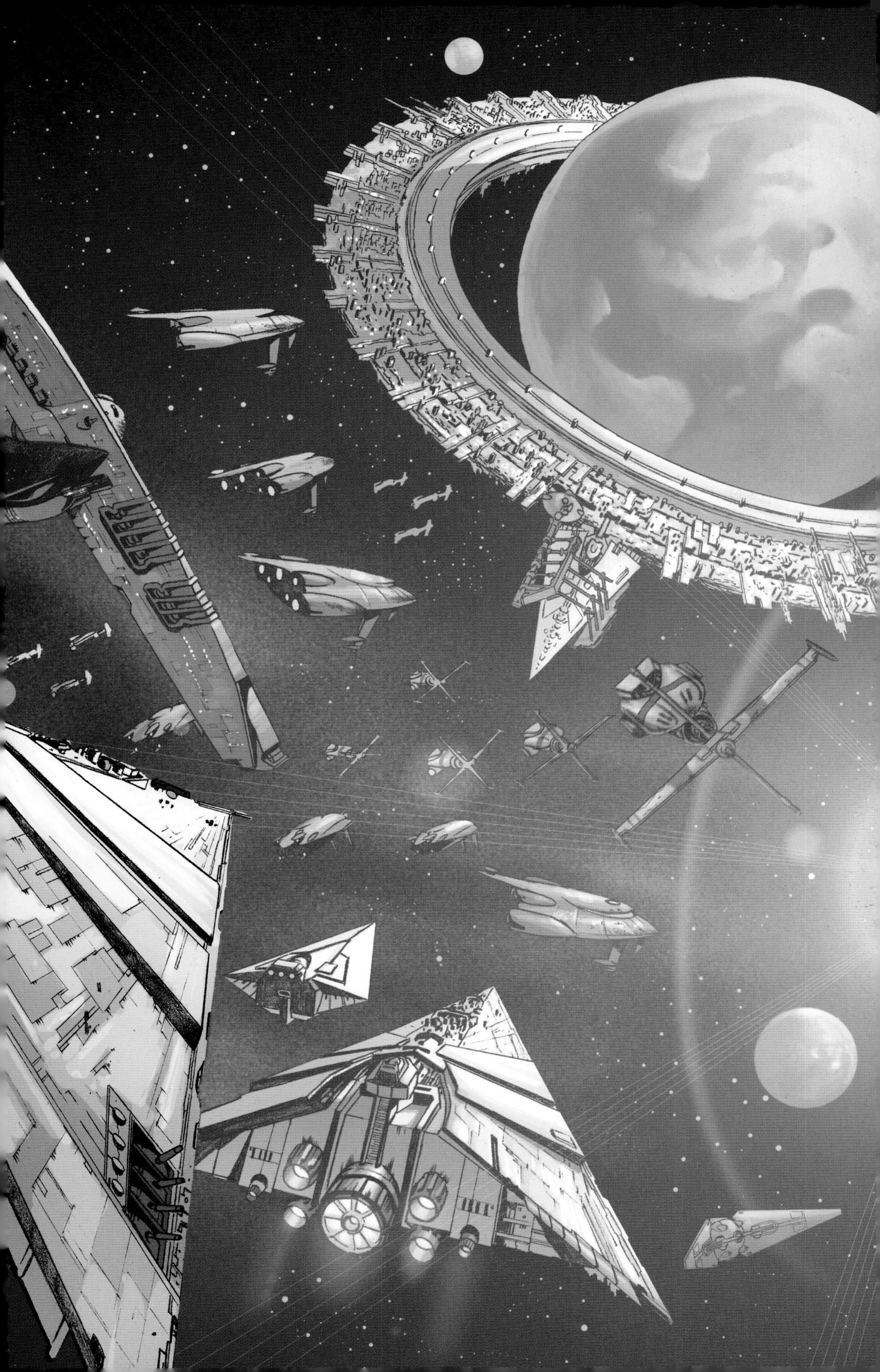

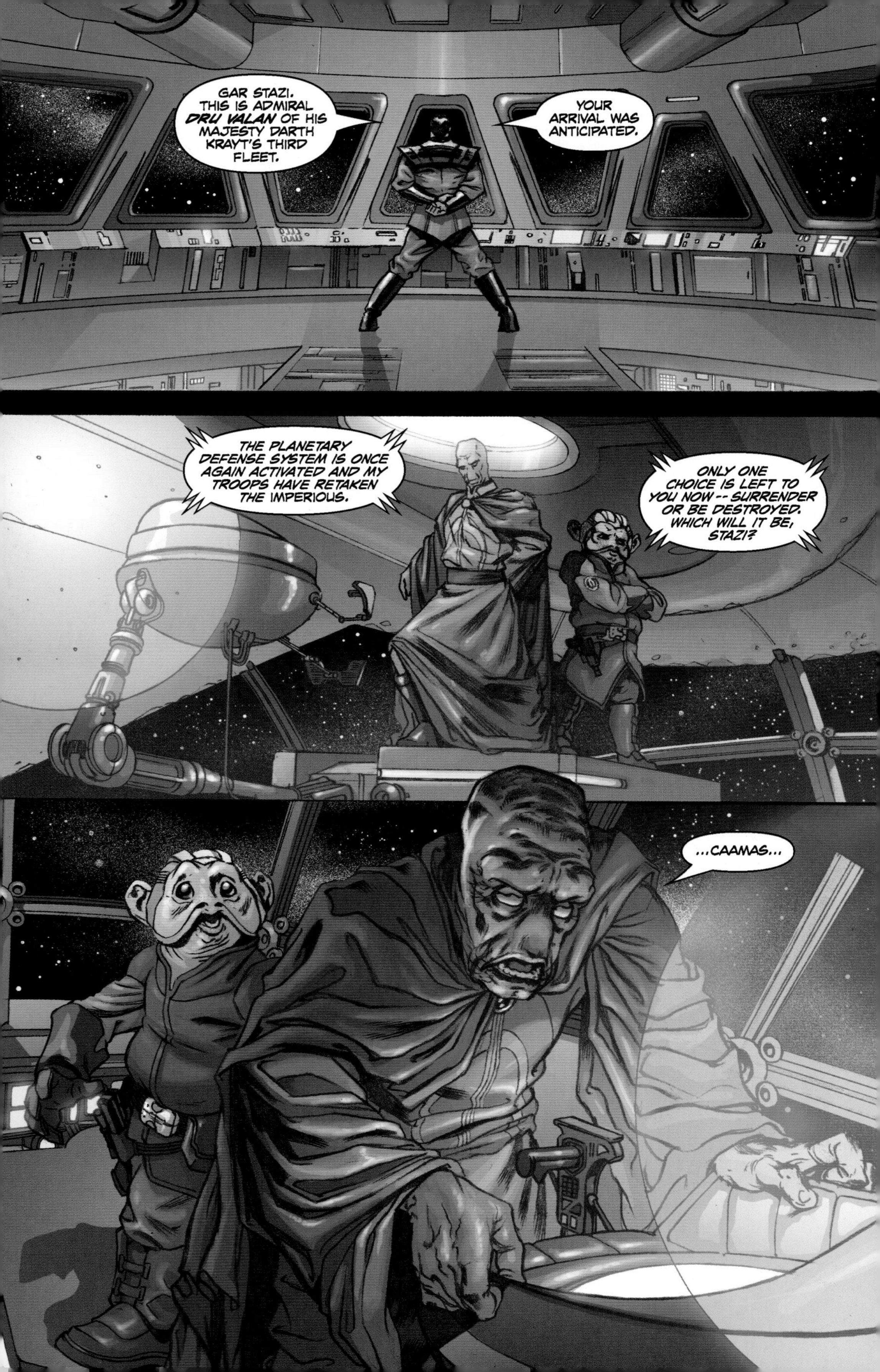
GAR STAZI. THIS IS ADMIRAL DRU VALAN OF HIS MAJESTY DARTH KRAYT'S THIRD FLEET.
YOUR ARRIVAL WAS ANTICIPATED.
THE PLANETARY DEFENSE SYSTEM IS ONCE AGAIN ACTIVATED AND MY TROOPS HAVE RETAKEN THE IMPERIOUS.
ONLY ONE CHOICE IS LEFT TO YOU NOW -- SURRENDER OR BE DESTROYED. WHICH WILL IT BE, STAZI?
...CAAMAS...

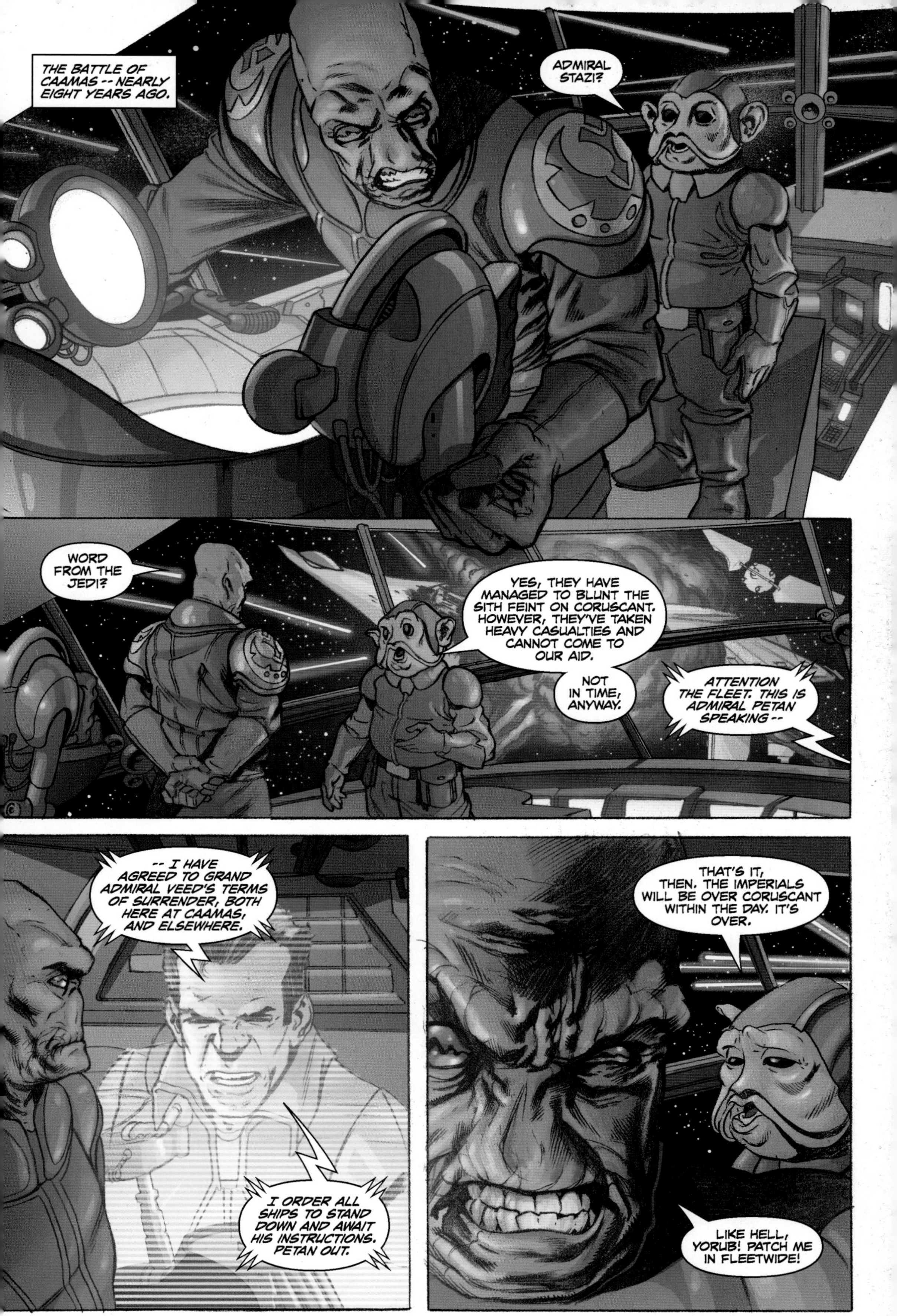

THE BATTLE OF CAAMAS -- NEARLY EIGHT YEARS AGO.
ADMIRAL STAZI?
WORD FROM THE JEDI?
YES, THEY HAVE MANAGED TO BLUNT THE SITH FEINT ON CORUSCANT. HOWEVER, THEY'VE TAKEN HEAVY CASUALTIES AND CANNOT COME TO OUR AID.
NOT IN TIME, ANYWAY.
ATTENTION THE FLEET. THIS IS ADMIRAL PETAN SPEAKING --
-- I HAVE AGREED TO GRAND ADMIRAL VEED'S TERMS OF SURRENDER, BOTH HERE AT CAAMAS, AND ELSEWHERE.
I ORDER ALL SHIPS TO STAND DOWN AND AWAIT HIS INSTRUCTIONS. PETAN OUT.
THAT'S IT, THEN. THE IMPERIALS WILL BE OVER CORUSCANT WITHIN THE DAY. IT'S OVER.
LIKE HELL, YORUB! PATCH ME IN FLEETWIDE!

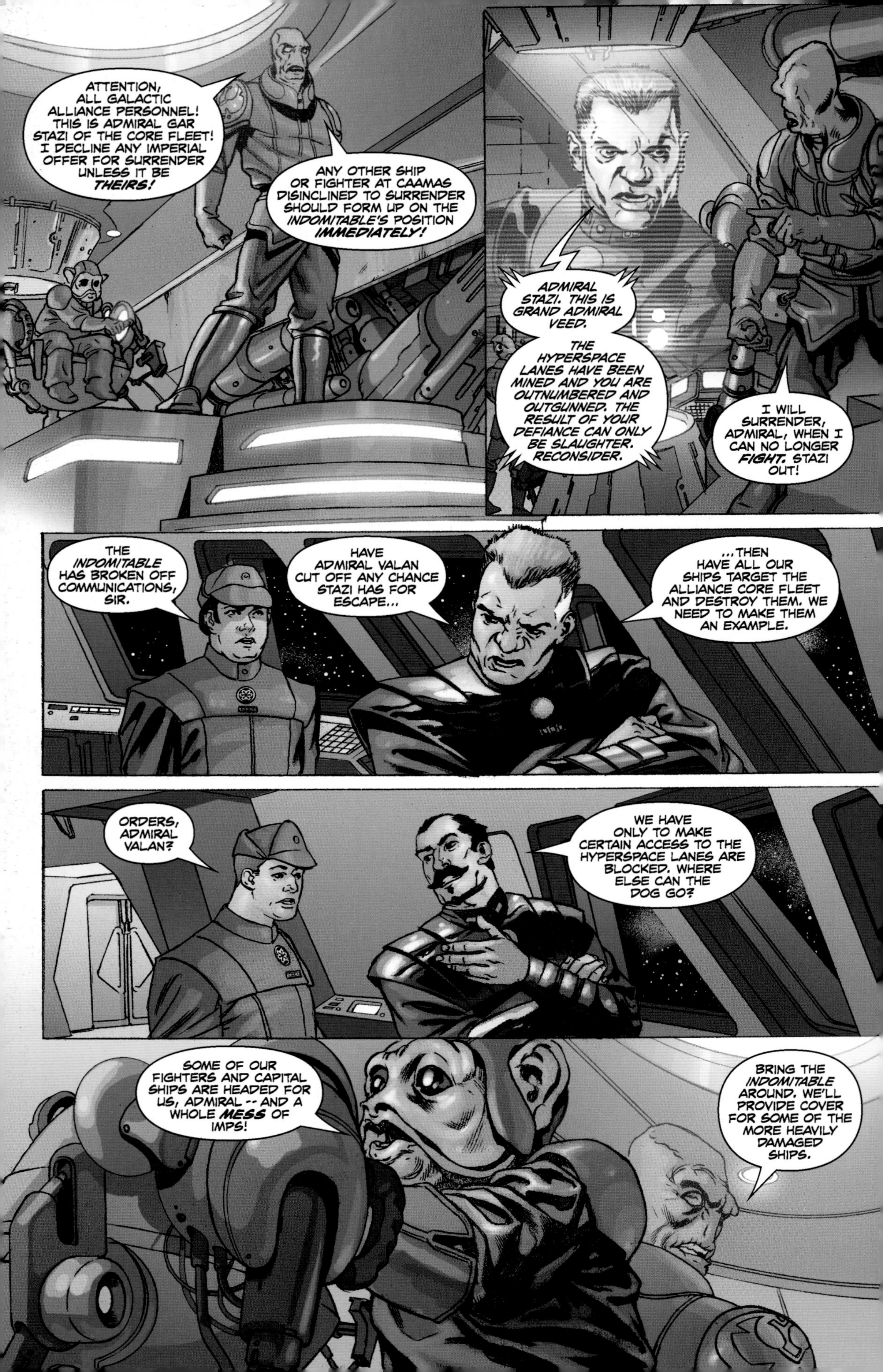
ATTENTION, ALL GALACTIC ALLIANCE PERSONNEL! THIS IS ADMIRAL GAR STAZI OF THE CORE FLEET! I DECLINE ANY IMPERIAL OFFER FOR SURRENDER UNLESS IT BE THEIRS!
ANY OTHER SHIP OR FIGHTER AT CAAMAS DISINCLINED TO SURRENDER SHOULD FORM UP ON THE INDOMITABLE'S POSITION IMMEDIATELY!
ADMIRAL STAZI. THIS IS GRAND ADMIRAL VEED.
THE HYPERSPACE LANES HAVE BEEN MINED AND YOU ARE OUTNUMBERED AND OUTGUNNED. THE RESULT OF YOUR DEFIANCE CAN ONLY BE SLAUGHTER. RECONSIDER.
I WILL SURRENDER, ADMIRAL, WHEN I CAN NO LONGER FIGHT. STAZI OUT!
THE INDOMITABLE HAS BROKEN OFF COMMUNICATIONS, SIR.
HAVE ADMIRAL VALAN CUT OFF ANY CHANCE STAZI HAS FOR ESCAPE...
...THEN HAVE ALL OUR SHIPS TARGET THE ALLIANCE CORE FLEET AND DESTROY THEM. WE NEED TO MAKE THEM AN EXAMPLE.
ORDERS, ADMIRAL VALAN?
WE HAVE ONLY TO MAKE CERTAIN ACCESS TO THE HYPERSPACE LANES ARE BLOCKED. WHERE ELSE CAN THE DOG GO?
SOME OF OUR FIGHTERS AND CAPITAL SHIPS ARE HEADED FOR US, ADMIRAL -- AND A WHOLE MESS OF IMPS!
BRING THE INDOMITABLE AROUND. WE'LL PROVIDE COVER FOR SOME OF THE MORE HEAVILY DAMAGED SHIPS.

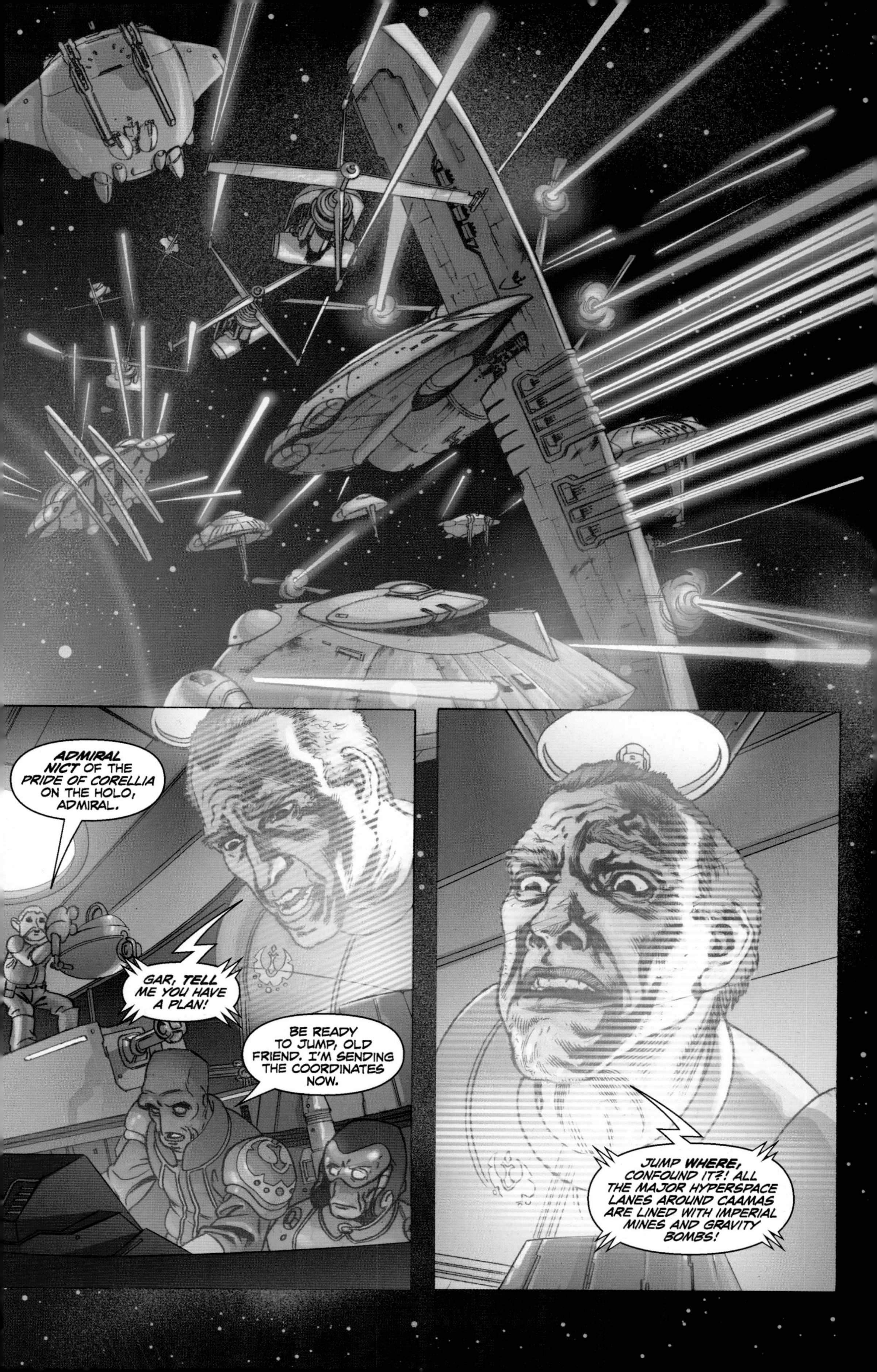
ADMIRAL NICT OF THE PRIDE OF CORELLIA ON THE HOLO, ADMIRAL.
GAR, TELL ME YOU HAVE A PLAN!
BE READY TO JUMP, OLD FRIEND. I'M SENDING THE COORDINATES NOW.
JUMP WHERE, CONFOUND IT?! ALL THE MAJOR HYPERSPACE LANES AROUND CAAMAS ARE LINED WITH IMPERIAL MINES AND GRAVITY BOMBS!

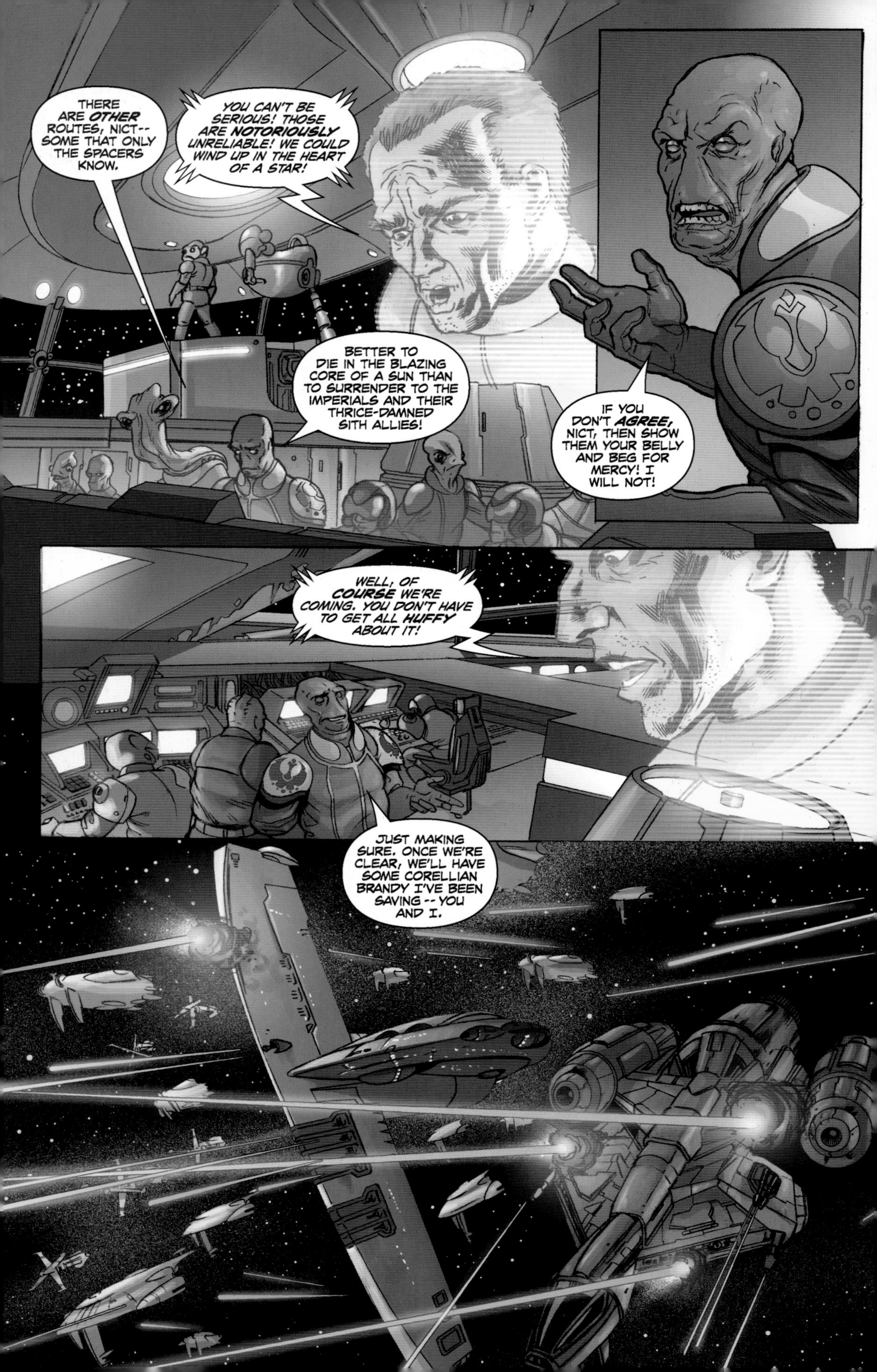
THERE ARE OTHER ROUTES, NICT-- SOME THAT ONLY THE SPACERS KNOW.
YOU CAN'T BE SERIOUS! THOSE ARE NOTORIOUSLY UNRELIABLE! WE COULD WIND UP IN THE HEART OF A STAR!
BETTER TO DIE IN THE BLAZING CORE OF A SUN THAN TO SURRENDER TO THE IMPERIALS AND THEIR THRICE-DAMNED SITH ALLIES!
IF YOU DON'T AGREE, NICT, THEN SHOW THEM YOUR BELLY AND BEG FOR MERCY! I WILL NOT!
WELL, OF COURSE WE'RE COMING. YOU DON'T HAVE TO GET ALL HUFFY ABOUT IT!
JUST MAKING SURE. ONCE WE'RE CLEAR, WE'LL HAVE SOME CORELLIAN BRANDY I'VE BEEN SAVING -- YOU AND I.

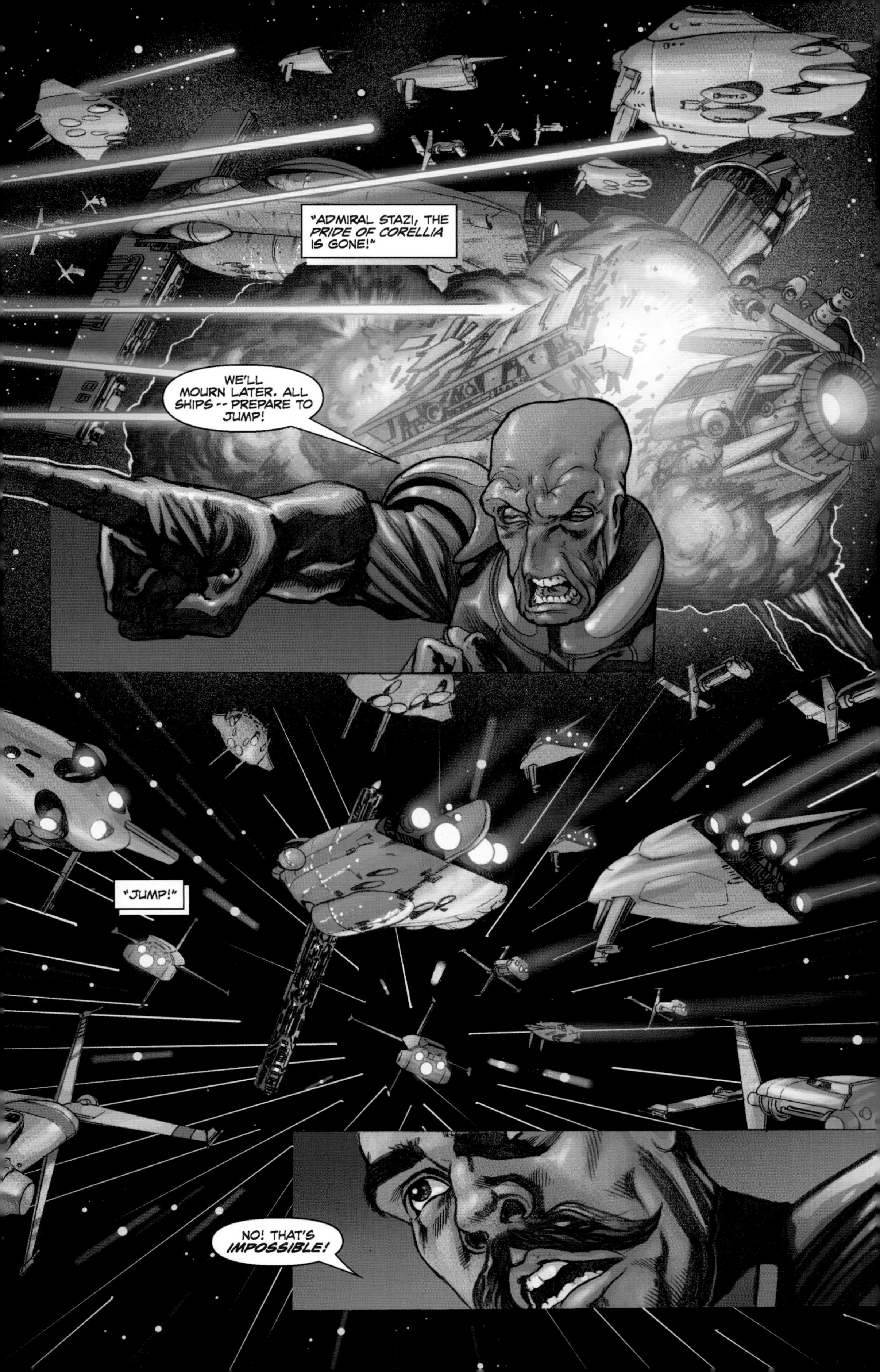
"ADMIRAL STAZI, THE *PRIDE OF CORELLIA* IS GONE!"
WE'LL MOURN LATER. ALL SHIPS -- PREPARE TO JUMP!
"JUMP!"
NO! THAT'S *IMPOSSIBLE!*

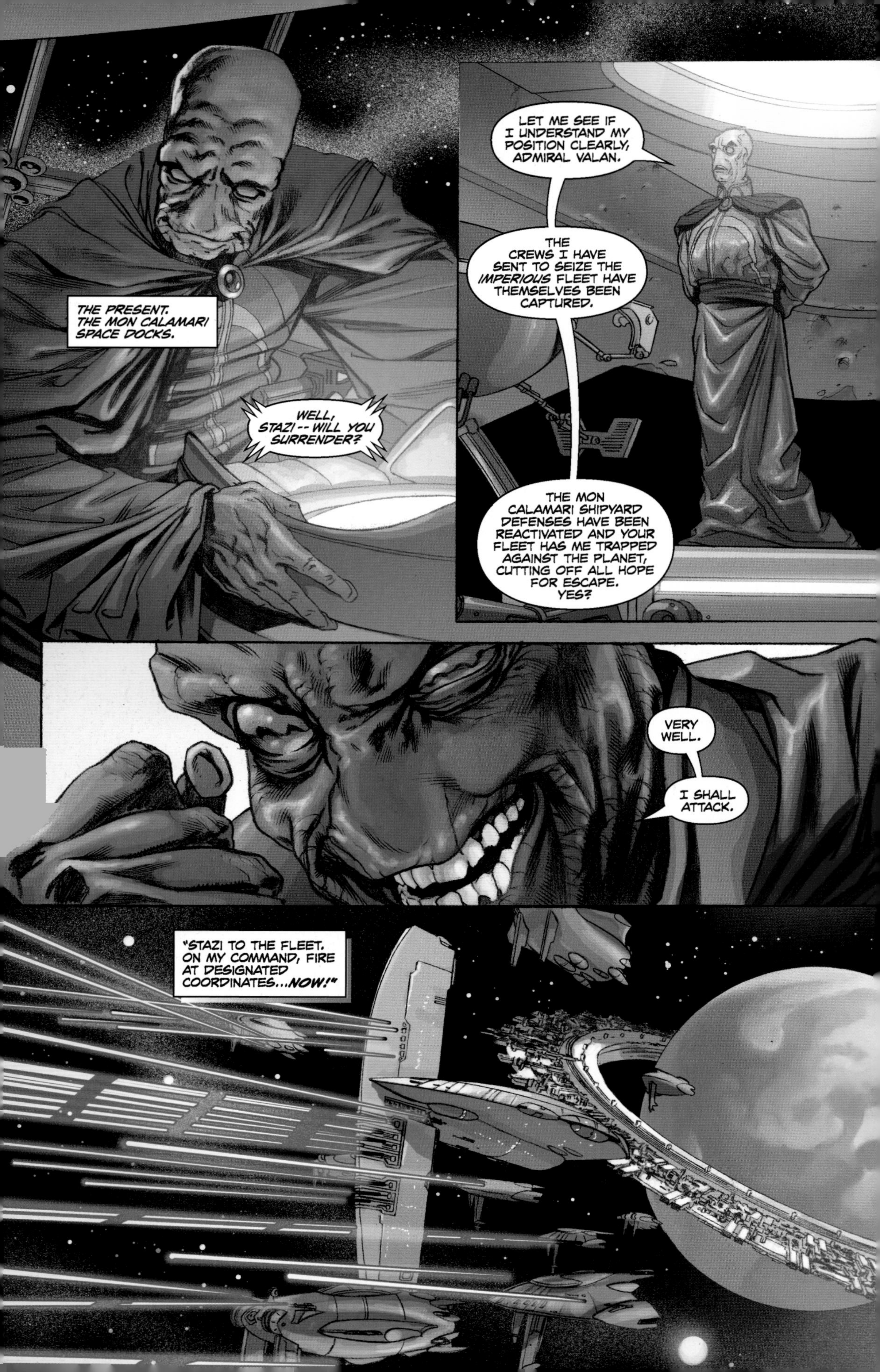
THE PRESENT. THE MON CALAMARI SPACE DOCKS.
WELL, STAZI -- WILL YOU SURRENDER?
LET ME SEE IF I UNDERSTAND MY POSITION CLEARLY, ADMIRAL VALAN.
THE CREWS I HAVE SENT TO SEIZE THE *IMPERIOUS* FLEET HAVE THEMSELVES BEEN CAPTURED.
THE MON CALAMARI SHIPYARD DEFENSES HAVE BEEN REACTIVATED AND YOUR FLEET HAS ME TRAPPED AGAINST THE PLANET, CUTTING OFF ALL HOPE FOR ESCAPE. YES?
VERY WELL.
I SHALL ATTACK.
"STAZI TO THE FLEET. ON MY COMMAND, FIRE AT DESIGNATED COORDINATES...*NOW!*"

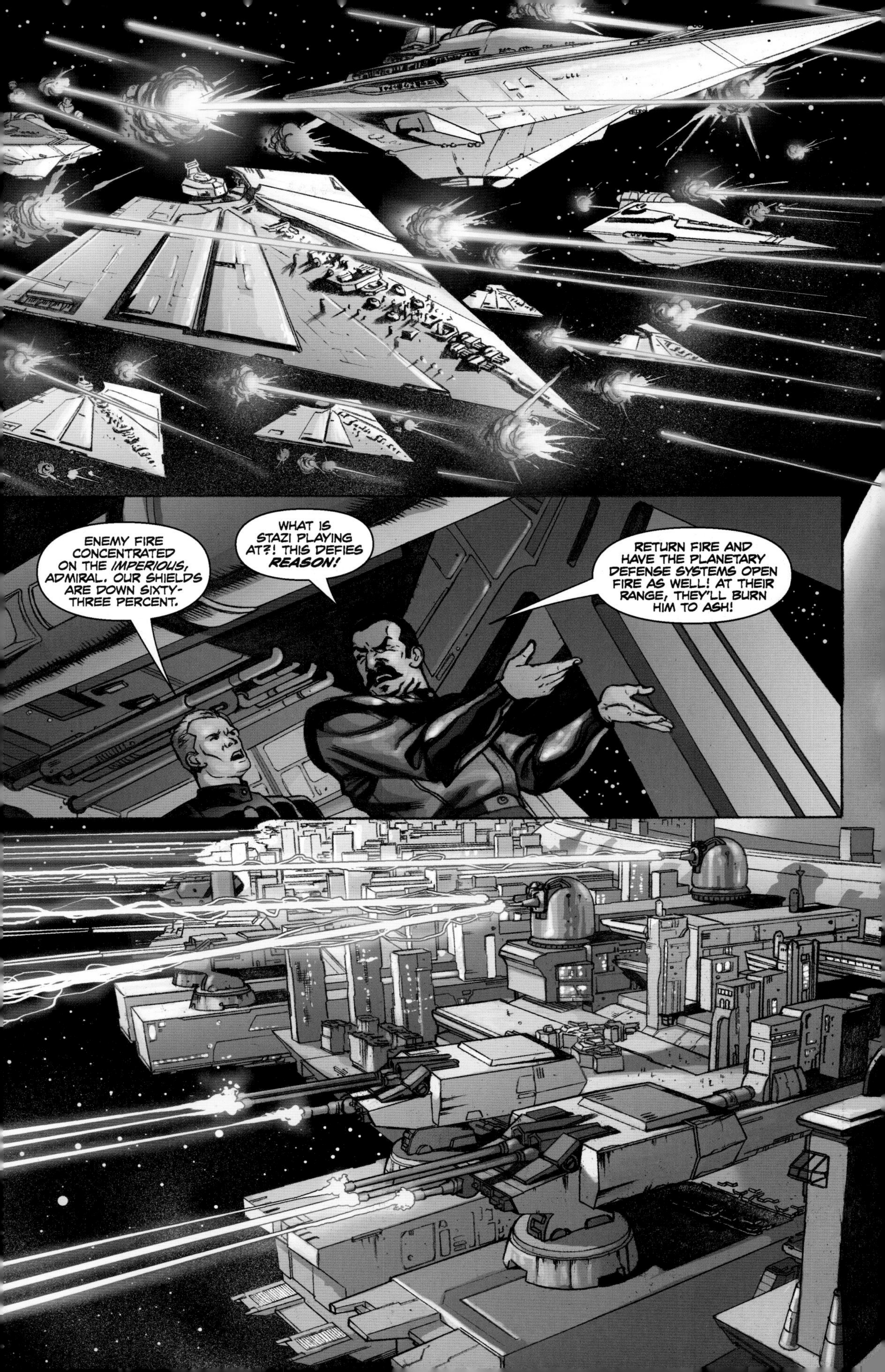
ENEMY FIRE CONCENTRATED ON THE *IMPERIOUS*, ADMIRAL. OUR SHIELDS ARE DOWN SIXTY-THREE PERCENT.
WHAT IS STAZI PLAYING AT?! THIS DEFIES ***REASON!***
RETURN FIRE AND HAVE THE PLANETARY DEFENSE SYSTEMS OPEN FIRE AS WELL! AT THEIR RANGE, THEY'LL BURN HIM TO ASH!

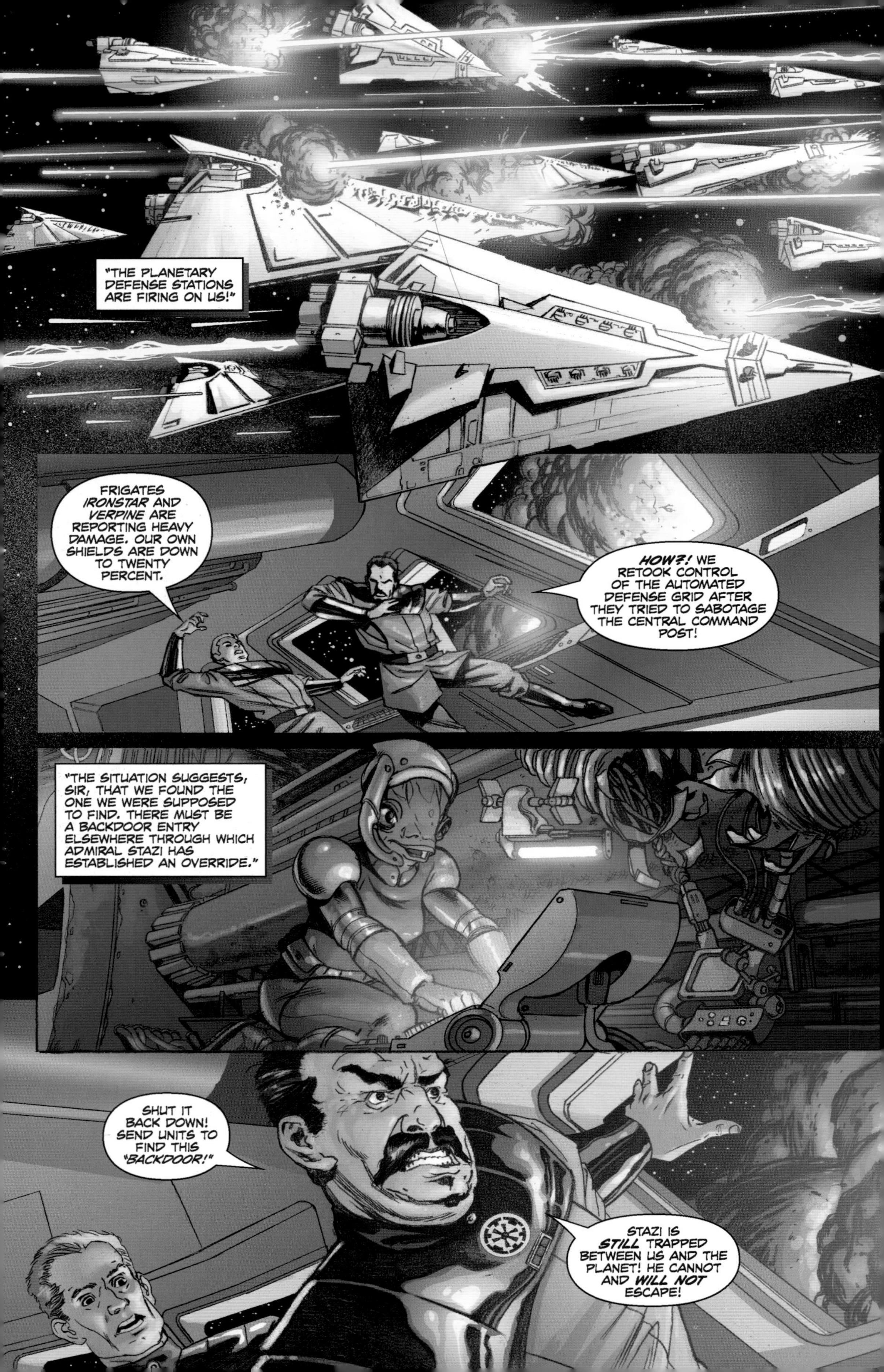
"THE PLANETARY DEFENSE STATIONS ARE FIRING ON US!"
FRIGATES *IRONSTAR* AND *VERPINE* ARE REPORTING HEAVY DAMAGE. OUR OWN SHIELDS ARE DOWN TO TWENTY PERCENT.
HOW?! WE RETOOK CONTROL OF THE AUTOMATED DEFENSE GRID AFTER THEY TRIED TO SABOTAGE THE CENTRAL COMMAND POST!
"THE SITUATION SUGGESTS, SIR, THAT WE FOUND THE ONE WE WERE SUPPOSED TO FIND. THERE MUST BE A BACKDOOR ENTRY ELSEWHERE THROUGH WHICH ADMIRAL STAZI HAS ESTABLISHED AN OVERRIDE."
SHUT IT BACK DOWN! SEND UNITS TO FIND THIS *"BACKDOOR!"*
STAZI IS *STILL* TRAPPED BETWEEN US AND THE PLANET! HE CANNOT AND *WILL NOT* ESCAPE!

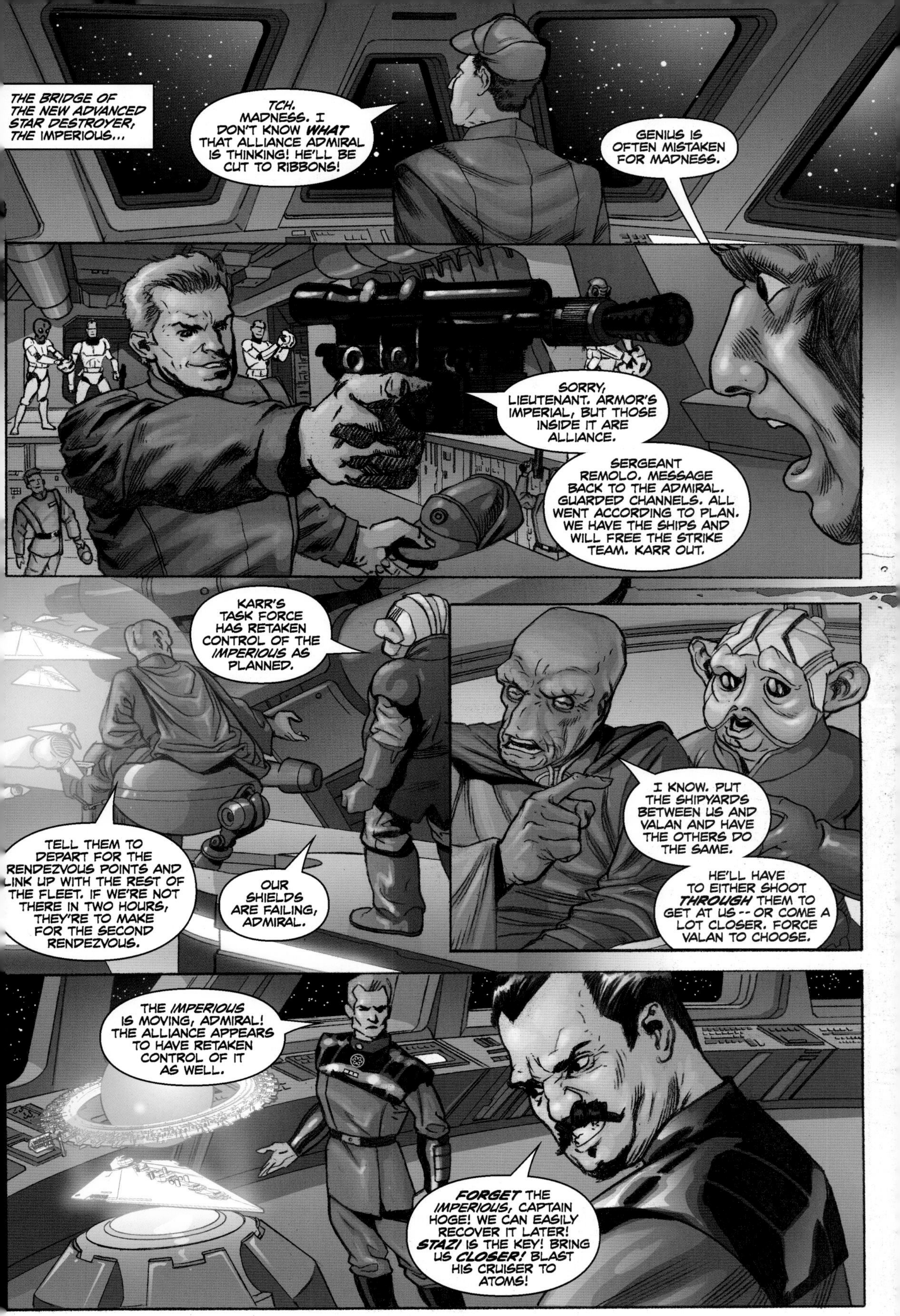
THE BRIDGE OF THE NEW ADVANCED STAR DESTROYER, THE IMPERIOUS...
TCH. MADNESS. I DON'T KNOW WHAT THAT ALLIANCE ADMIRAL IS THINKING! HE'LL BE CUT TO RIBBONS!
GENIUS IS OFTEN MISTAKEN FOR MADNESS.
SORRY, LIEUTENANT. ARMOR'S IMPERIAL, BUT THOSE INSIDE IT ARE ALLIANCE.
SERGEANT REMOLO. MESSAGE BACK TO THE ADMIRAL. GUARDED CHANNELS. ALL WENT ACCORDING TO PLAN. WE HAVE THE SHIPS AND WILL FREE THE STRIKE TEAM. KARR OUT.
KARR'S TASK FORCE HAS RETAKEN CONTROL OF THE IMPERIOUS AS PLANNED.
TELL THEM TO DEPART FOR THE RENDEZVOUS POINTS AND LINK UP WITH THE REST OF THE FLEET. IF WE'RE NOT THERE IN TWO HOURS, THEY'RE TO MAKE FOR THE SECOND RENDEZVOUS.
OUR SHIELDS ARE FAILING, ADMIRAL.
I KNOW. PUT THE SHIPYARDS BETWEEN US AND VALAN AND HAVE THE OTHERS DO THE SAME.
HE'LL HAVE TO EITHER SHOOT THROUGH THEM TO GET AT US -- OR COME A LOT CLOSER. FORCE VALAN TO CHOOSE.
THE IMPERIOUS IS MOVING, ADMIRAL! THE ALLIANCE APPEARS TO HAVE RETAKEN CONTROL OF IT AS WELL.
FORGET THE IMPERIOUS, CAPTAIN HOGE! WE CAN EASILY RECOVER IT LATER! STAZI IS THE KEY! BRING US CLOSER! BLAST HIS CRUISER TO ATOMS!

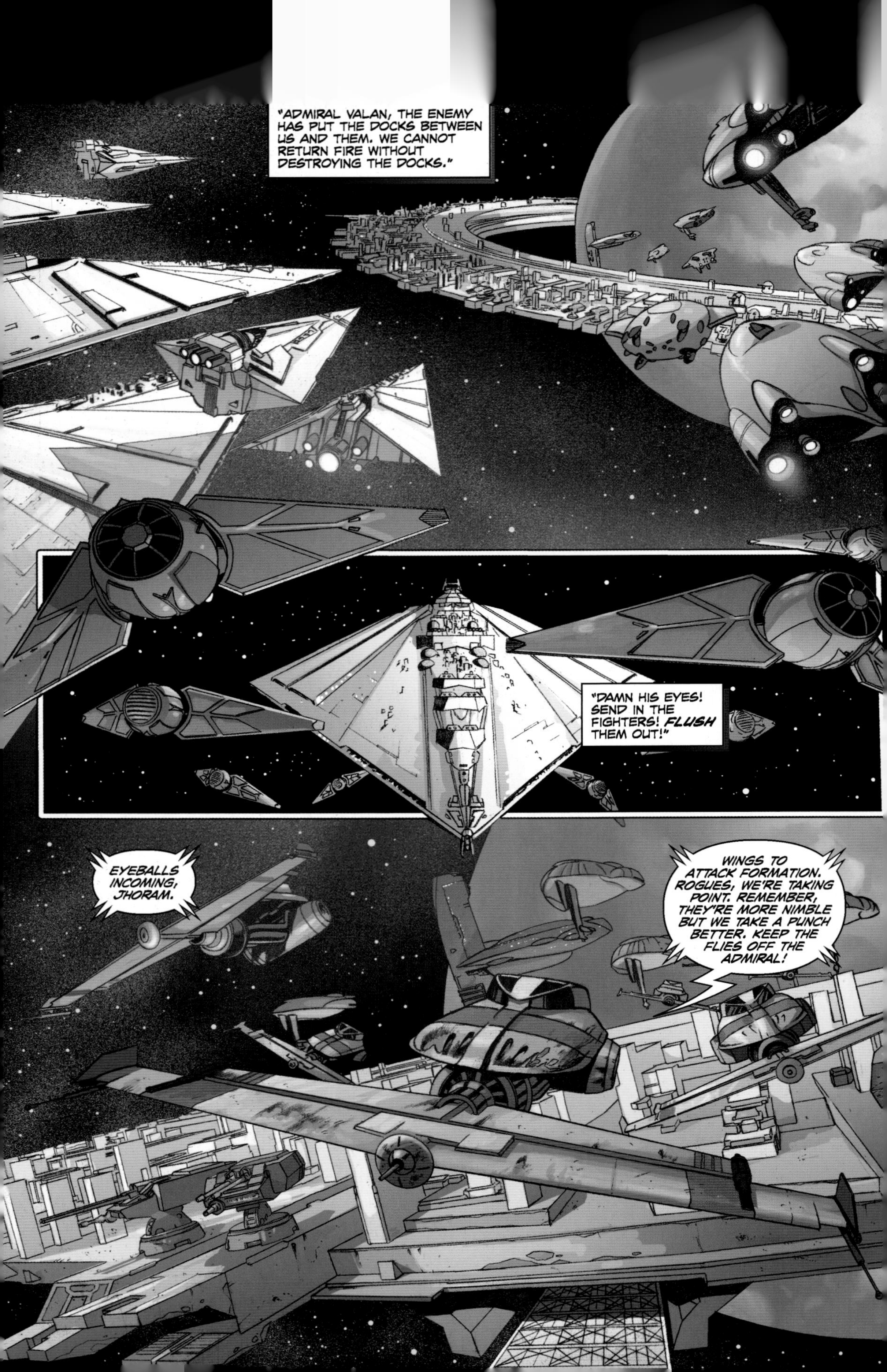
"ADMIRAL VALAN, THE ENEMY HAS PUT THE DOCKS BETWEEN US AND THEM. WE CANNOT RETURN FIRE WITHOUT DESTROYING THE DOCKS."
"DAMN HIS EYES! SEND IN THE FIGHTERS! FLUSH THEM OUT!"
EYEBALLS INCOMING, JHORAM.
WINGS TO ATTACK FORMATION. ROGUES, WE'RE TAKING POINT. REMEMBER, THEY'RE MORE NIMBLE BUT WE TAKE A PUNCH BETTER. KEEP THE FLIES OFF THE ADMIRAL!

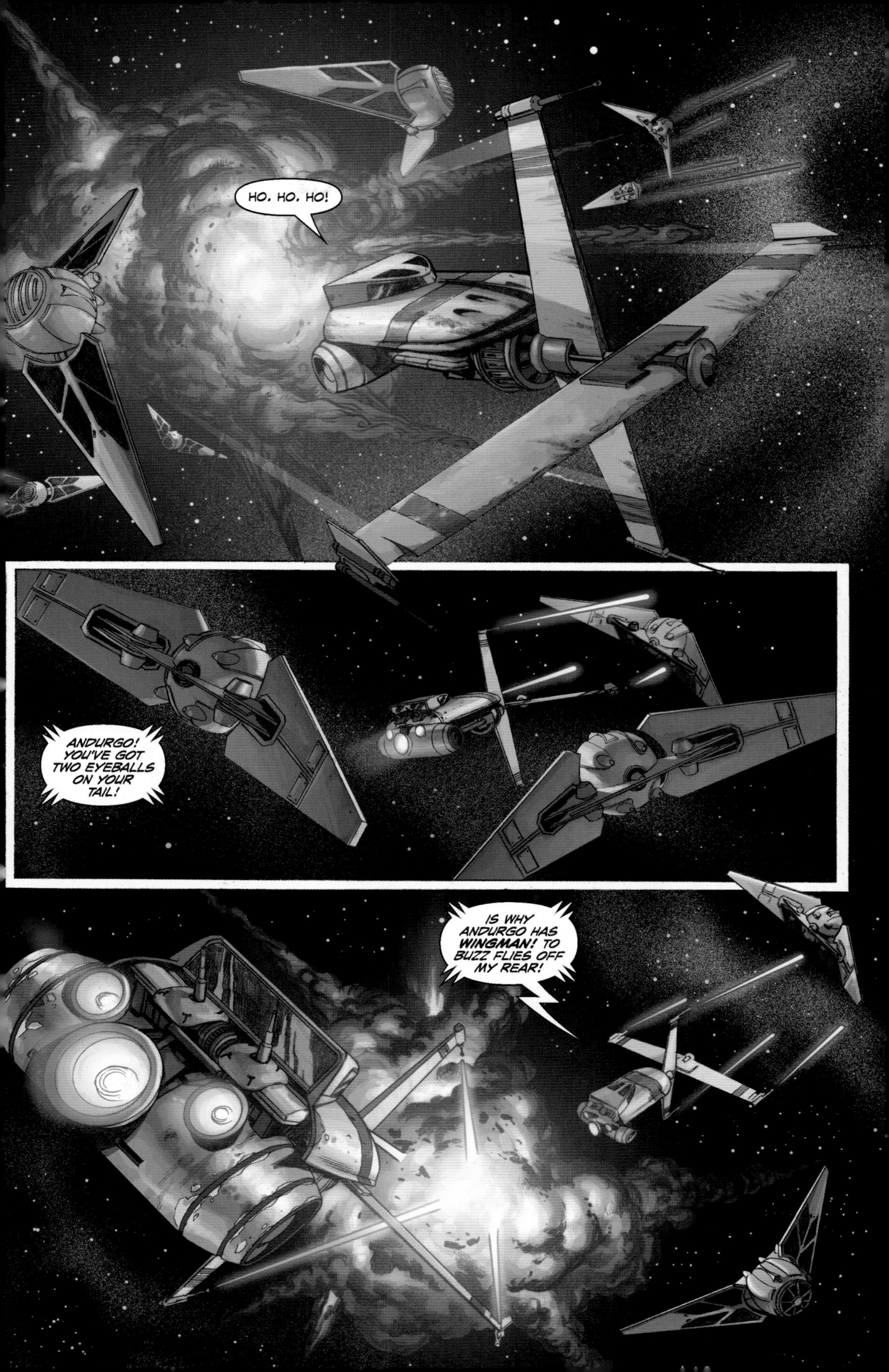
HO. HO. HO!
ANDURGO! YOU'VE GOT TWO EYEBALLS ON YOUR TAIL!
IS WHY ANDURGO HAS **WINGMAN!** TO BUZZ FLIES OFF MY REAR!

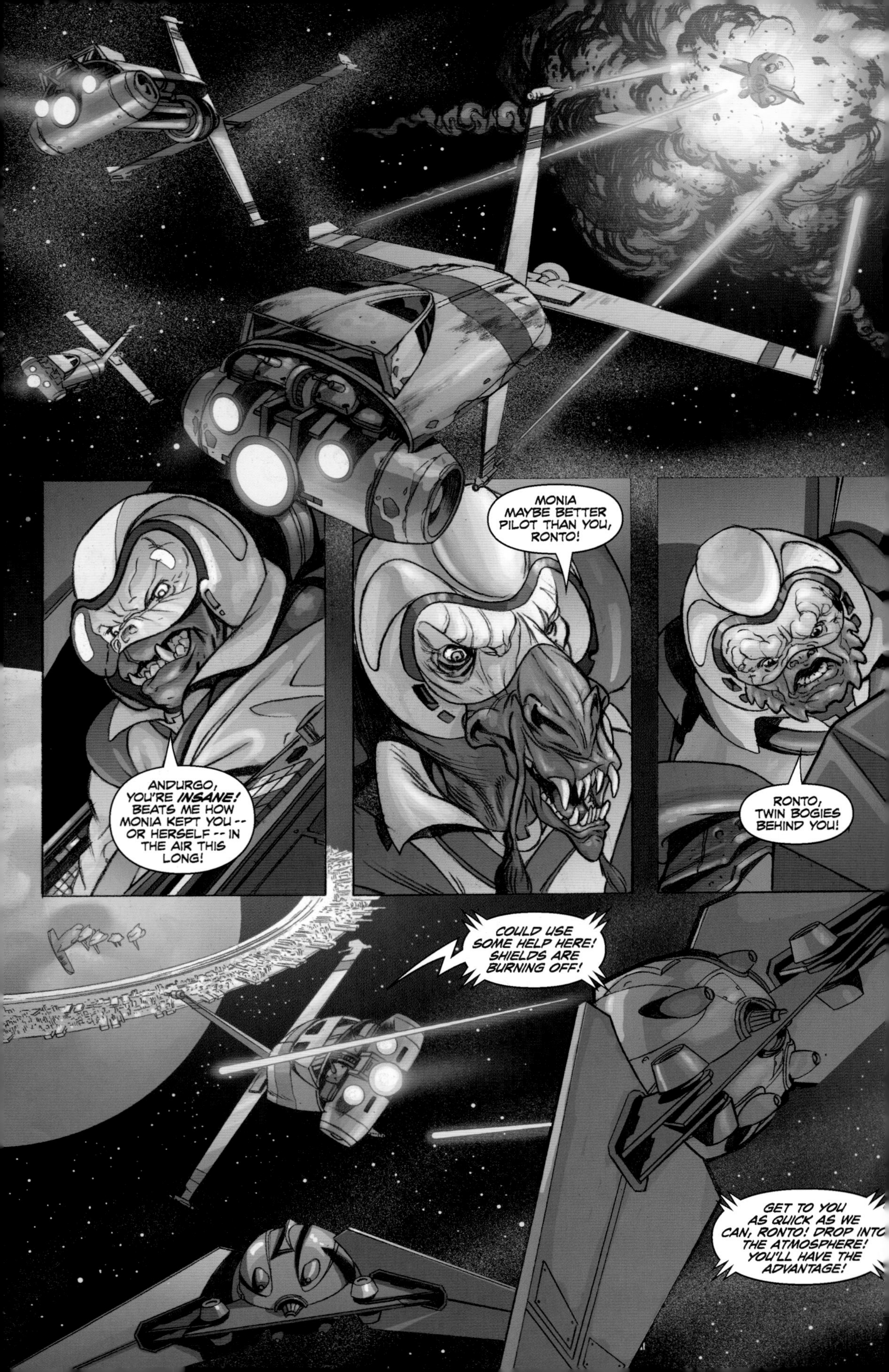
ANDURGO, YOU'RE *INSANE!* BEATS ME HOW MONIA KEPT YOU -- OR HERSELF -- IN THE AIR THIS LONG!
MONIA MAYBE BETTER PILOT THAN YOU, RONTO!
RONTO, TWIN BOGIES BEHIND YOU!
COULD USE SOME HELP HERE! SHIELDS ARE BURNING OFF!
GET TO YOU AS QUICK AS WE CAN, RONTO! DROP INTO THE ATMOSPHERE! YOU'LL HAVE THE ADVANTAGE!

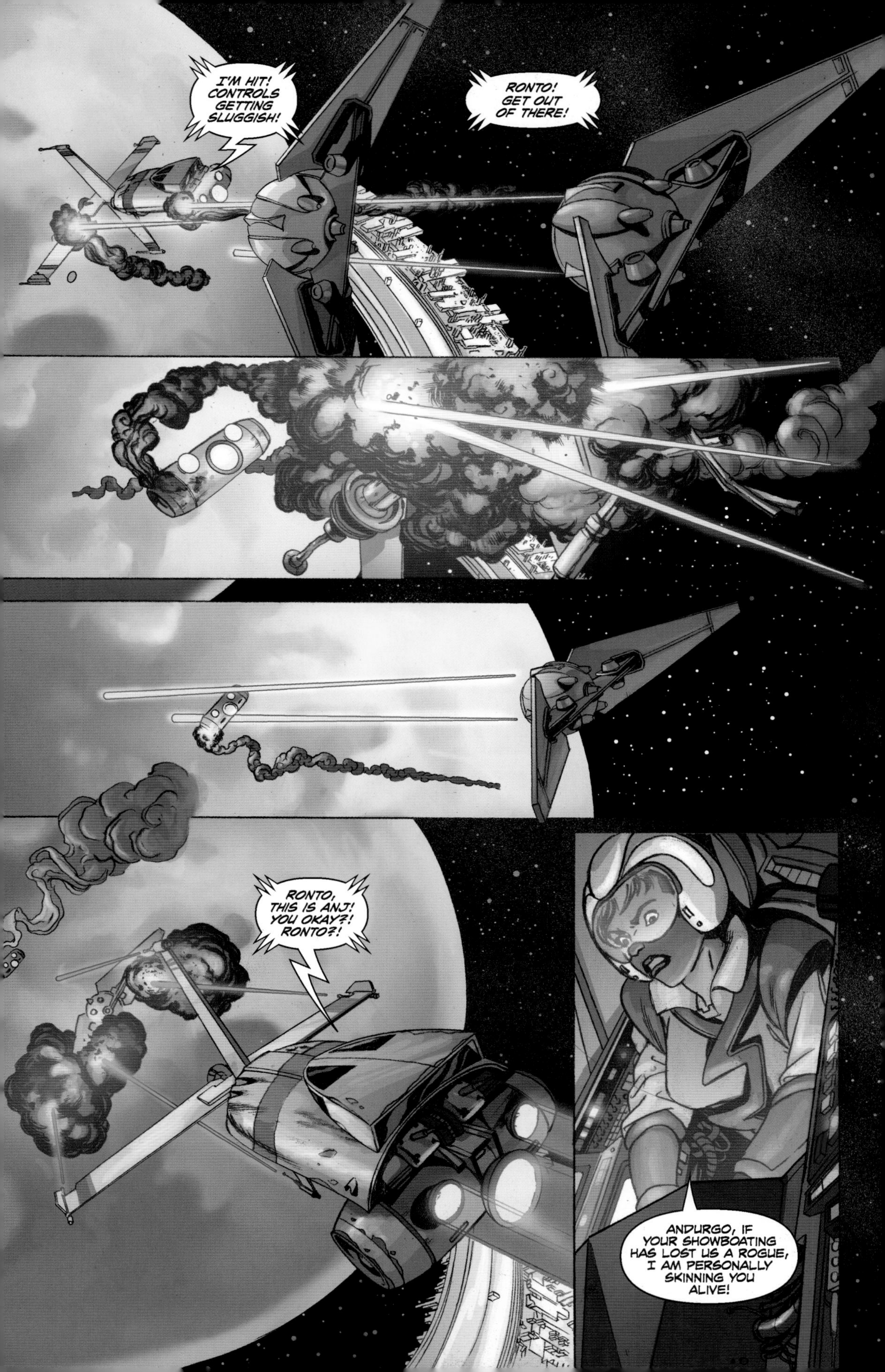
I'M HIT! CONTROLS GETTING SLUGGISH!
RONTO! GET OUT OF THERE!
RONTO, THIS IS ANJ! YOU OKAY?! RONTO?!
ANDURGO, IF YOUR SHOWBOATING HAS LOST US A ROGUE, I AM PERSONALLY SKINNING YOU ALIVE!

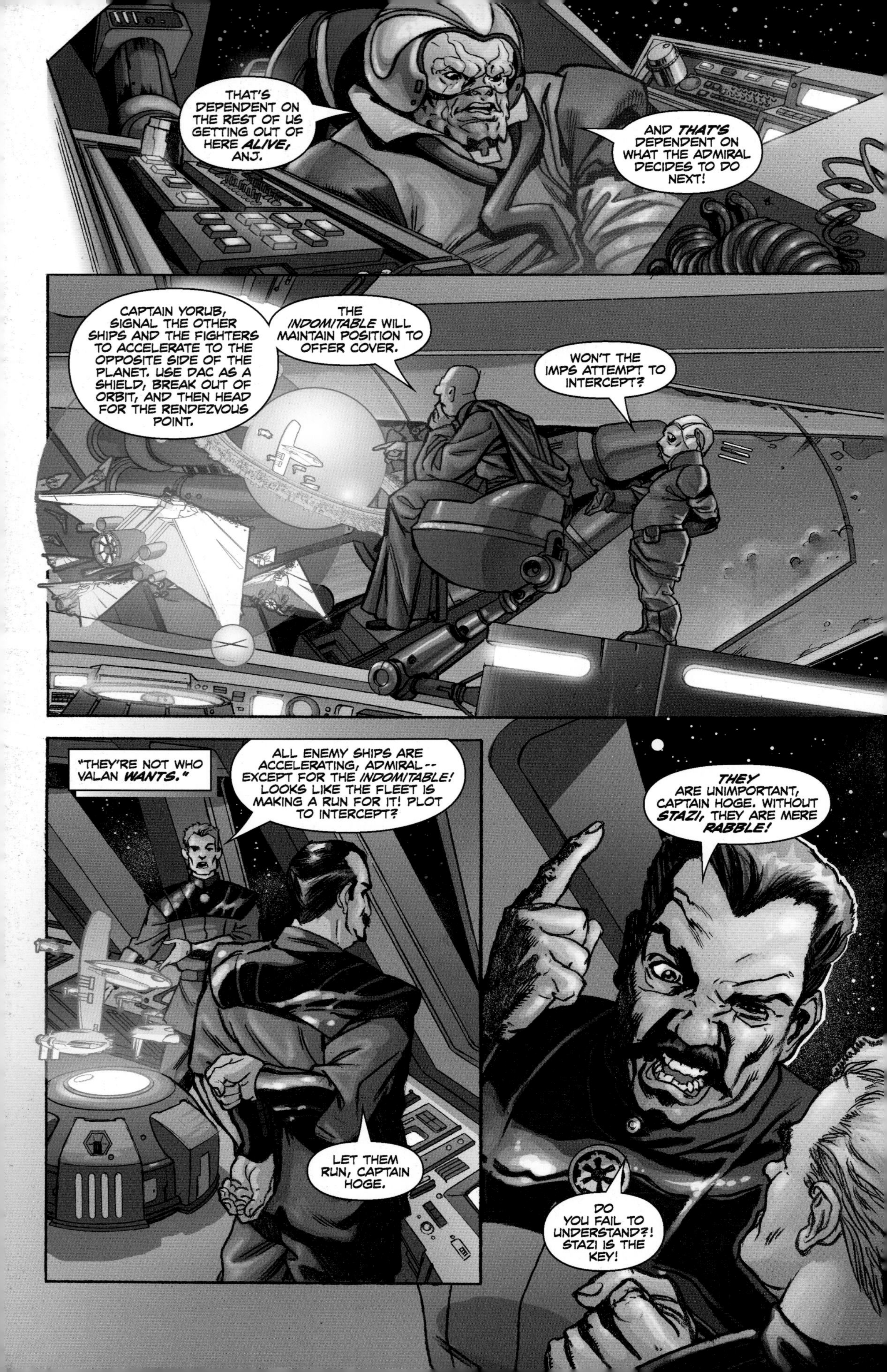
THAT'S DEPENDENT ON THE REST OF US GETTING OUT OF HERE ALIVE, ANJ.
AND THAT'S DEPENDENT ON WHAT THE ADMIRAL DECIDES TO DO NEXT!
CAPTAIN YORUB, SIGNAL THE OTHER SHIPS AND THE FIGHTERS TO ACCELERATE TO THE OPPOSITE SIDE OF THE PLANET. USE DAC AS A SHIELD, BREAK OUT OF ORBIT, AND THEN HEAD FOR THE RENDEZVOUS POINT.
THE INDOMITABLE WILL MAINTAIN POSITION TO OFFER COVER.
WON'T THE IMPS ATTEMPT TO INTERCEPT?
"THEY'RE NOT WHO VALAN WANTS."
ALL ENEMY SHIPS ARE ACCELERATING, ADMIRAL-- EXCEPT FOR THE INDOMITABLE! LOOKS LIKE THE FLEET IS MAKING A RUN FOR IT! PLOT TO INTERCEPT?
LET THEM RUN, CAPTAIN HOGE.
THEY ARE UNIMPORTANT, CAPTAIN HOGE. WITHOUT STAZI, THEY ARE MERE RABBLE!
DO YOU FAIL TO UNDERSTAND?! STAZI IS THE KEY!

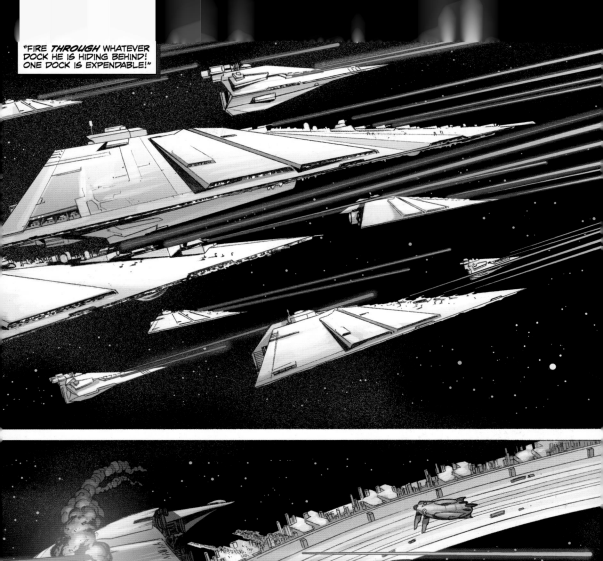

"FIRE *THROUGH* WHATEVER DOCK HE IS HIDING BEHIND! ONE DOCK IS EXPENDABLE!"

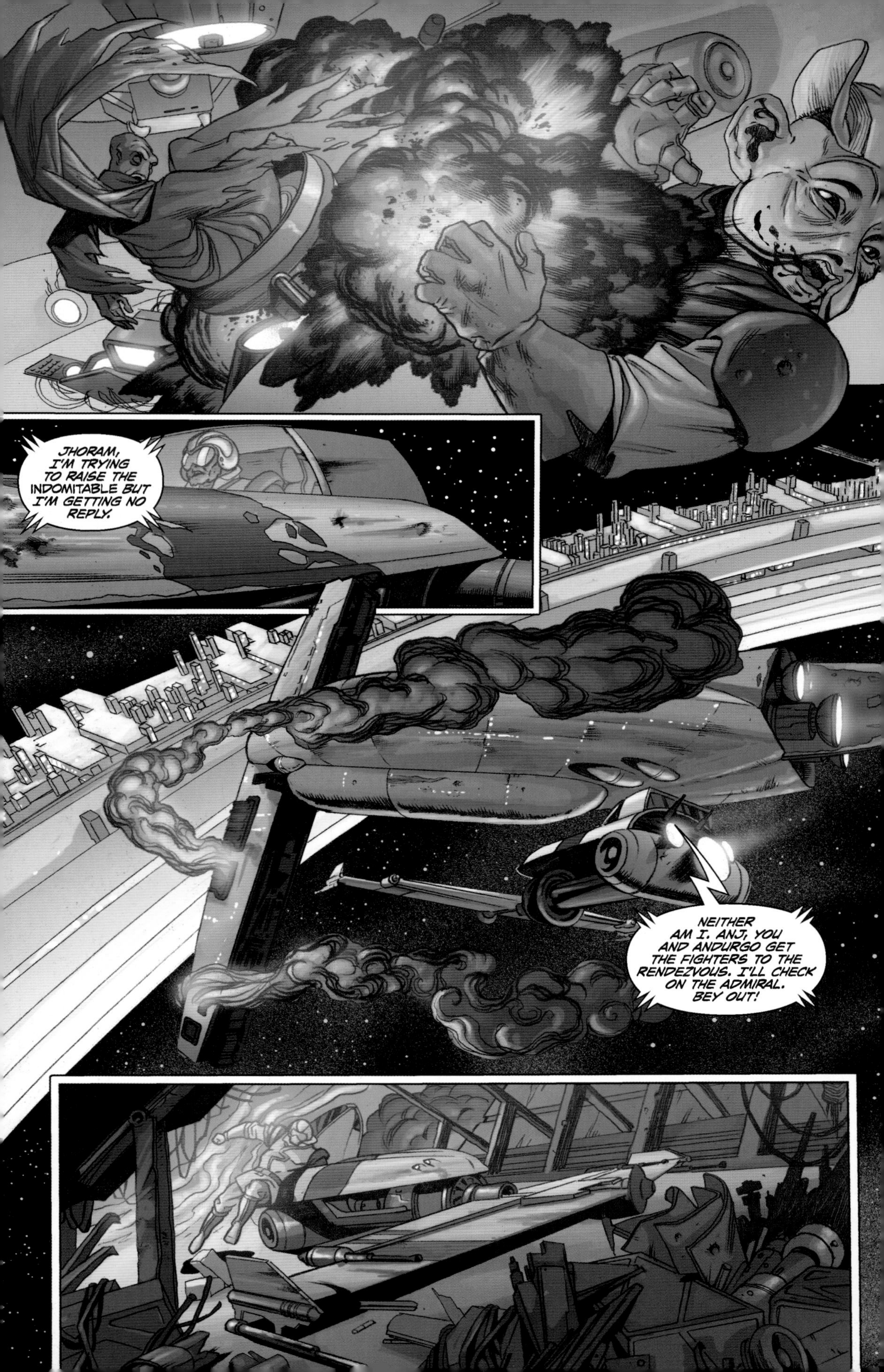
JHORAM, I'M TRYING TO RAISE THE INDOMITABLE BUT I'M GETTING NO REPLY.
NEITHER AM I. ANJ, YOU AND ANDURGO GET THE FIGHTERS TO THE RENDEZVOUS. I'LL CHECK ON THE ADMIRAL. BEY OUT!

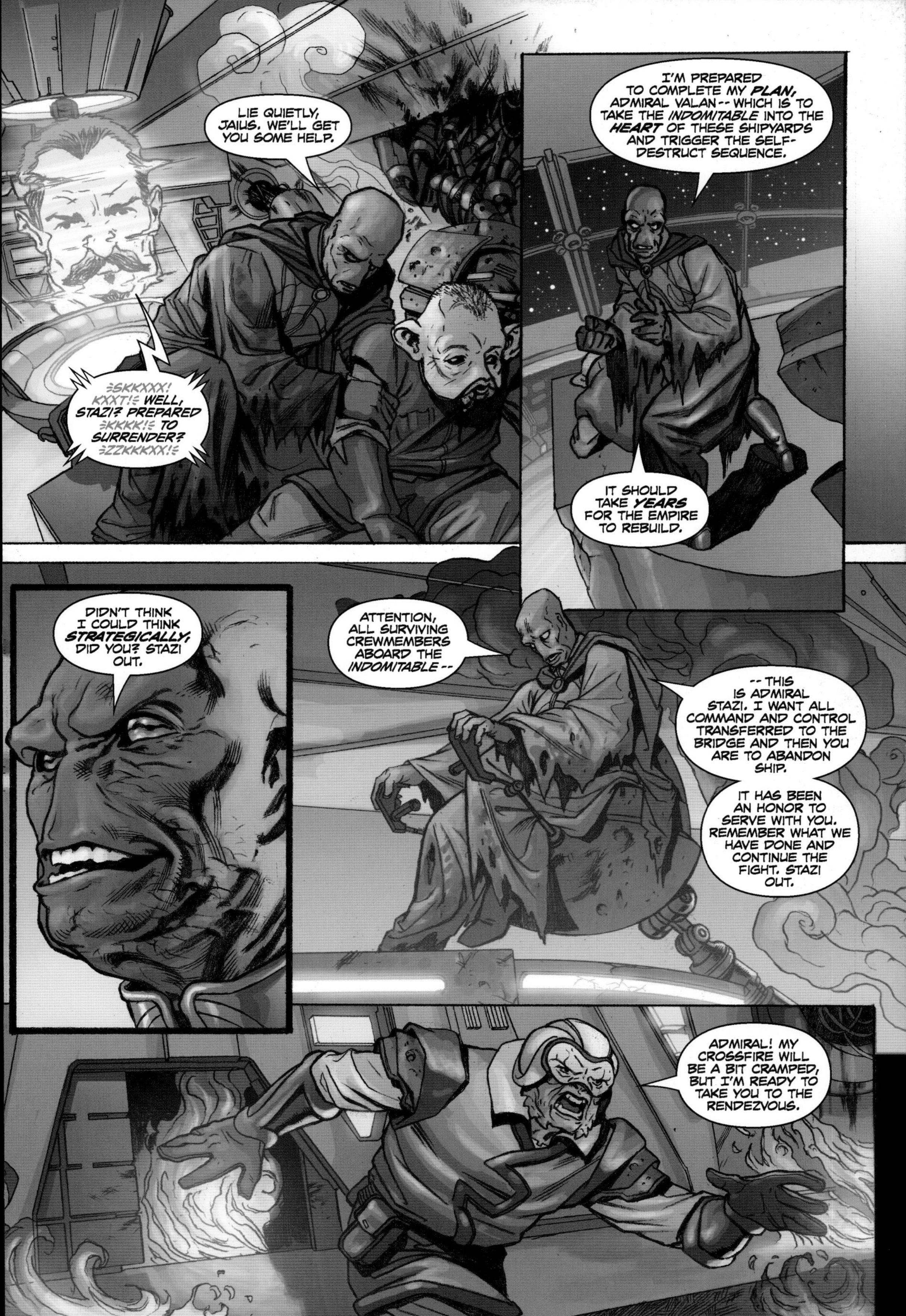

LIE QUIETLY, JAIUS. WE'LL GET YOU SOME HELP.
≡SKKXXX! KXXT!≡ WELL, STAZI? PREPARED ≡KKKK!≡ TO SURRENDER? ≡ZZKKKXX!≡
I'M PREPARED TO COMPLETE MY PLAN, ADMIRAL VALAN -- WHICH IS TO TAKE THE INDOMITABLE INTO THE HEART OF THESE SHIPYARDS AND TRIGGER THE SELF-DESTRUCT SEQUENCE.
IT SHOULD TAKE YEARS FOR THE EMPIRE TO REBUILD.
DIDN'T THINK I COULD THINK STRATEGICALLY, DID YOU? STAZI OUT.
ATTENTION, ALL SURVIVING CREWMEMBERS ABOARD THE INDOMITABLE --
-- THIS IS ADMIRAL STAZI. I WANT ALL COMMAND AND CONTROL TRANSFERRED TO THE BRIDGE AND THEN YOU ARE TO ABANDON SHIP.
IT HAS BEEN AN HONOR TO SERVE WITH YOU. REMEMBER WHAT WE HAVE DONE AND CONTINUE THE FIGHT. STAZI OUT.
ADMIRAL! MY CROSSFIRE WILL BE A BIT CRAMPED, BUT I'M READY TO TAKE YOU TO THE RENDEZVOUS.

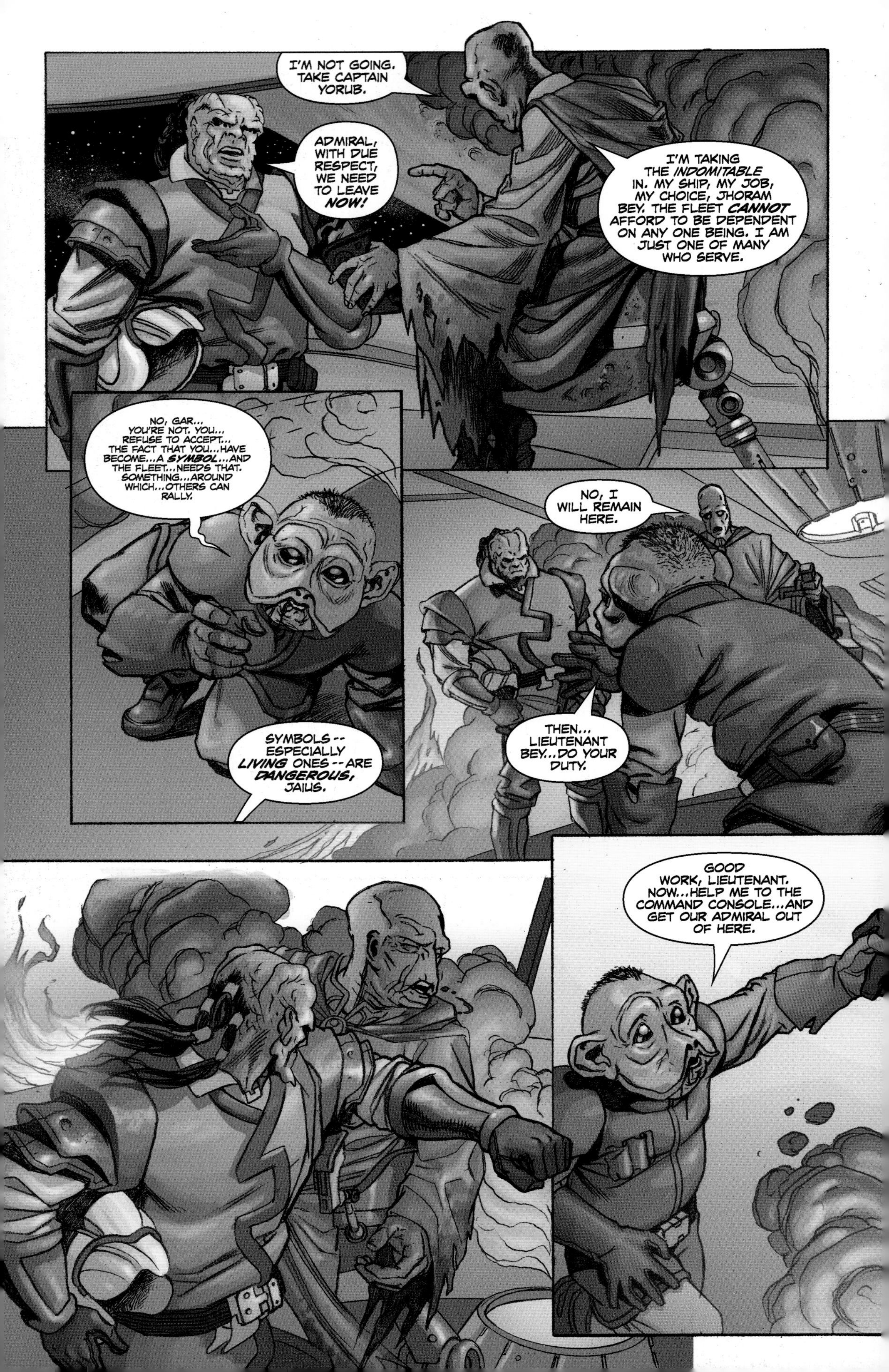
I'M NOT GOING. TAKE CAPTAIN YORUB.
ADMIRAL, WITH DUE RESPECT, WE NEED TO LEAVE NOW!
I'M TAKING THE INDOMITABLE IN. MY SHIP, MY JOB, MY CHOICE, JHORAM BEY. THE FLEET CANNOT AFFORD TO BE DEPENDENT ON ANY ONE BEING. I AM JUST ONE OF MANY WHO SERVE.
NO, GAR... YOU'RE NOT. YOU... REFUSE TO ACCEPT... THE FACT THAT YOU...HAVE BECOME...A SYMBOL...AND THE FLEET...NEEDS THAT. SOMETHING...AROUND WHICH...OTHERS CAN RALLY.
SYMBOLS -- ESPECIALLY LIVING ONES -- ARE DANGEROUS, JAIUS.
NO, I WILL REMAIN HERE.
THEN... LIEUTENANT BEY...DO YOUR DUTY.
GOOD WORK, LIEUTENANT. NOW...HELP ME TO THE COMMAND CONSOLE...AND GET OUR ADMIRAL OUT OF HERE.

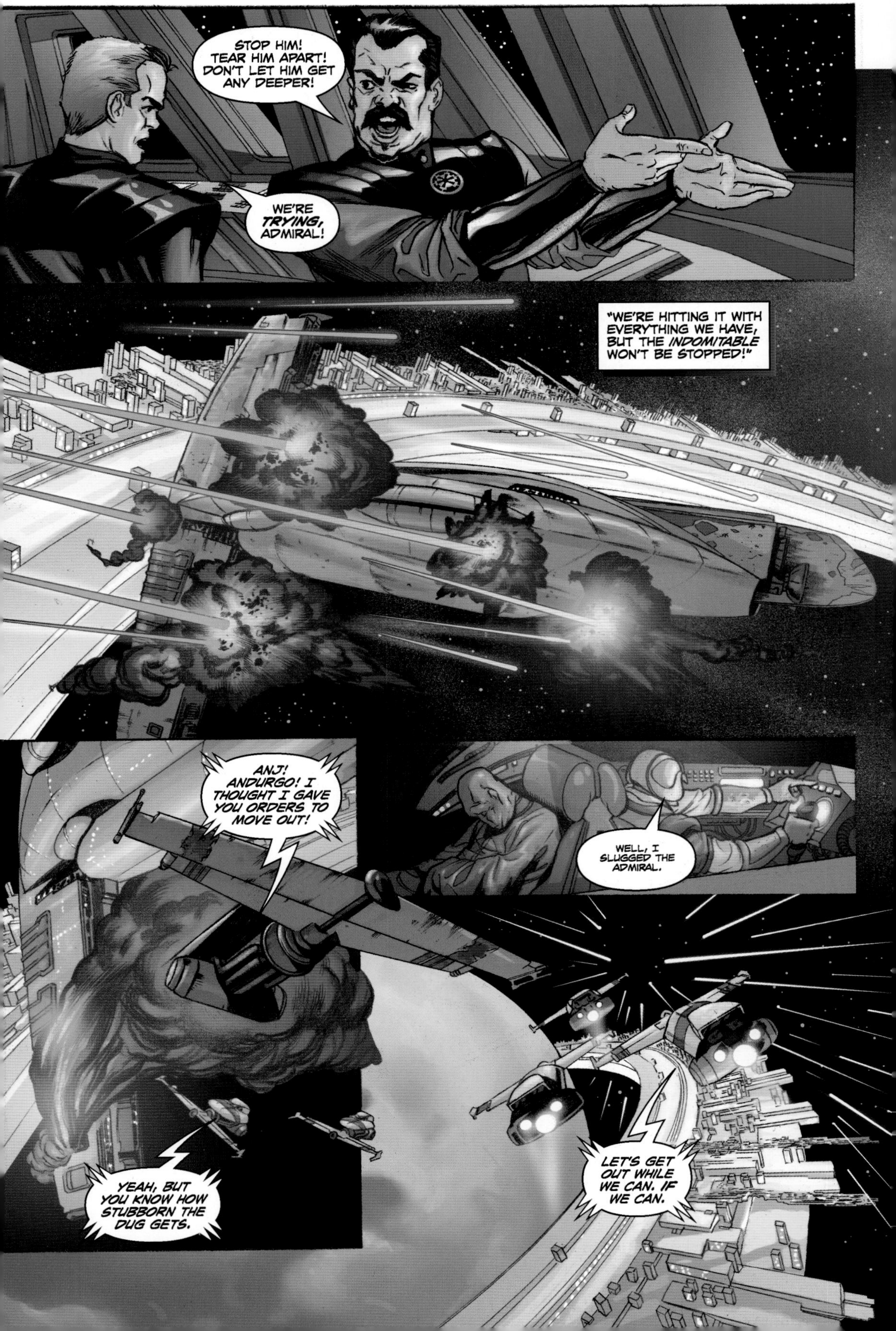
STOP HIM! TEAR HIM APART! DON'T LET HIM GET ANY DEEPER!
WE'RE *TRYING*, ADMIRAL!
"WE'RE HITTING IT WITH EVERYTHING WE HAVE, BUT THE *INDOMITABLE* WON'T BE STOPPED!"
ANJ! ANDURGO! I THOUGHT I GAVE YOU ORDERS TO MOVE OUT!
WELL, I SLUGGED THE ADMIRAL.
YEAH, BUT YOU KNOW HOW STUBBORN THE DUG GETS.
LET'S GET OUT WHILE WE CAN. IF WE CAN.

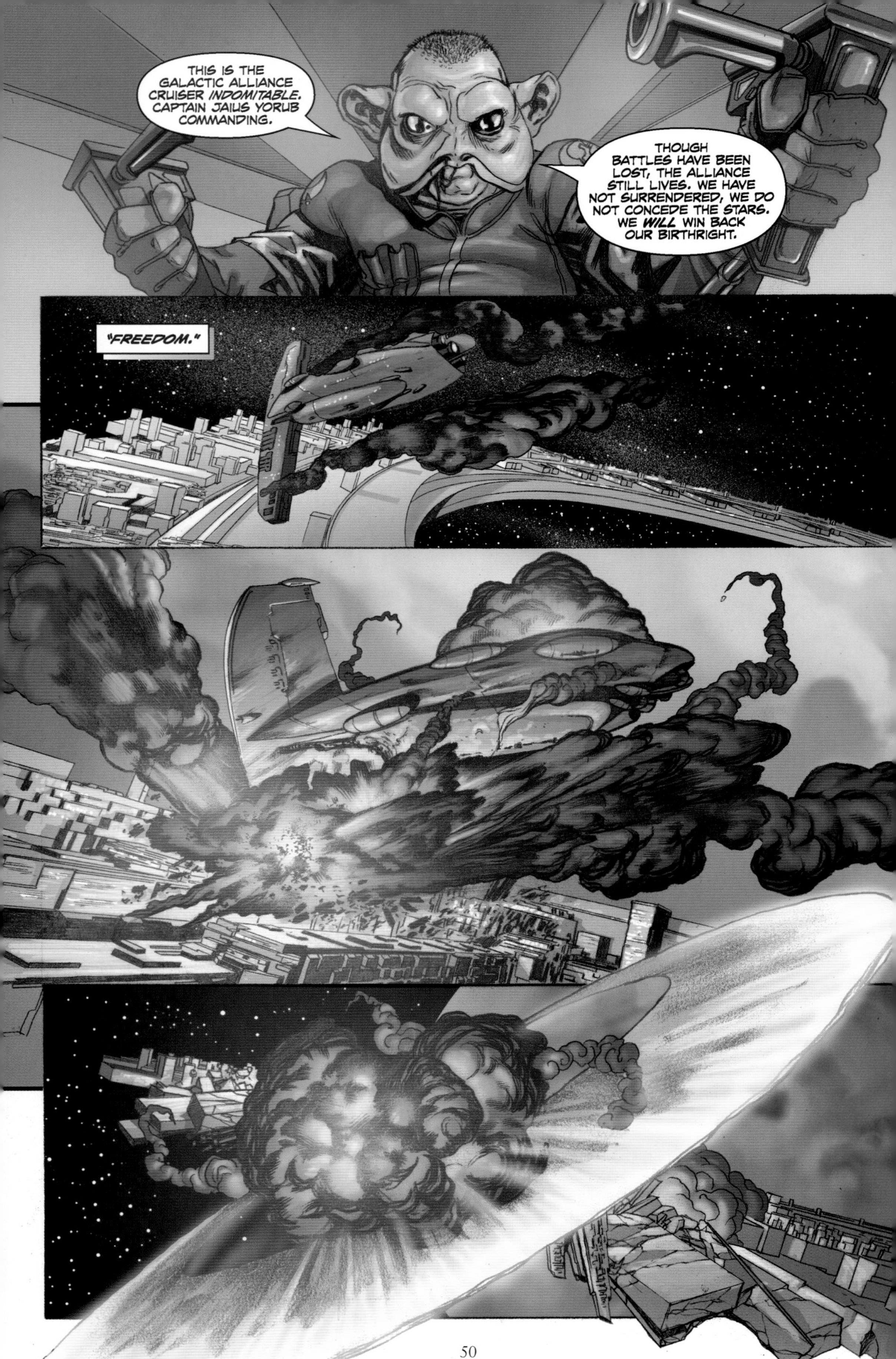
THIS IS THE GALACTIC ALLIANCE CRUISER *INDOMITABLE*. CAPTAIN JAIUS YORUB COMMANDING.
THOUGH BATTLES HAVE BEEN LOST, THE ALLIANCE STILL LIVES. WE HAVE NOT SURRENDERED, WE DO NOT CONCEDE THE STARS. WE ***WILL*** WIN BACK OUR BIRTHRIGHT.
"FREEDOM."

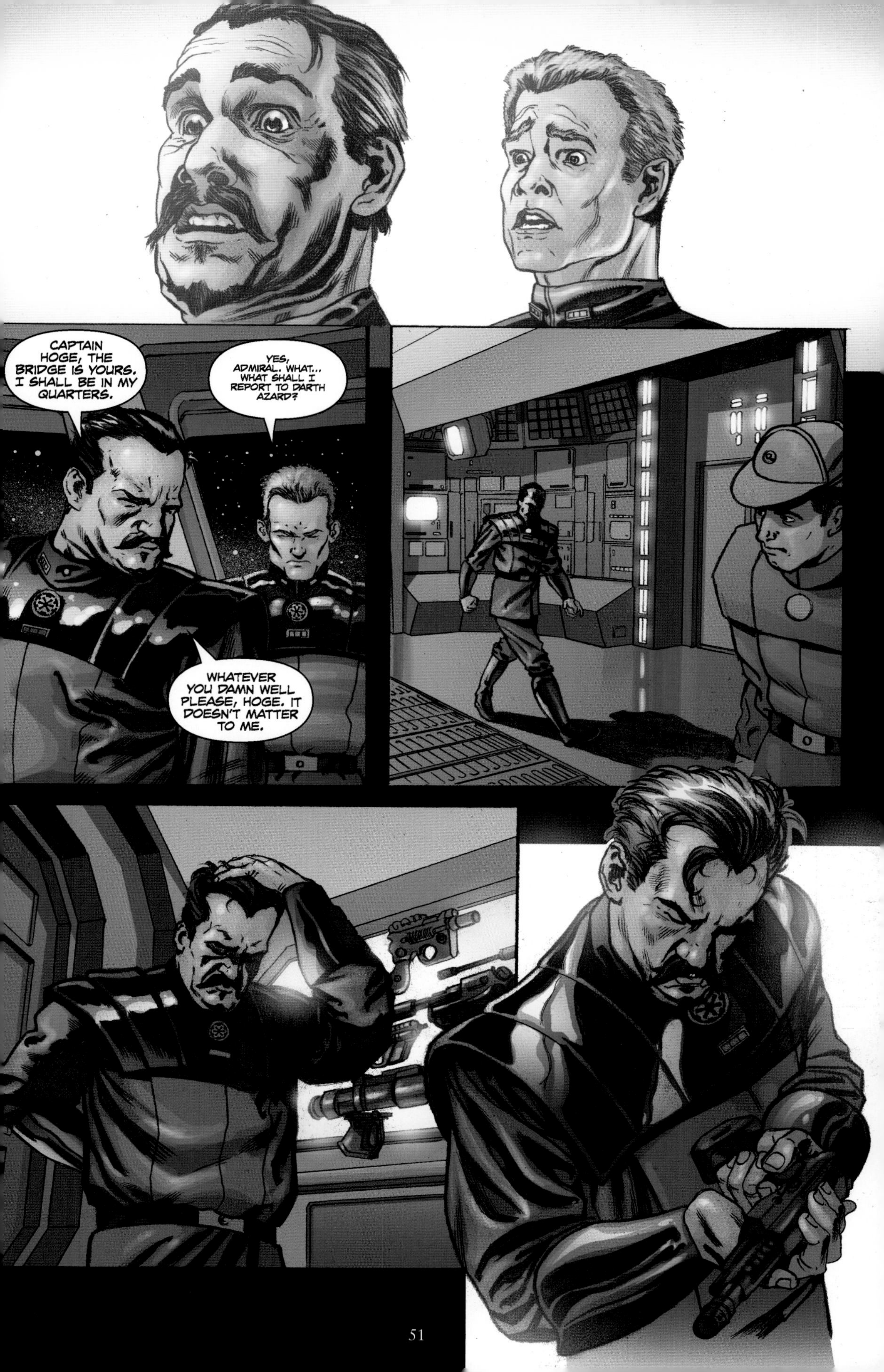
CAPTAIN HOGE, THE BRIDGE IS YOURS. I SHALL BE IN MY QUARTERS.
YES, ADMIRAL. WHAT... WHAT SHALL I REPORT TO DARTH AZARD?
WHATEVER YOU DAMN WELL PLEASE, HOGE. IT DOESN'T MATTER TO ME.

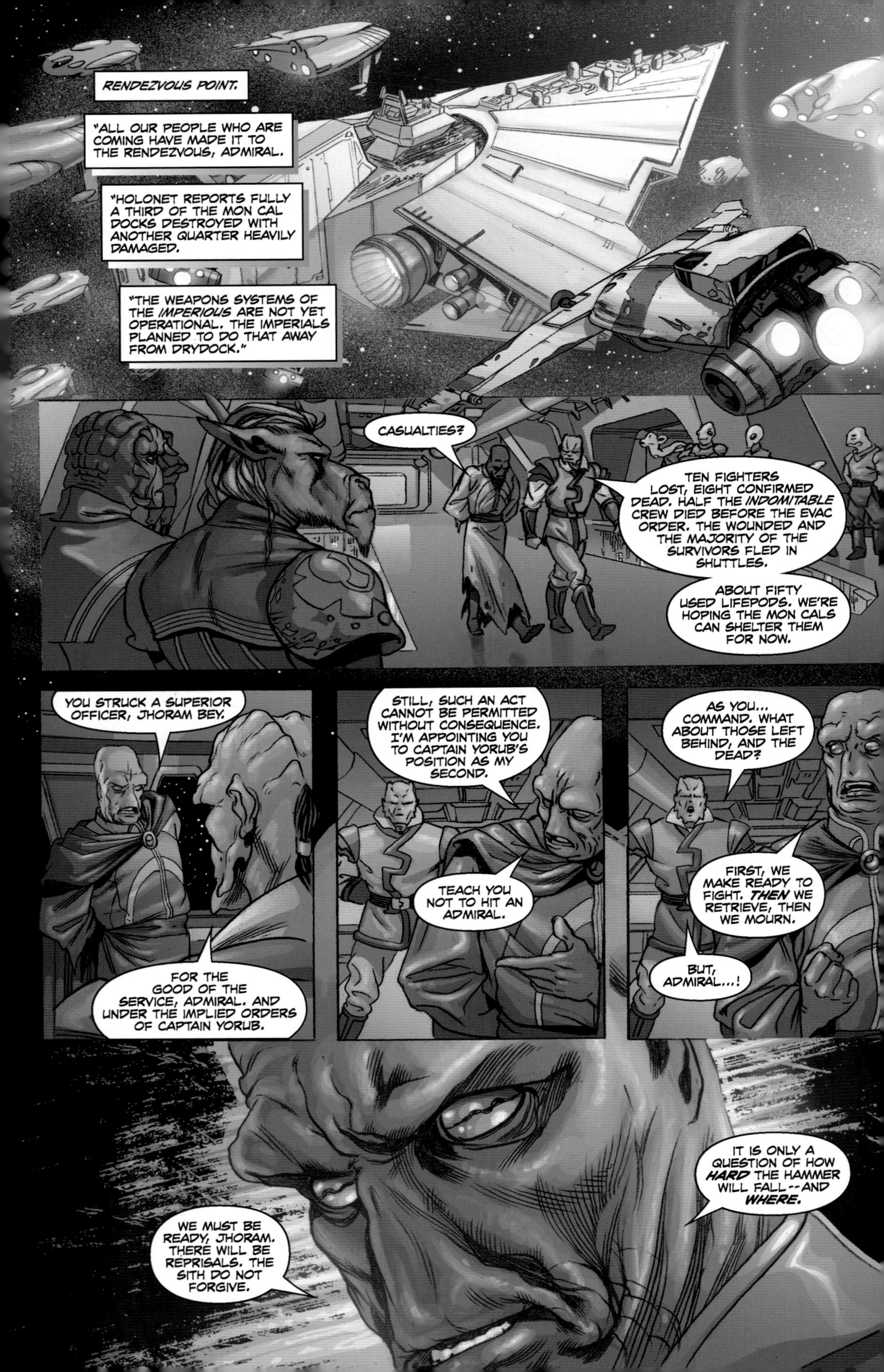
RENDEZVOUS POINT.
"ALL OUR PEOPLE WHO ARE COMING HAVE MADE IT TO THE RENDEZVOUS, ADMIRAL.
"HOLONET REPORTS FULLY A THIRD OF THE MON CAL DOCKS DESTROYED WITH ANOTHER QUARTER HEAVILY DAMAGED.
"THE WEAPONS SYSTEMS OF THE *IMPERIOUS* ARE NOT YET OPERATIONAL. THE IMPERIALS PLANNED TO DO THAT AWAY FROM DRYDOCK."
CASUALTIES?
TEN FIGHTERS LOST, EIGHT CONFIRMED DEAD. HALF THE *INDOMITABLE* CREW DIED BEFORE THE EVAC ORDER. THE WOUNDED AND THE MAJORITY OF THE SURVIVORS FLED IN SHUTTLES.
ABOUT FIFTY USED LIFEPODS. WE'RE HOPING THE MON CALS CAN SHELTER THEM FOR NOW.
YOU STRUCK A SUPERIOR OFFICER, JHORAM BEY.
FOR THE GOOD OF THE SERVICE, ADMIRAL. AND UNDER THE IMPLIED ORDERS OF CAPTAIN YORUB.
STILL, SUCH AN ACT CANNOT BE PERMITTED WITHOUT CONSEQUENCE. I'M APPOINTING YOU TO CAPTAIN YORUB'S POSITION AS MY SECOND.
TEACH YOU NOT TO HIT AN ADMIRAL.
AS YOU... COMMAND. WHAT ABOUT THOSE LEFT BEHIND, AND THE DEAD?
FIRST, WE MAKE READY TO FIGHT. ***THEN*** WE RETRIEVE, THEN WE MOURN.
BUT, ADMIRAL...!
WE MUST BE READY, JHORAM. THERE WILL BE REPRISALS. THE SITH DO NOT FORGIVE.
IT IS ONLY A QUESTION OF HOW ***HARD*** THE HAMMER WILL FALL--AND ***WHERE.***

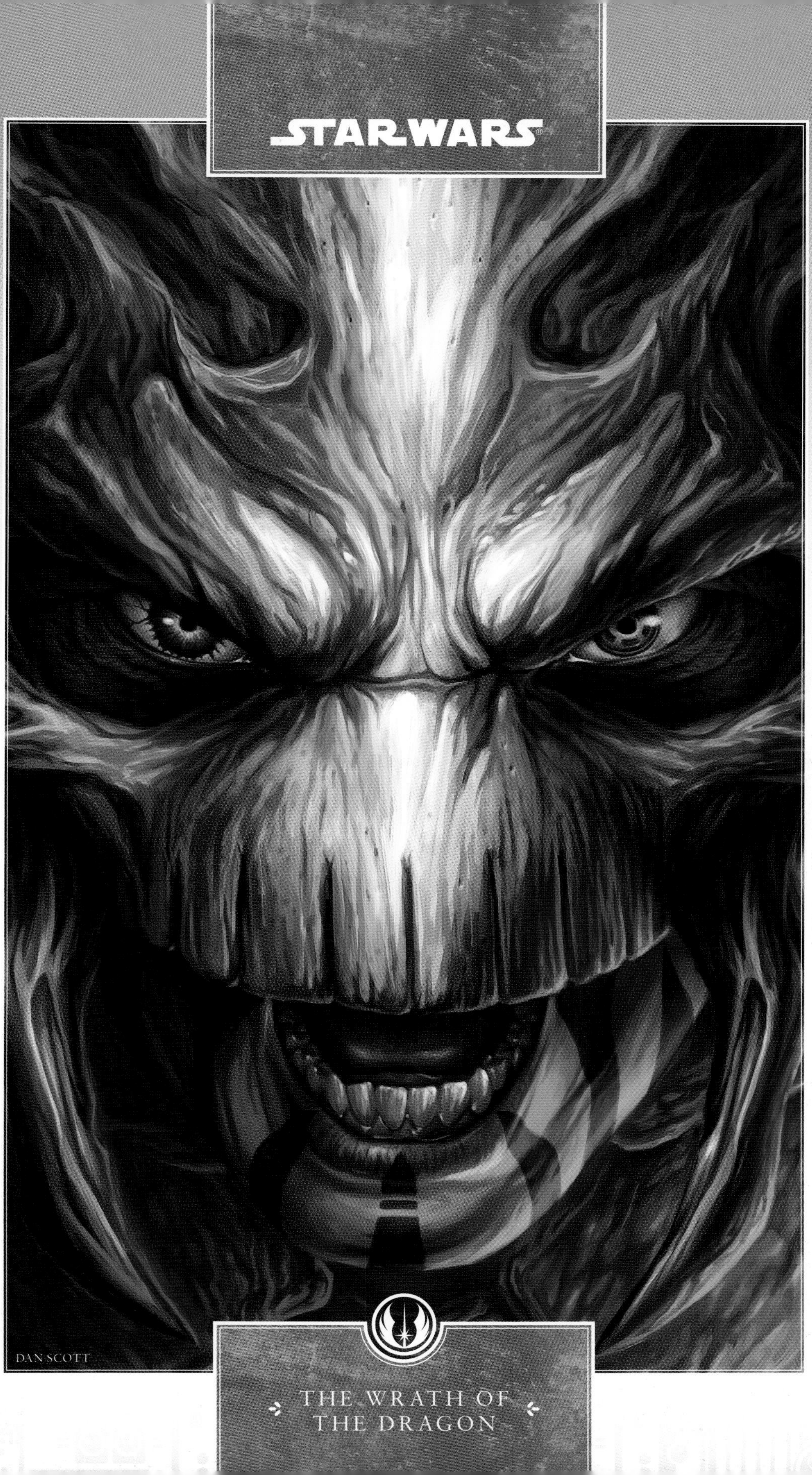
STAR WARS
DAN SCOTT
THE WRATH OF
THE DRAGON

THE WRATH OF THE DRAGON

SCRIPT
John Ostrander

ART
Alan Robinson

COLORS
Brad Anderson

LETTERS
Michael Heisler

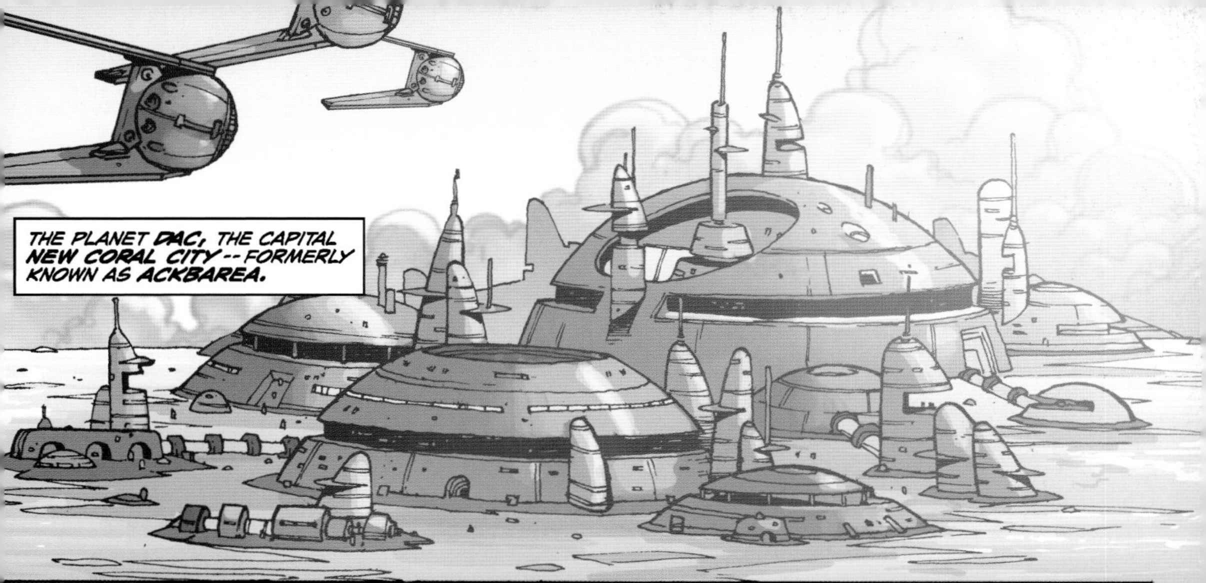
THE PLANET DAC, THE CAPITAL NEW CORAL CITY -- FORMERLY KNOWN AS ACKBAREA.

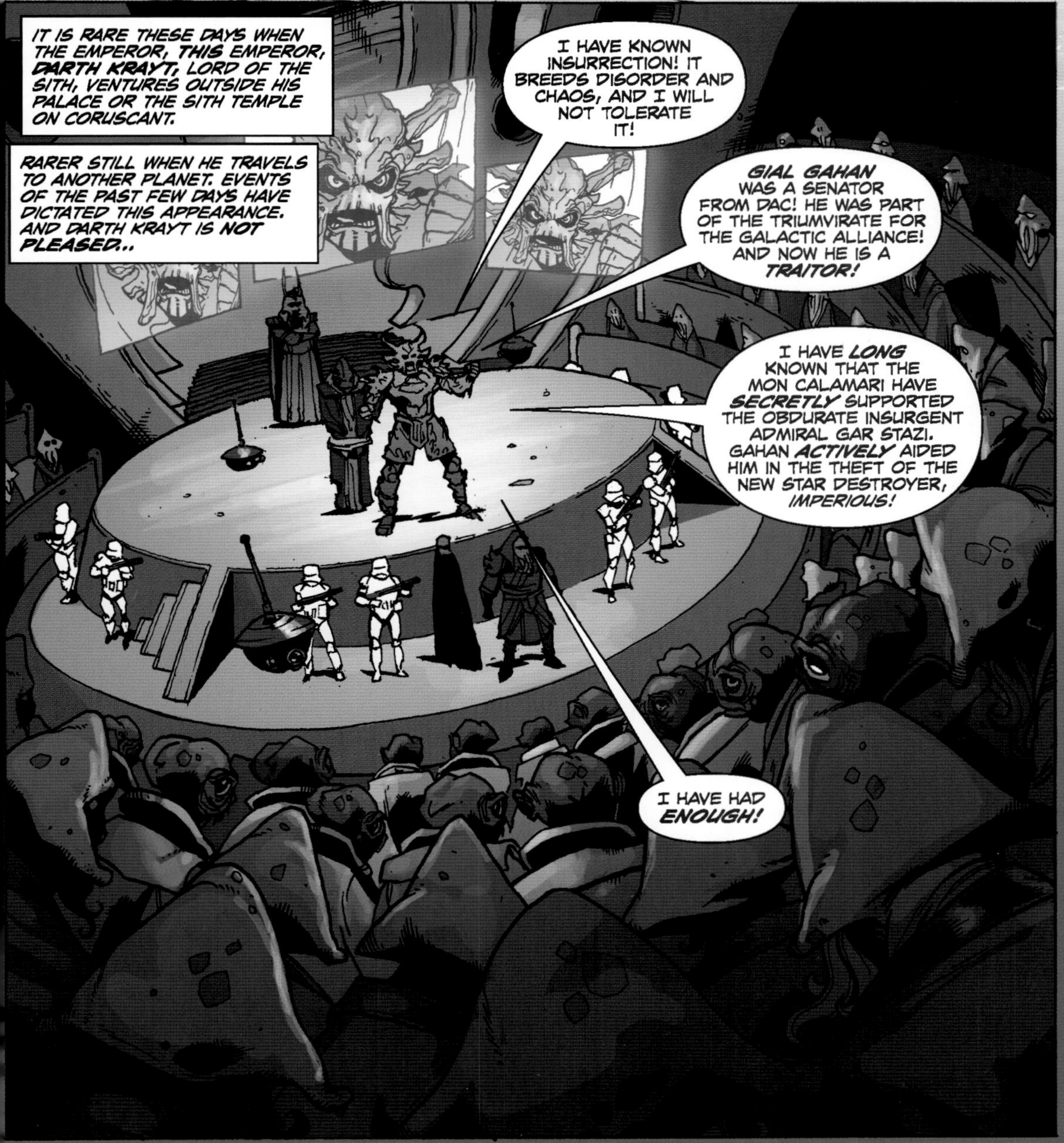
IT IS RARE THESE DAYS WHEN THE EMPEROR, THIS EMPEROR, DARTH KRAYT, LORD OF THE SITH, VENTURES OUTSIDE HIS PALACE OR THE SITH TEMPLE ON CORUSCANT.
RARER STILL WHEN HE TRAVELS TO ANOTHER PLANET. EVENTS OF THE PAST FEW DAYS HAVE DICTATED THIS APPEARANCE. AND DARTH KRAYT IS NOT PLEASED...
I HAVE KNOWN INSURRECTION! IT BREEDS DISORDER AND CHAOS, AND I WILL NOT TOLERATE IT!
GIAL GAHAN WAS A SENATOR FROM DAC! HE WAS PART OF THE TRIUMVIRATE FOR THE GALACTIC ALLIANCE! AND NOW HE IS A TRAITOR!
I HAVE LONG KNOWN THAT THE MON CALAMARI HAVE SECRETLY SUPPORTED THE OBDURATE INSURGENT ADMIRAL GAR STAZI. GAHAN ACTIVELY AIDED HIM IN THE THEFT OF THE NEW STAR DESTROYER, IMPERIOUS!
I HAVE HAD ENOUGH!

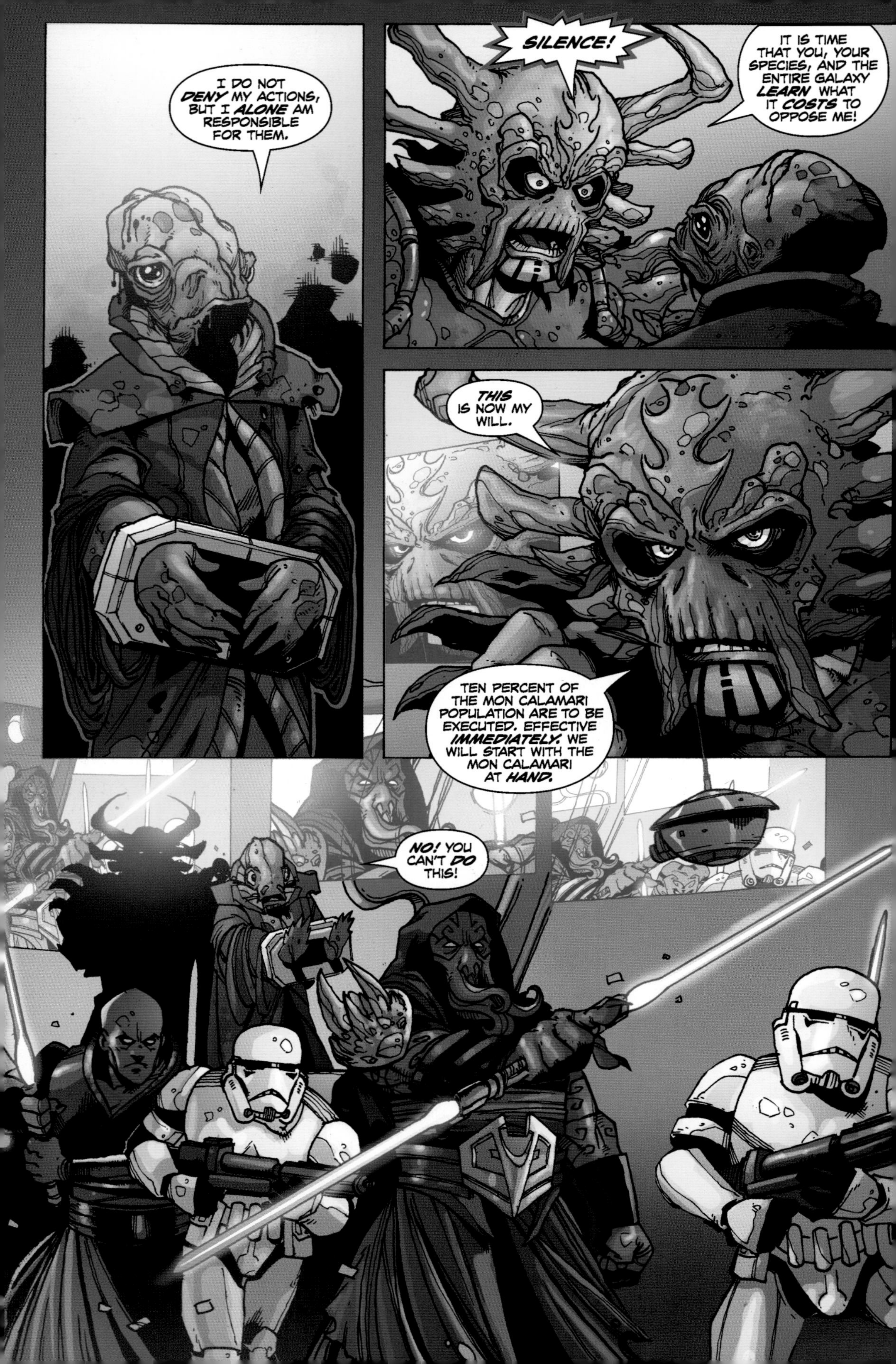
I DO NOT DENY MY ACTIONS, BUT I ALONE AM RESPONSIBLE FOR THEM.
SILENCE!
IT IS TIME THAT YOU, YOUR SPECIES, AND THE ENTIRE GALAXY LEARN WHAT IT COSTS TO OPPOSE ME!
THIS IS NOW MY WILL.
TEN PERCENT OF THE MON CALAMARI POPULATION ARE TO BE EXECUTED. EFFECTIVE IMMEDIATELY. WE WILL START WITH THE MON CALAMARI AT HAND.
NO! YOU CAN'T DO THIS!

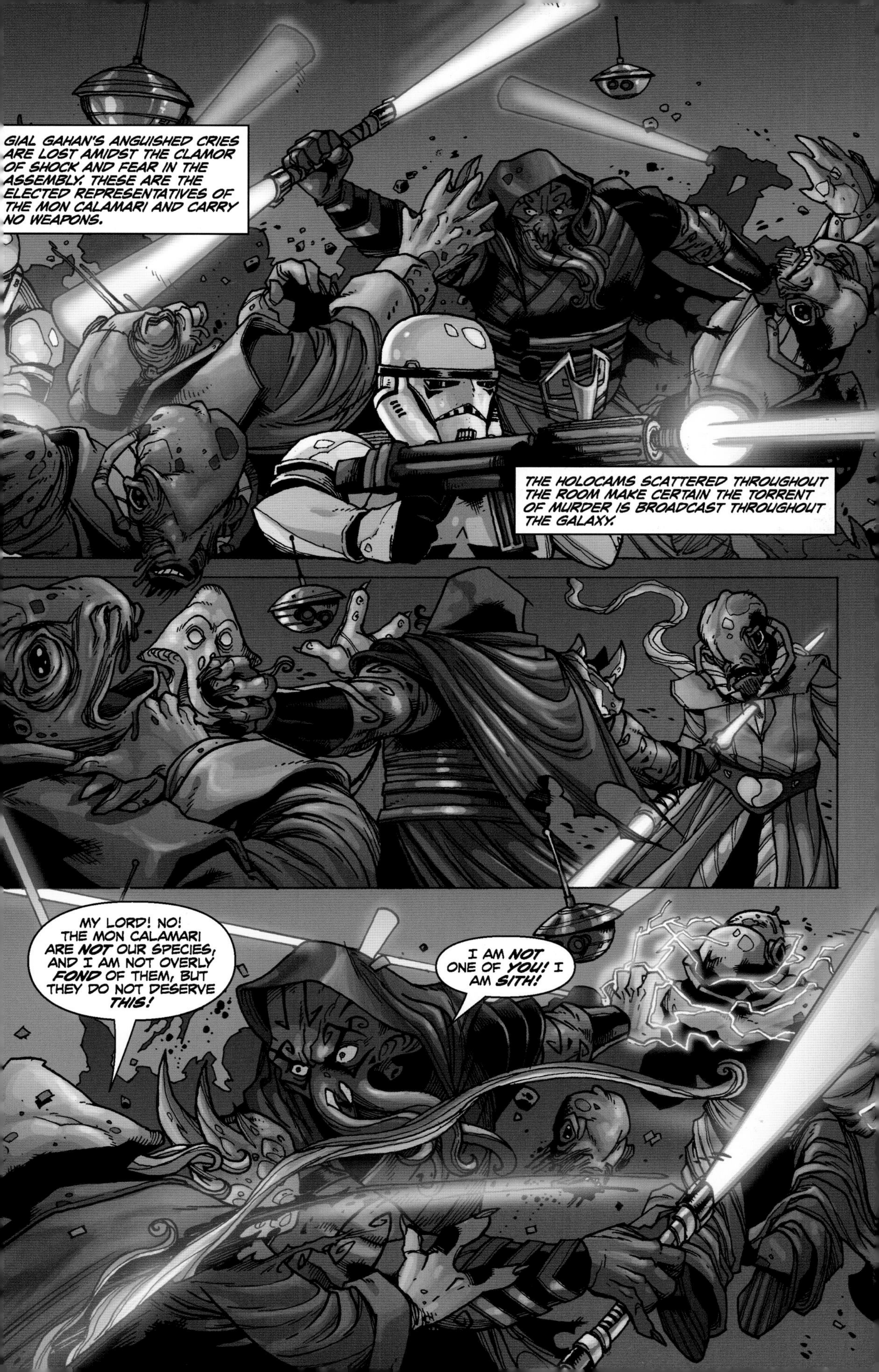
GIAL GAHAN'S ANGUISHED CRIES ARE LOST AMIDST THE CLAMOR OF SHOCK AND FEAR IN THE ASSEMBLY. THESE ARE THE ELECTED REPRESENTATIVES OF THE MON CALAMARI AND CARRY NO WEAPONS.
THE HOLOCAMS SCATTERED THROUGHOUT THE ROOM MAKE CERTAIN THE TORRENT OF MURDER IS BROADCAST THROUGHOUT THE GALAXY.
MY LORD! NO! THE MON CALAMARI ARE NOT OUR SPECIES, AND I AM NOT OVERLY FOND OF THEM, BUT THEY DO NOT DESERVE THIS!
I AM NOT ONE OF YOU! I AM SITH!

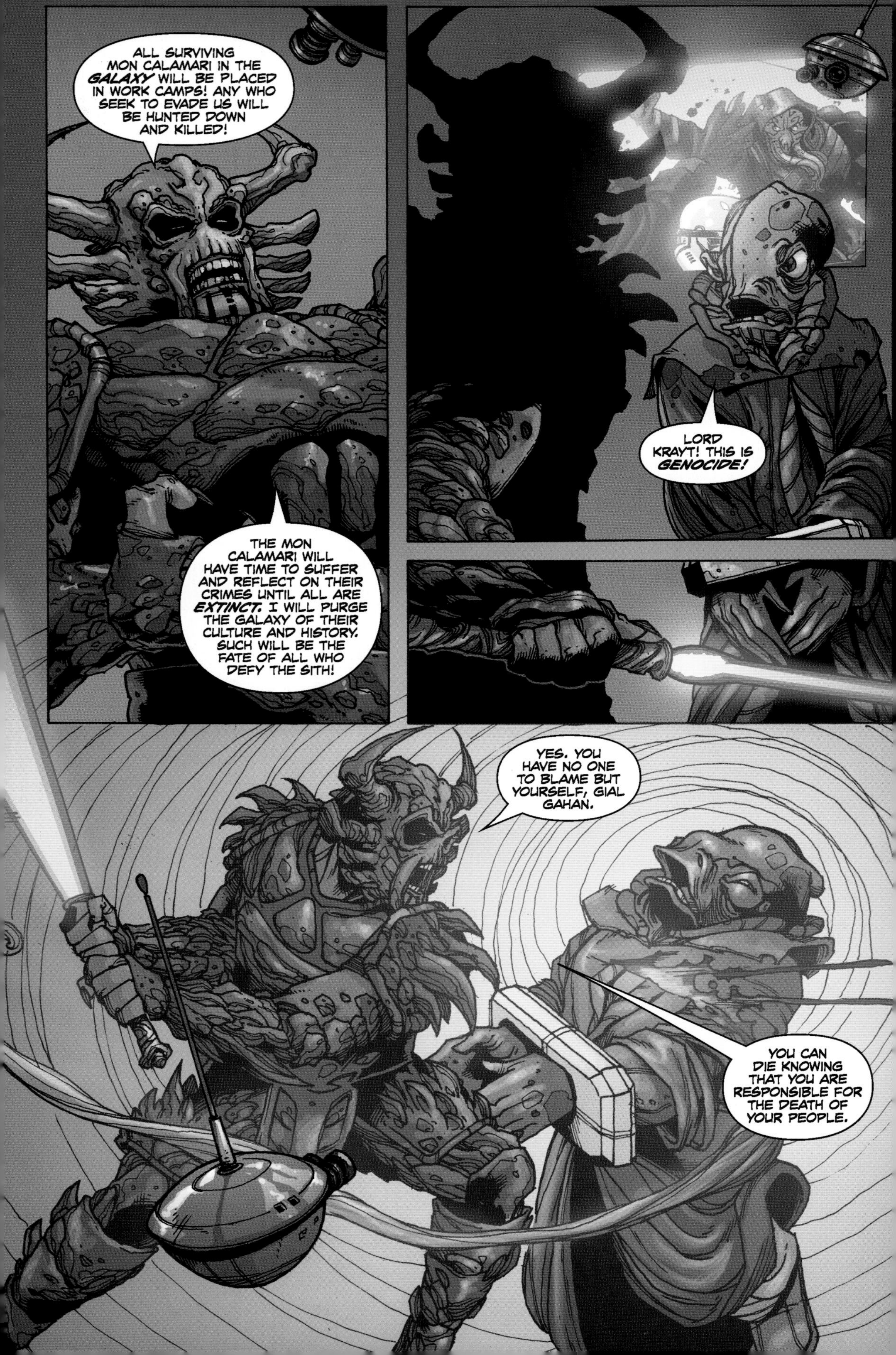

ALL SURVIVING MON CALAMARI IN THE GALAXY WILL BE PLACED IN WORK CAMPS! ANY WHO SEEK TO EVADE US WILL BE HUNTED DOWN AND KILLED!
LORD KRAYT! THIS IS GENOCIDE!
THE MON CALAMARI WILL HAVE TIME TO SUFFER AND REFLECT ON THEIR CRIMES UNTIL ALL ARE EXTINCT. I WILL PURGE THE GALAXY OF THEIR CULTURE AND HISTORY. SUCH WILL BE THE FATE OF ALL WHO DEFY THE SITH!
YES. YOU HAVE NO ONE TO BLAME BUT YOURSELF, GIAL GAHAN.
YOU CAN DIE KNOWING THAT YOU ARE RESPONSIBLE FOR THE DEATH OF YOUR PEOPLE.

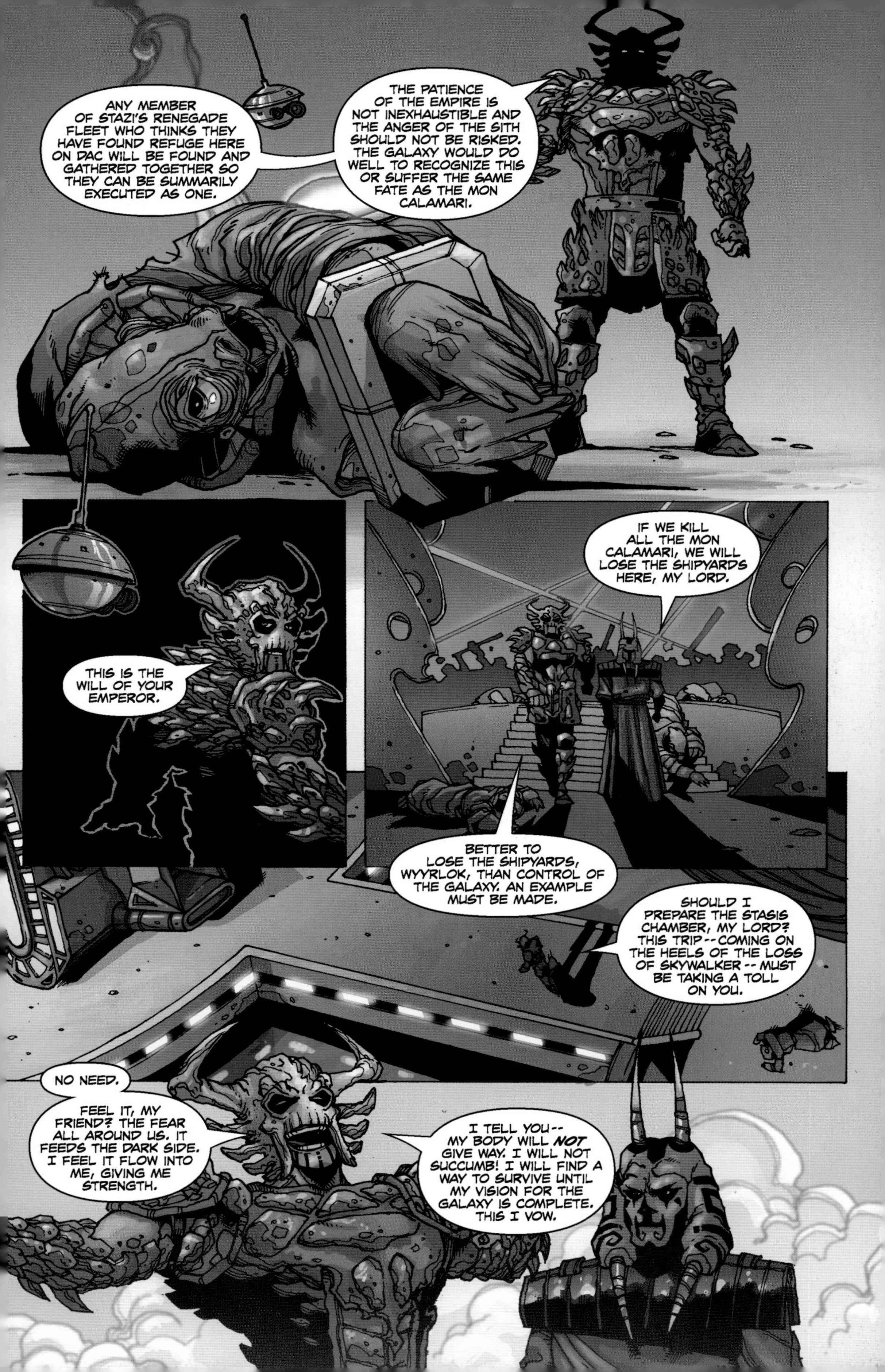
ANY MEMBER OF STAZI'S RENEGADE FLEET WHO THINKS THEY HAVE FOUND REFUGE HERE ON DAC WILL BE FOUND AND GATHERED TOGETHER SO THEY CAN BE SUMMARILY EXECUTED AS ONE.
THE PATIENCE OF THE EMPIRE IS NOT INEXHAUSTIBLE AND THE ANGER OF THE SITH SHOULD NOT BE RISKED. THE GALAXY WOULD DO WELL TO RECOGNIZE THIS OR SUFFER THE SAME FATE AS THE MON CALAMARI.
THIS IS THE WILL OF YOUR EMPEROR.
IF WE KILL ALL THE MON CALAMARI, WE WILL LOSE THE SHIPYARDS HERE, MY LORD.
BETTER TO LOSE THE SHIPYARDS, WYYRLOK, THAN CONTROL OF THE GALAXY. AN EXAMPLE MUST BE MADE.
SHOULD I PREPARE THE STASIS CHAMBER, MY LORD? THIS TRIP--COMING ON THE HEELS OF THE LOSS OF SKYWALKER--MUST BE TAKING A TOLL ON YOU.
NO NEED.
FEEL IT, MY FRIEND? THE FEAR ALL AROUND US. IT FEEDS THE DARK SIDE. I FEEL IT FLOW INTO ME, GIVING ME STRENGTH.
I TELL YOU--MY BODY WILL NOT GIVE WAY. I WILL NOT SUCCUMB! I WILL FIND A WAY TO SURVIVE UNTIL MY VISION FOR THE GALAXY IS COMPLETE. THIS I VOW.

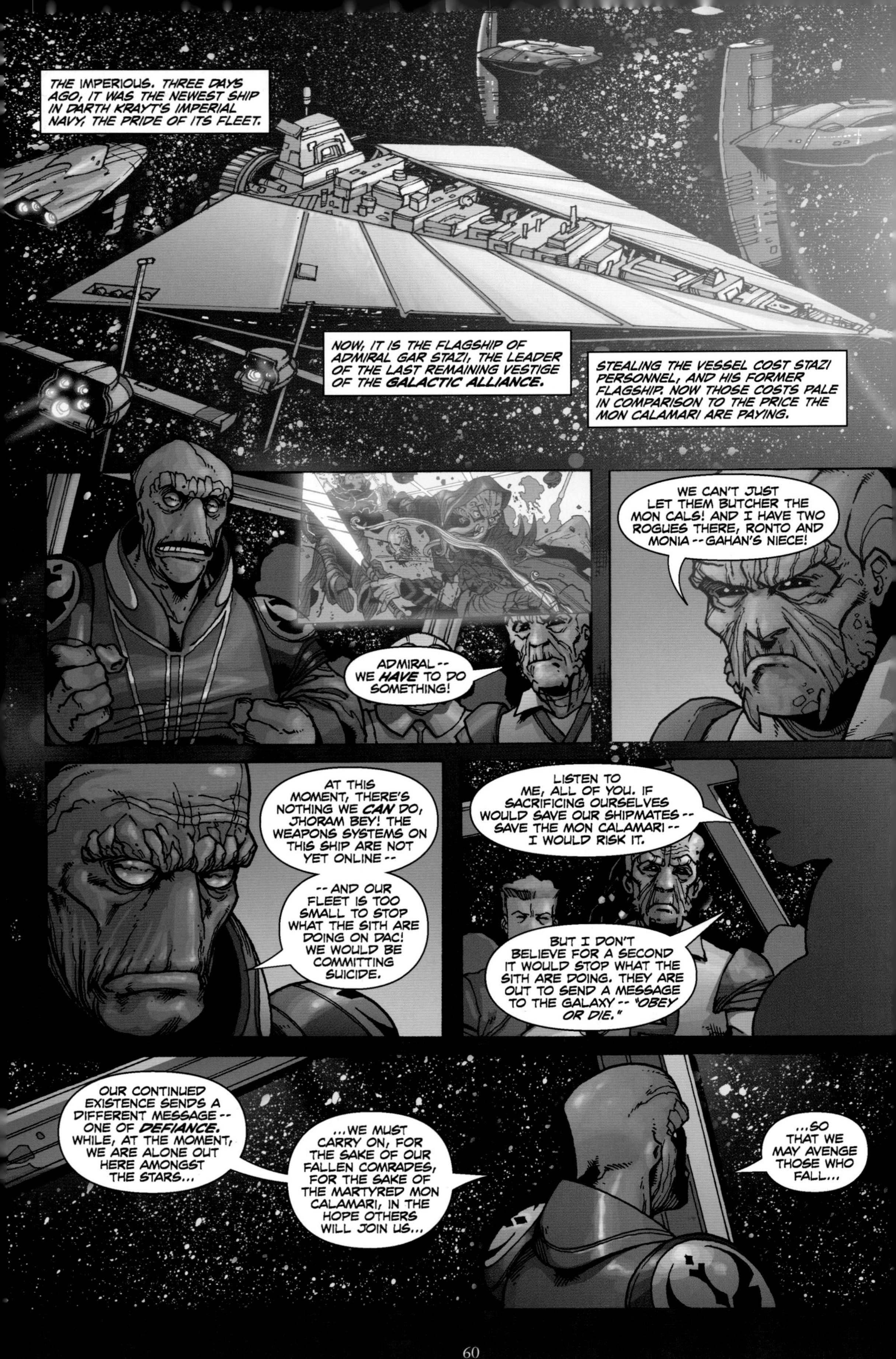
THE IMPERIOUS. THREE DAYS AGO, IT WAS THE NEWEST SHIP IN DARTH KRAYT'S IMPERIAL NAVY, THE PRIDE OF ITS FLEET.
NOW, IT IS THE FLAGSHIP OF ADMIRAL GAR STAZI, THE LEADER OF THE LAST REMAINING VESTIGE OF THE GALACTIC ALLIANCE.
STEALING THE VESSEL COST STAZI PERSONNEL, AND HIS FORMER FLAGSHIP. NOW THOSE COSTS PALE IN COMPARISON TO THE PRICE THE MON CALAMARI ARE PAYING.
ADMIRAL -- WE HAVE TO DO SOMETHING!
WE CAN'T JUST LET THEM BUTCHER THE MON CALS! AND I HAVE TWO ROGUES THERE, RONTO AND MONIA -- GAHAN'S NIECE!
AT THIS MOMENT, THERE'S NOTHING WE CAN DO, JHORAM BEY! THE WEAPONS SYSTEMS ON THIS SHIP ARE NOT YET ONLINE --
-- AND OUR FLEET IS TOO SMALL TO STOP WHAT THE SITH ARE DOING ON DAC! WE WOULD BE COMMITTING SUICIDE.
LISTEN TO ME, ALL OF YOU. IF SACRIFICING OURSELVES WOULD SAVE OUR SHIPMATES -- SAVE THE MON CALAMARI -- I WOULD RISK IT.
BUT I DON'T BELIEVE FOR A SECOND IT WOULD STOP WHAT THE SITH ARE DOING. THEY ARE OUT TO SEND A MESSAGE TO THE GALAXY -- "OBEY OR DIE."
OUR CONTINUED EXISTENCE SENDS A DIFFERENT MESSAGE -- ONE OF DEFIANCE. WHILE, AT THE MOMENT, WE ARE ALONE OUT HERE AMONGST THE STARS...
...WE MUST CARRY ON, FOR THE SAKE OF OUR FALLEN COMRADES, FOR THE SAKE OF THE MARTYRED MON CALAMARI, IN THE HOPE OTHERS WILL JOIN US...
...SO THAT WE MAY AVENGE THOSE WHO FALL...

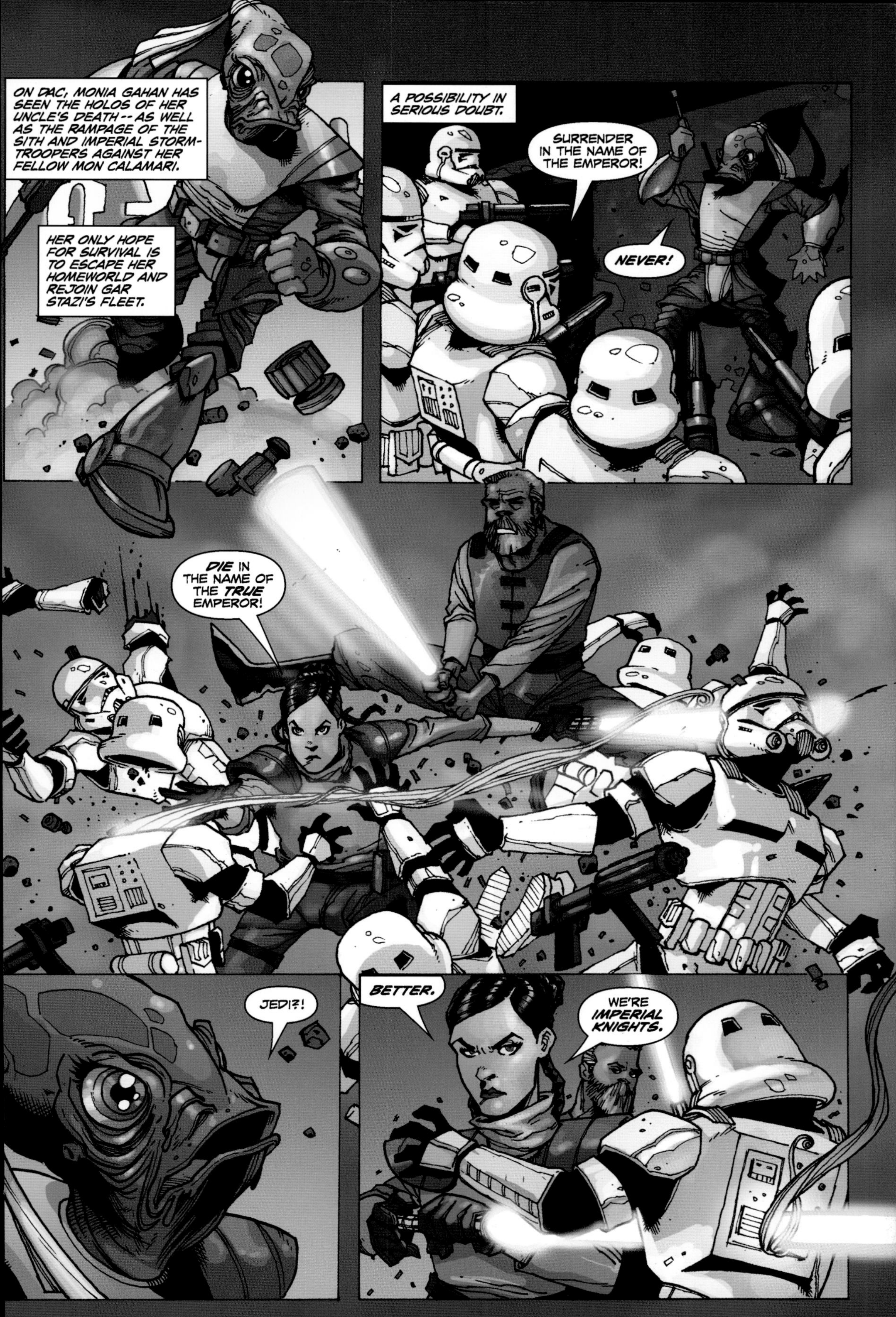

ON DAC, MONIA GAHAN HAS SEEN THE HOLOS OF HER UNCLE'S DEATH -- AS WELL AS THE RAMPAGE OF THE SITH AND IMPERIAL STORM-TROOPERS AGAINST HER FELLOW MON CALAMARI.
HER ONLY HOPE FOR SURVIVAL IS TO ESCAPE HER HOMEWORLD AND REJOIN GAR STAZI'S FLEET.
A POSSIBILITY IN SERIOUS DOUBT.
SURRENDER IN THE NAME OF THE EMPEROR!
NEVER!
DIE IN THE NAME OF THE TRUE EMPEROR!
JEDI?!
BETTER.
WE'RE IMPERIAL KNIGHTS.

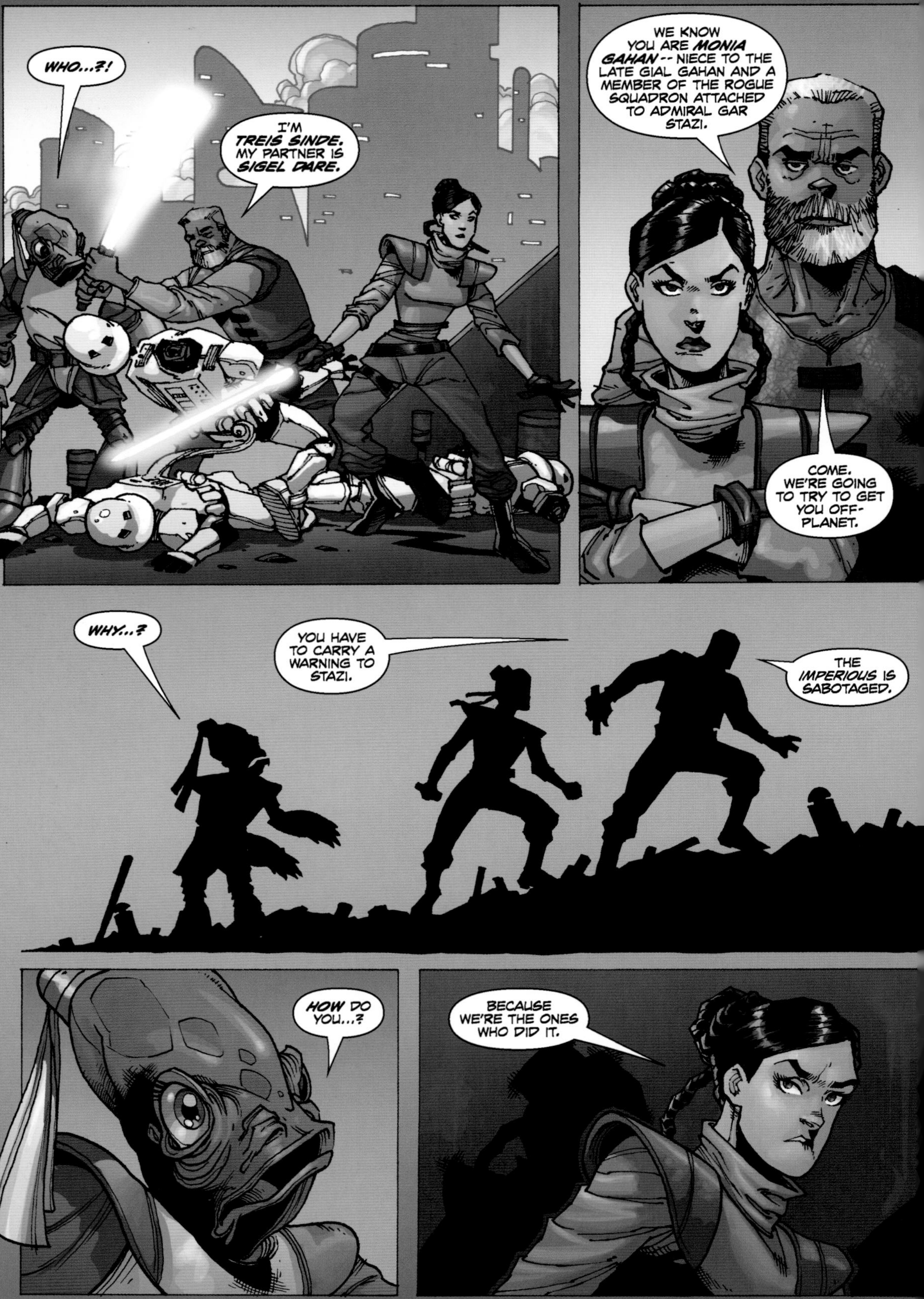
WHO...?!
I'M TREIS SINDE. MY PARTNER IS SIGEL DARE.
WE KNOW YOU ARE MONIA GAHAN -- NIECE TO THE LATE GIAL GAHAN AND A MEMBER OF THE ROGUE SQUADRON ATTACHED TO ADMIRAL GAR STAZI.
COME. WE'RE GOING TO TRY TO GET YOU OFF-PLANET.
WHY...?
YOU HAVE TO CARRY A WARNING TO STAZI.
THE IMPERIOUS IS SABOTAGED.
HOW DO YOU...?
BECAUSE WE'RE THE ONES WHO DID IT.

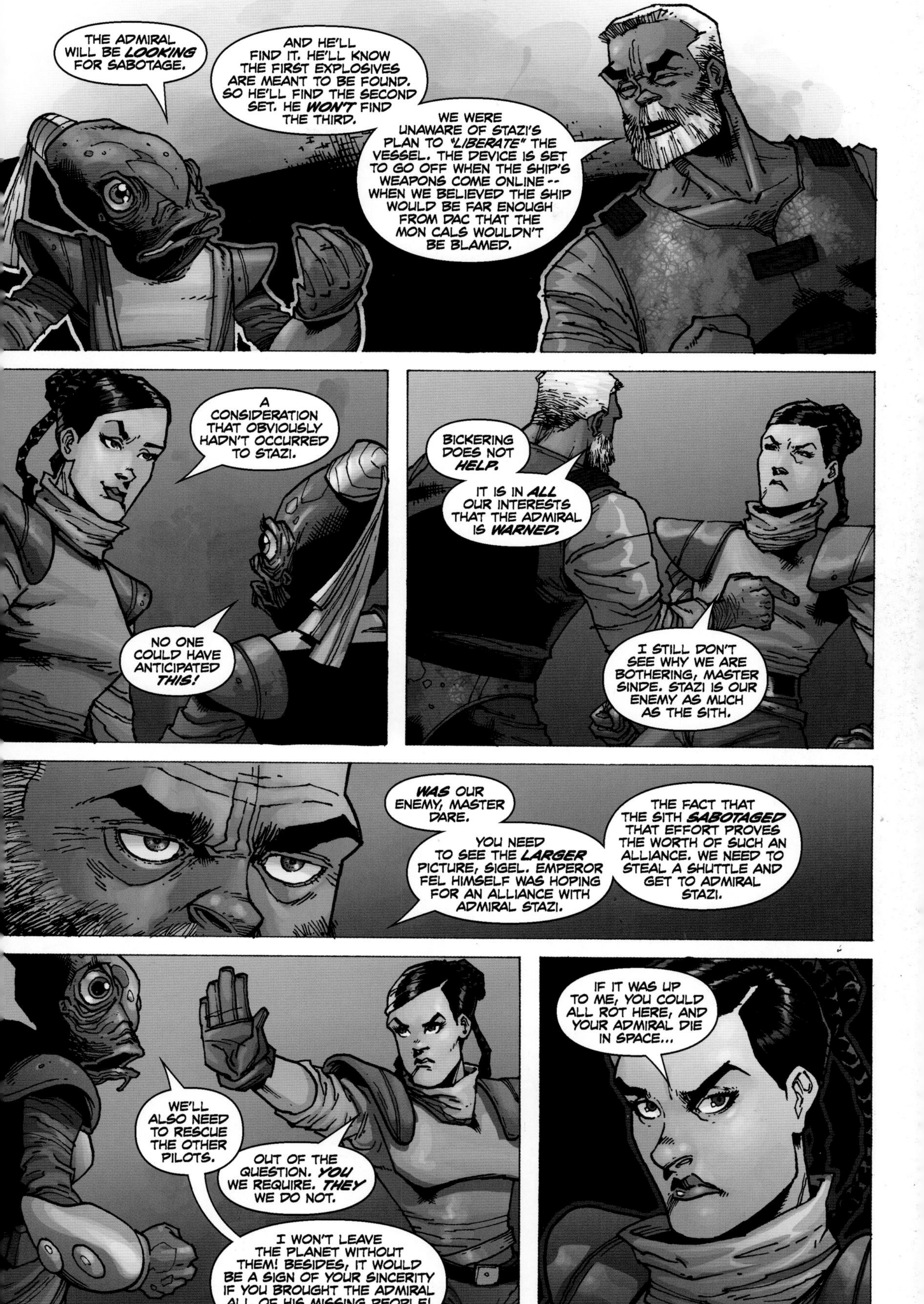
THE ADMIRAL WILL BE LOOKING FOR SABOTAGE.
AND HE'LL FIND IT. HE'LL KNOW THE FIRST EXPLOSIVES ARE MEANT TO BE FOUND. SO HE'LL FIND THE SECOND SET. HE WON'T FIND THE THIRD.
WE WERE UNAWARE OF STAZI'S PLAN TO "LIBERATE" THE VESSEL. THE DEVICE IS SET TO GO OFF WHEN THE SHIP'S WEAPONS COME ONLINE-- WHEN WE BELIEVED THE SHIP WOULD BE FAR ENOUGH FROM DAC THAT THE MON CALS WOULDN'T BE BLAMED.
A CONSIDERATION THAT OBVIOUSLY HADN'T OCCURRED TO STAZI.
NO ONE COULD HAVE ANTICIPATED THIS!
BICKERING DOES NOT HELP.
IT IS IN ALL OUR INTERESTS THAT THE ADMIRAL IS WARNED.
I STILL DON'T SEE WHY WE ARE BOTHERING, MASTER SINDE. STAZI IS OUR ENEMY AS MUCH AS THE SITH.
WAS OUR ENEMY, MASTER DARE.
YOU NEED TO SEE THE LARGER PICTURE, SIGEL. EMPEROR FEL HIMSELF WAS HOPING FOR AN ALLIANCE WITH ADMIRAL STAZI.
THE FACT THAT THE SITH SABOTAGED THAT EFFORT PROVES THE WORTH OF SUCH AN ALLIANCE. WE NEED TO STEAL A SHUTTLE AND GET TO ADMIRAL STAZI.
WE'LL ALSO NEED TO RESCUE THE OTHER PILOTS.
OUT OF THE QUESTION. YOU WE REQUIRE. THEY WE DO NOT.
I WON'T LEAVE THE PLANET WITHOUT THEM! BESIDES, IT WOULD BE A SIGN OF YOUR SINCERITY IF YOU BROUGHT THE ADMIRAL ALL OF HIS MISSING PEOPLE!
IF IT WAS UP TO ME, YOU COULD ALL ROT HERE, AND YOUR ADMIRAL DIE IN SPACE...

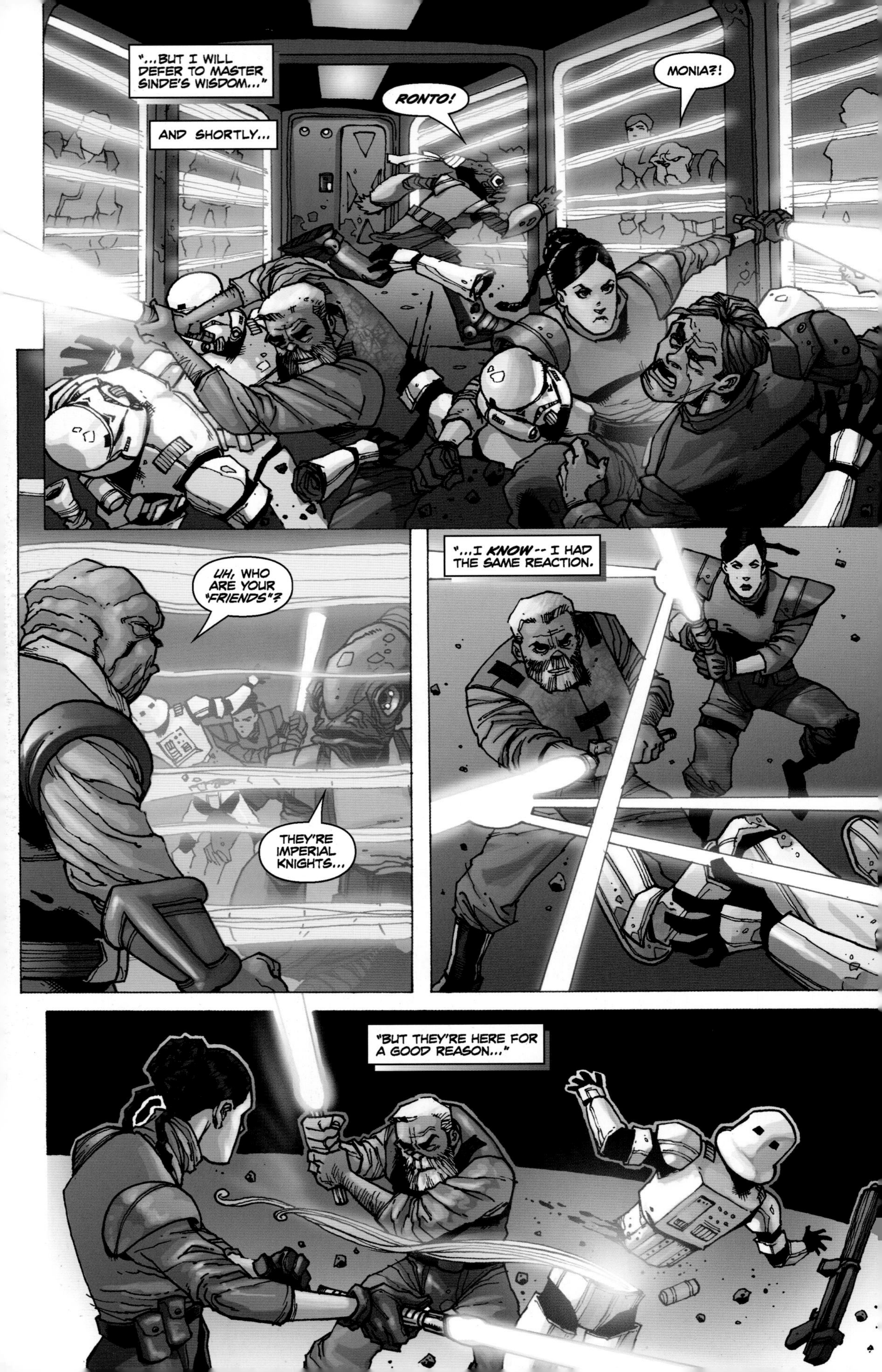
"...BUT I WILL DEFER TO MASTER SINDE'S WISDOM..."
AND SHORTLY...
RONTO!
MONIA?!
UH, WHO ARE YOUR "FRIENDS"?
THEY'RE IMPERIAL KNIGHTS...
"...I KNOW -- I HAD THE SAME REACTION.
"BUT THEY'RE HERE FOR A GOOD REASON..."

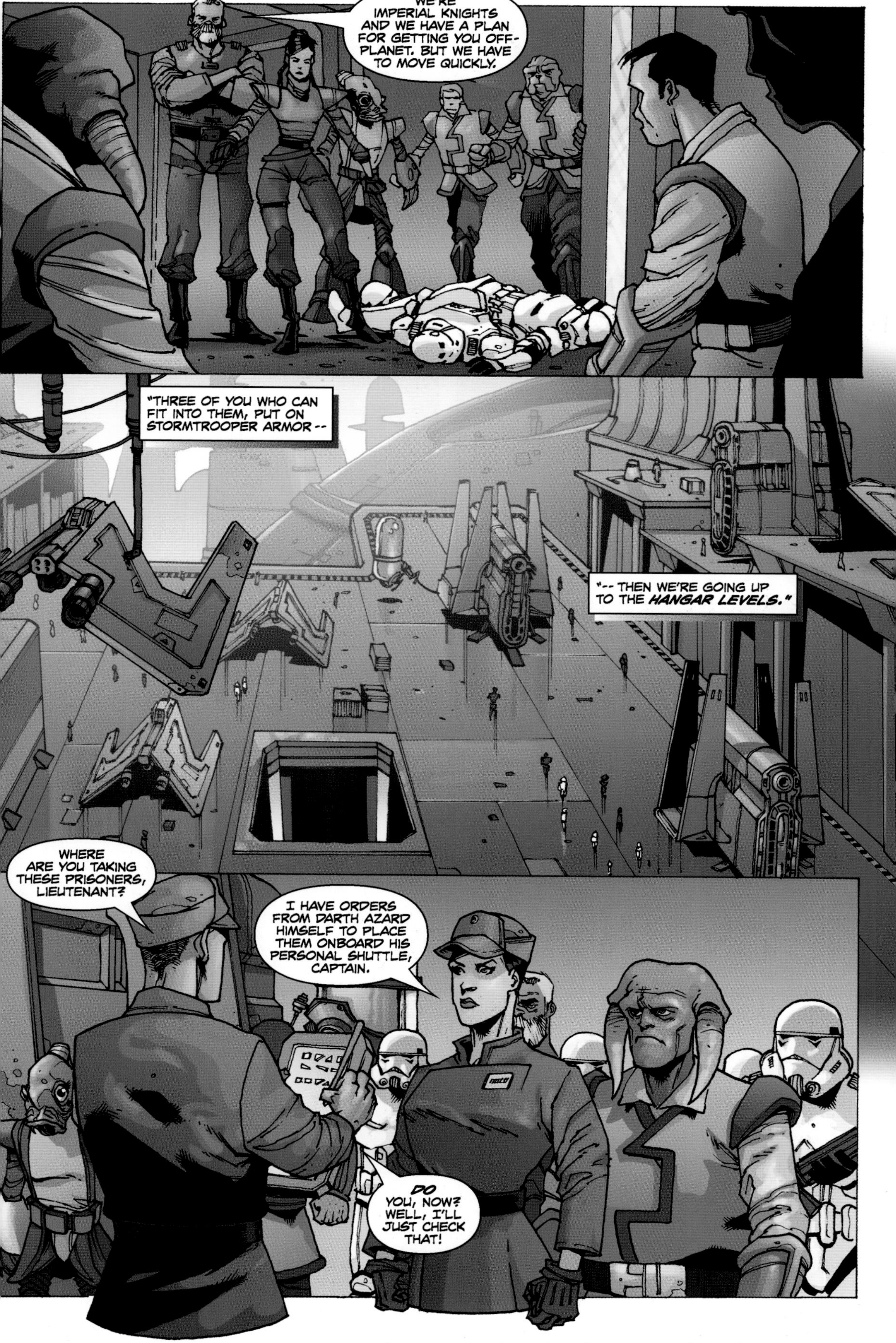
WE'RE IMPERIAL KNIGHTS AND WE HAVE A PLAN FOR GETTING YOU OFF-PLANET. BUT WE HAVE TO MOVE QUICKLY.
"THREE OF YOU WHO CAN FIT INTO THEM, PUT ON STORMTROOPER ARMOR --
"-- THEN WE'RE GOING UP TO THE *HANGAR LEVELS.*"
WHERE ARE YOU TAKING THESE PRISONERS, LIEUTENANT?
I HAVE ORDERS FROM DARTH AZARD HIMSELF TO PLACE THEM ONBOARD HIS PERSONAL SHUTTLE, CAPTAIN.
DO YOU, NOW? WELL, I'LL JUST CHECK THAT!

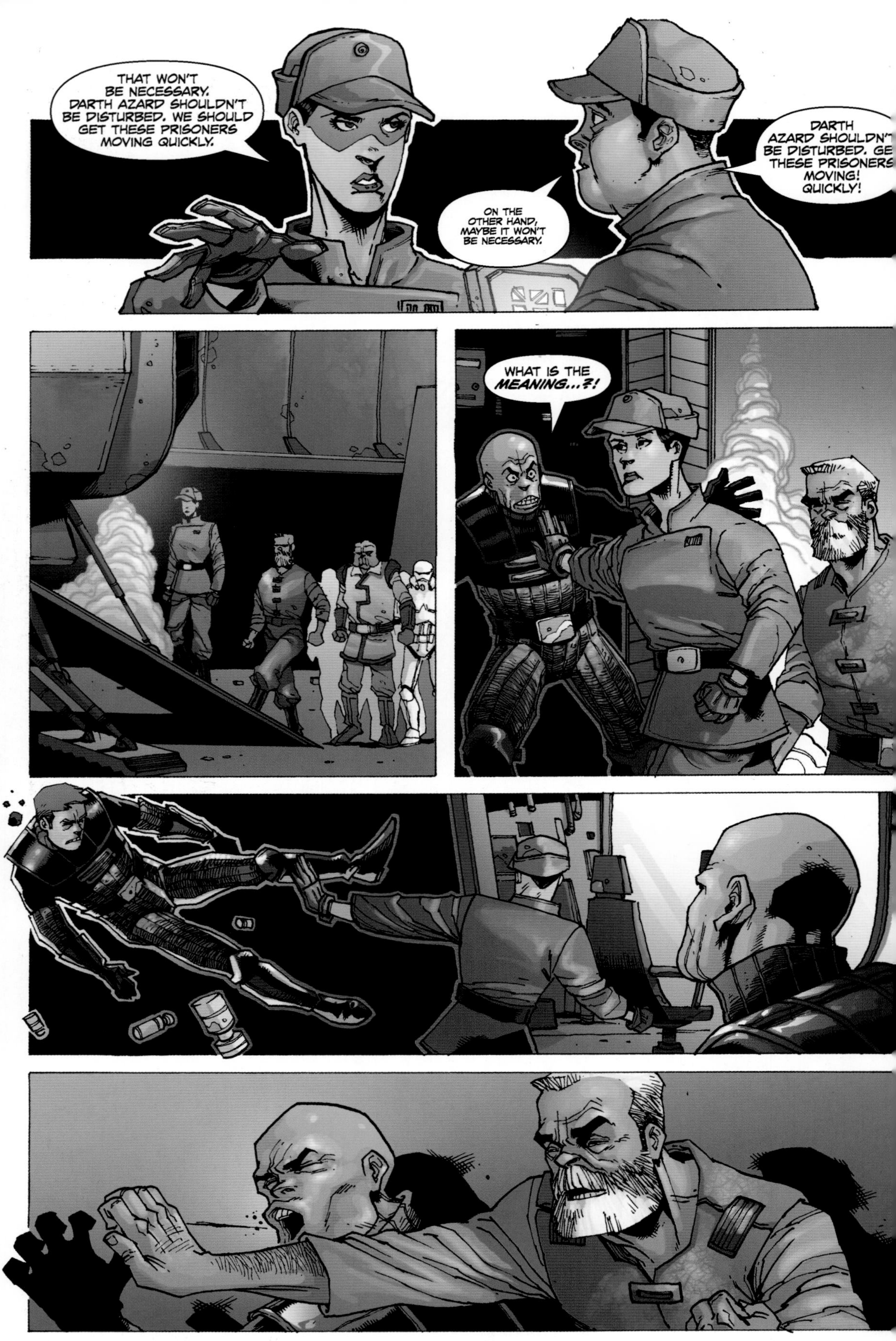
THAT WON'T BE NECESSARY. DARTH AZARD SHOULDN'T BE DISTURBED. WE SHOULD GET THESE PRISONERS MOVING QUICKLY.
DARTH AZARD SHOULDN'T BE DISTURBED. GE THESE PRISONERS MOVING! QUICKLY!
ON THE OTHER HAND, MAYBE IT WON'T BE NECESSARY.
WHAT IS THE *MEANING...?!*

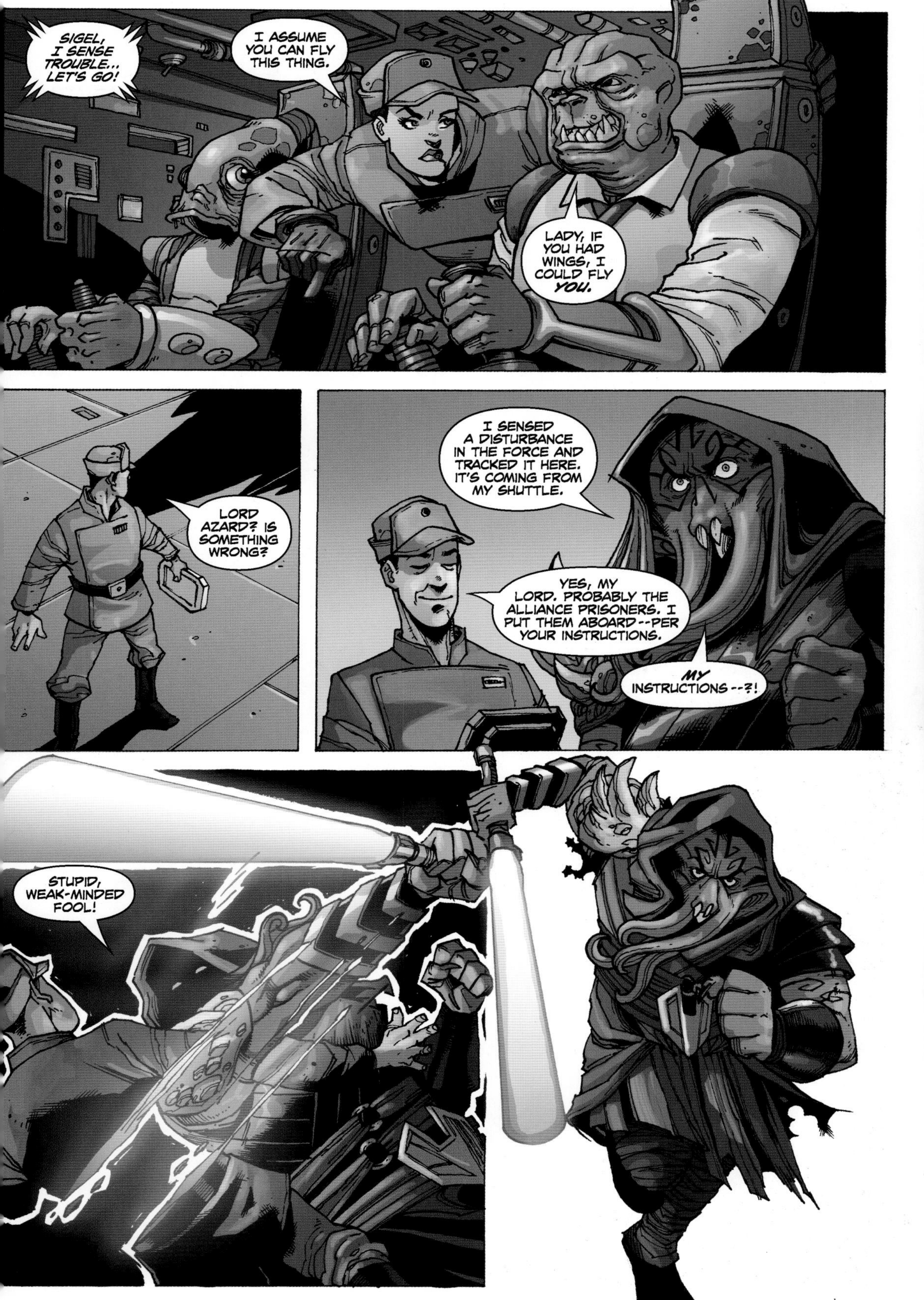
SIGEL, I SENSE TROUBLE... LET'S GO!
I ASSUME YOU CAN FLY THIS THING.
LADY, IF YOU HAD WINGS, I COULD FLY YOU.
LORD AZARD? IS SOMETHING WRONG?
I SENSED A DISTURBANCE IN THE FORCE AND TRACKED IT HERE. IT'S COMING FROM MY SHUTTLE.
YES, MY LORD. PROBABLY THE ALLIANCE PRISONERS. I PUT THEM ABOARD--PER YOUR INSTRUCTIONS.
MY INSTRUCTIONS--?!
STUPID, WEAK-MINDED FOOL!

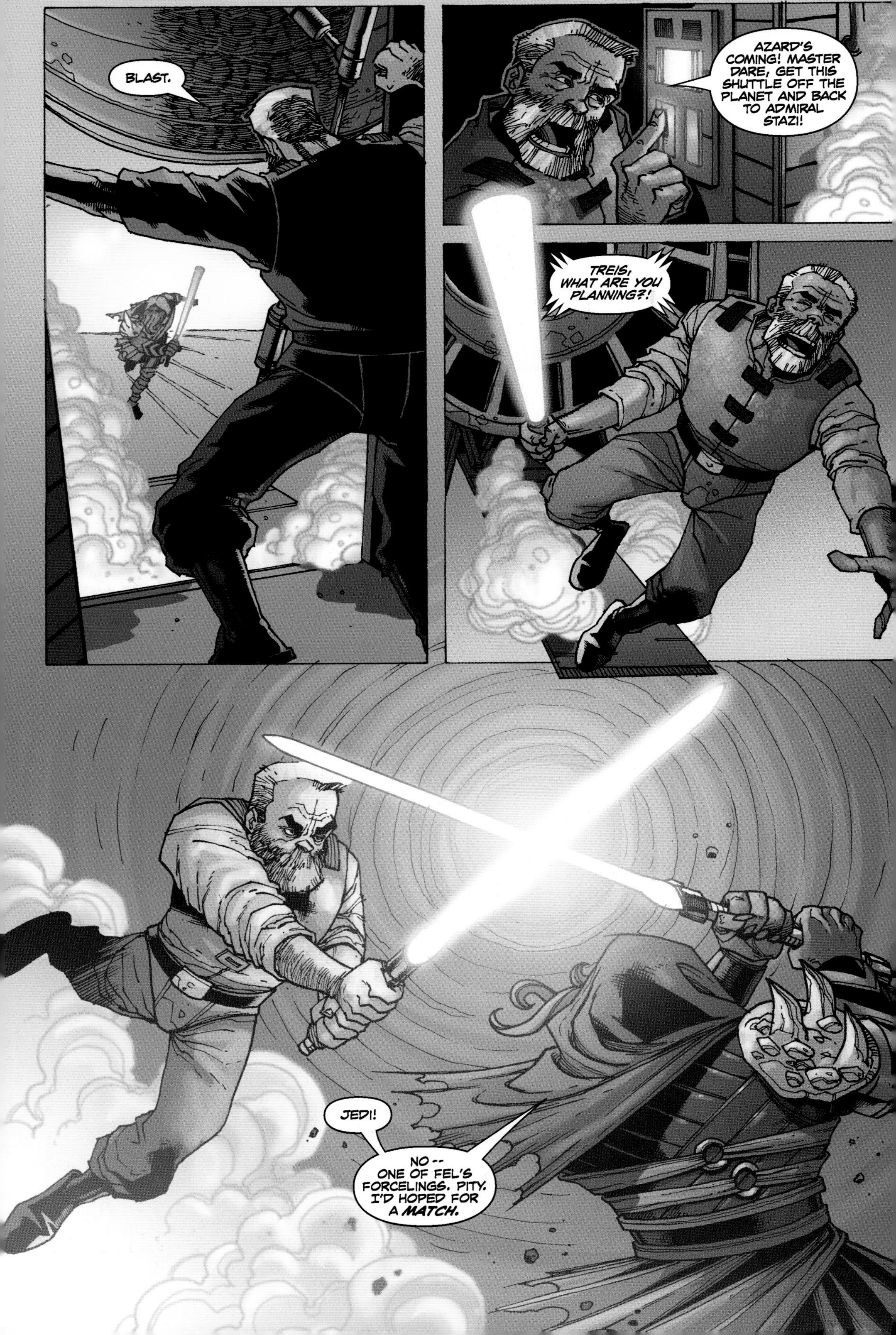
BLAST.
AZARD'S COMING! MASTER DARE, GET THIS SHUTTLE OFF THE PLANET AND BACK TO ADMIRAL STAZI!
TREIS, WHAT ARE YOU PLANNING?!
JEDI!
NO -- ONE OF FEL'S FORCELINGS. PITY. I'D HOPED FOR A *MATCH*.

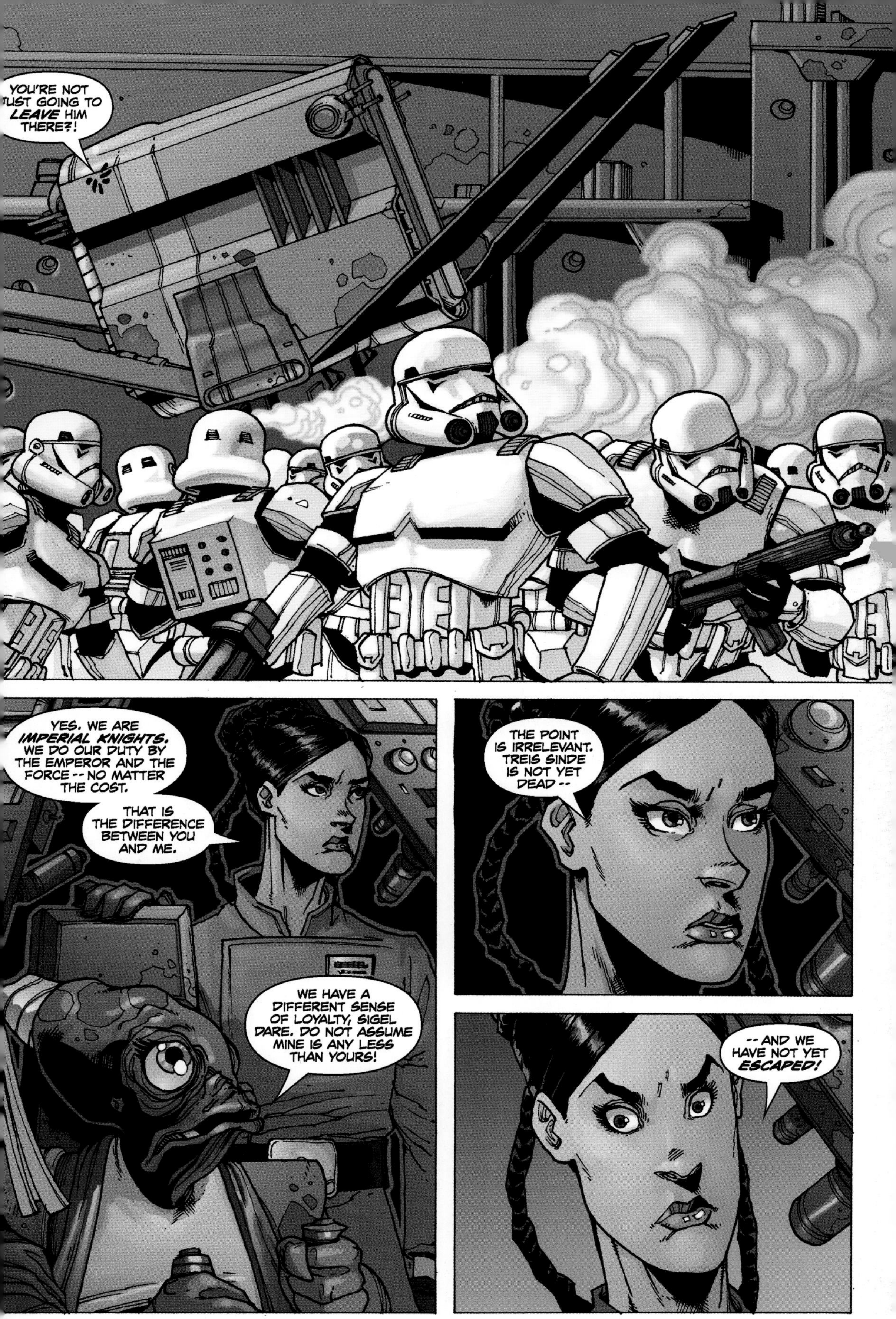
YOU'RE NOT JUST GOING TO LEAVE HIM THERE?!
YES. WE ARE IMPERIAL KNIGHTS. WE DO OUR DUTY BY THE EMPEROR AND THE FORCE -- NO MATTER THE COST.
THAT IS THE DIFFERENCE BETWEEN YOU AND ME.
WE HAVE A DIFFERENT SENSE OF LOYALTY, SIGEL DARE. DO NOT ASSUME MINE IS ANY LESS THAN YOURS!
THE POINT IS IRRELEVANT. TREIS SINDE IS NOT YET DEAD --
-- AND WE HAVE NOT YET ESCAPED!

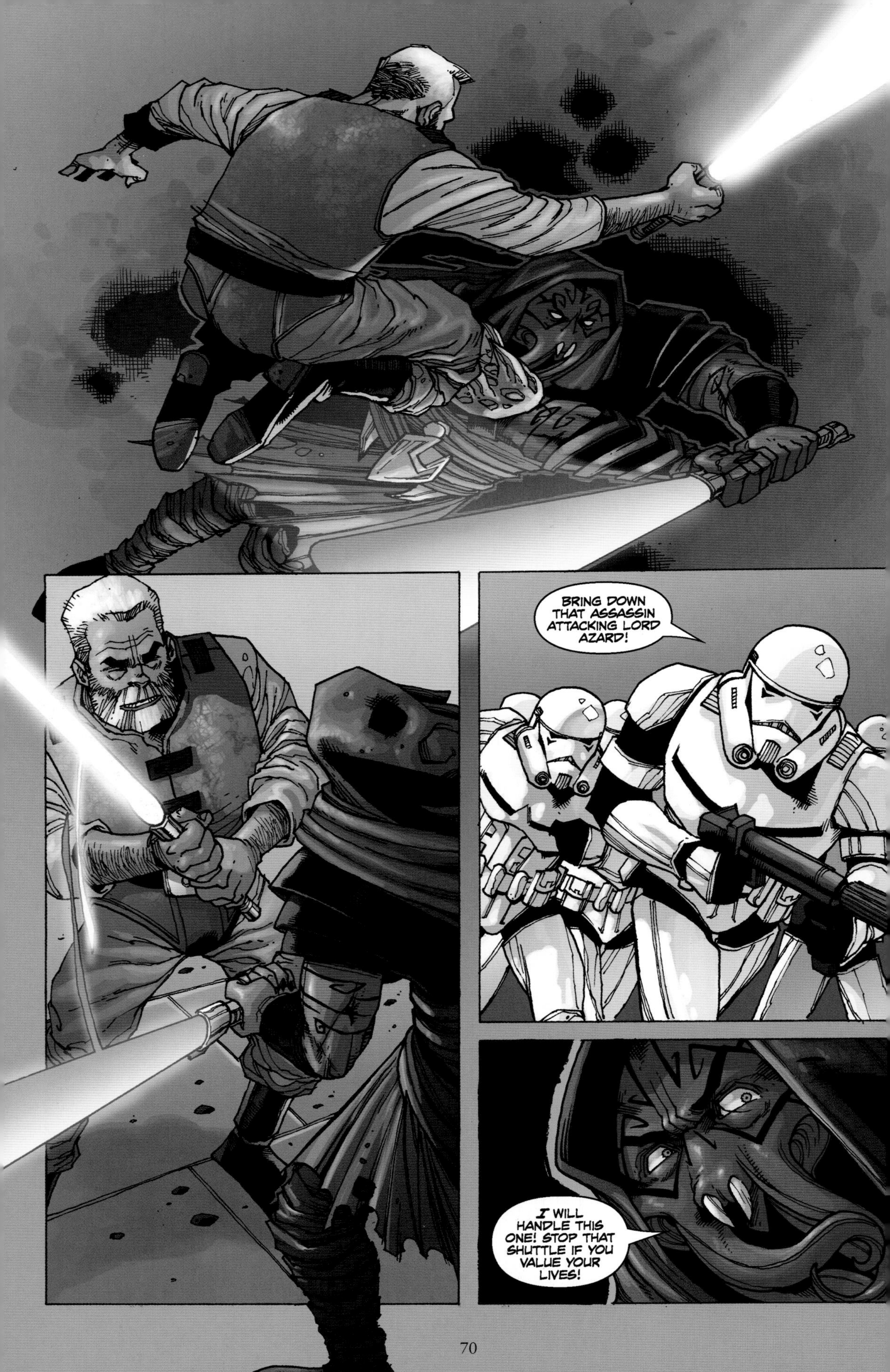
BRING DOWN THAT ASSASSIN ATTACKING LORD AZARD!
I WILL HANDLE THIS ONE! STOP THAT SHUTTLE IF YOU VALUE YOUR LIVES!

IMPRESSIVE -- FOR ONE OF YOUR KIND.

RUDIMENTARY. YOU SHOULD GET OUT MORE. MEET MORE OF MY KIND.

YOU CANNOT DEFEAT ME. WE BOTH KNOW IT.

KILLING YOU WOULD BE A PLEASURE, BUT IT'S NOT THE POINT.

I KNOW. YOU THINK TO DELAY ME LONG ENOUGH TO KEEP ME FROM GIVING THE ALARM ABOUT THE SHUTTLE.

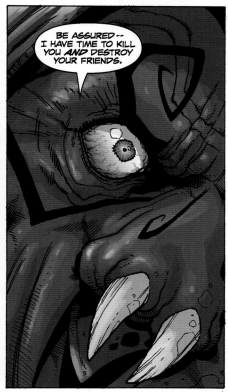

BE ASSURED -- I HAVE TIME TO KILL YOU *AND* DESTROY YOUR FRIENDS.

THIS SHUTTLE HAS SOME WEAPONRY, YES?

NOT A LOT, BUT -- FRONT AND REAR, YEAH! YOU GOT A *TARGET* IN MIND?

IN MY MIND -- YES. GET SOMEONE ON THE REAR GUNS --

-- AND HAVE THEM READY TO SHOOT ON MY COMMAND!

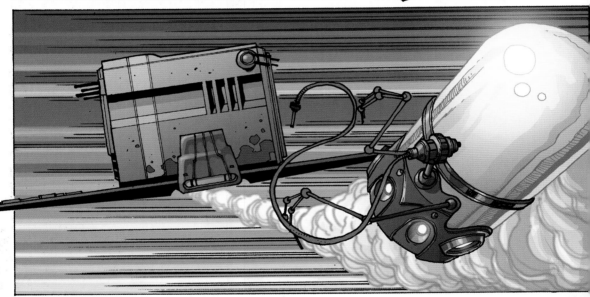

NOW!

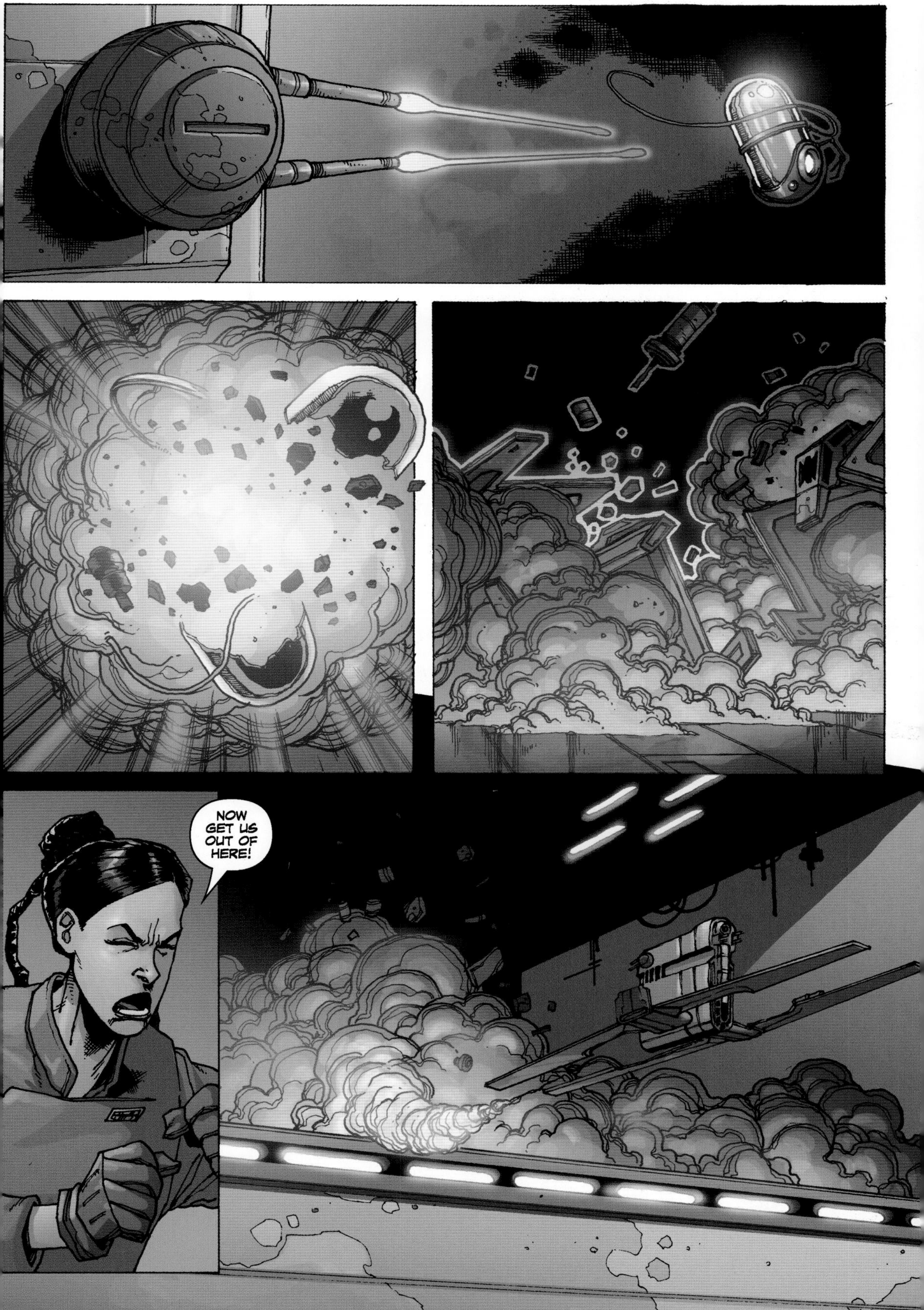
NOW GET US OUT OF HERE!

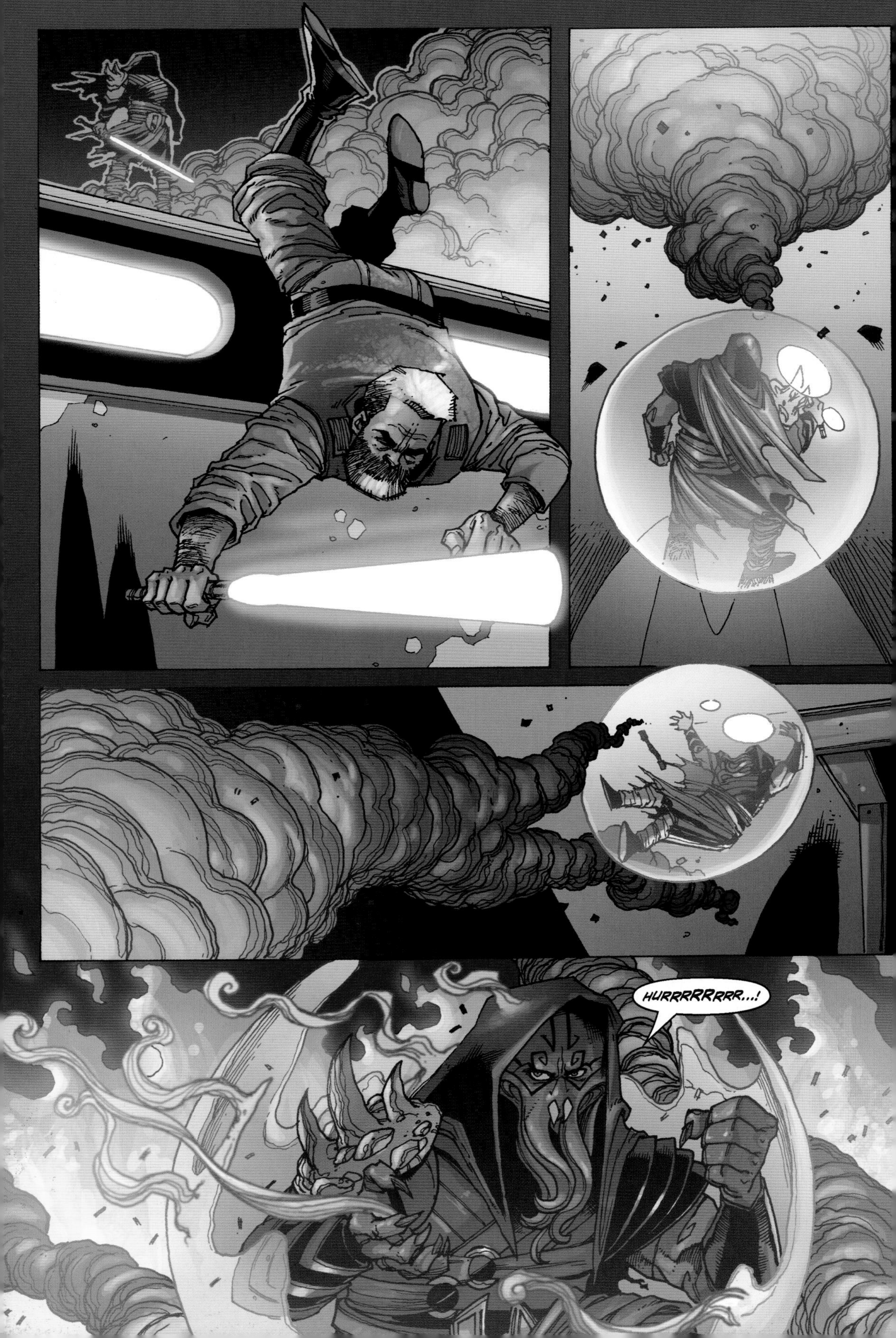
HURRRRRRRR...!

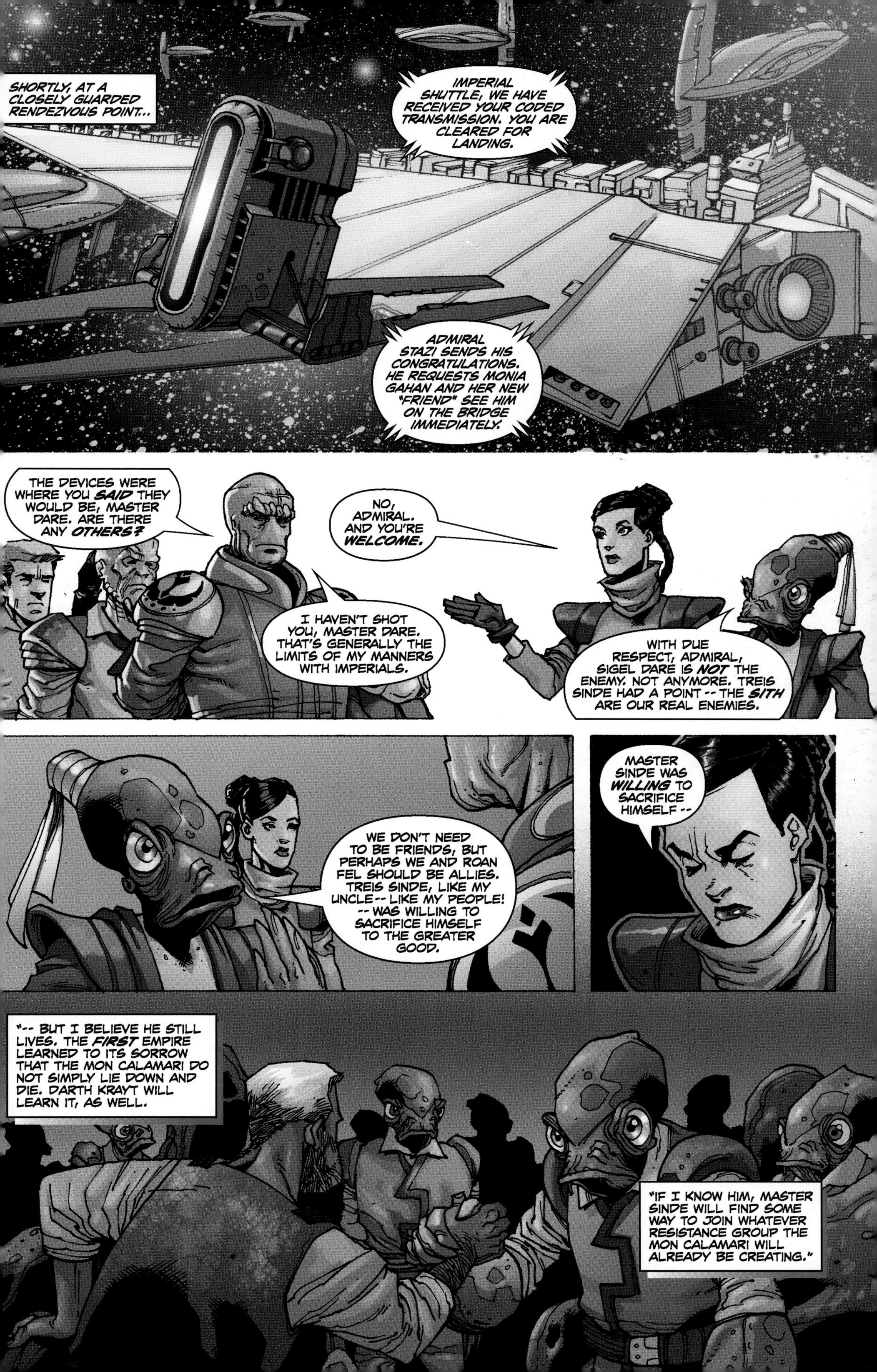
SHORTLY, AT A CLOSELY GUARDED RENDEZVOUS POINT...
IMPERIAL SHUTTLE, WE HAVE RECEIVED YOUR CODED TRANSMISSION. YOU ARE CLEARED FOR LANDING.
ADMIRAL STAZI SENDS HIS CONGRATULATIONS. HE REQUESTS MONIA GAHAN AND HER NEW "FRIEND" SEE HIM ON THE BRIDGE IMMEDIATELY.
THE DEVICES WERE WHERE YOU SAID THEY WOULD BE, MASTER DARE. ARE THERE ANY OTHERS?
NO, ADMIRAL. AND YOU'RE WELCOME.
I HAVEN'T SHOT YOU, MASTER DARE. THAT'S GENERALLY THE LIMITS OF MY MANNERS WITH IMPERIALS.
WITH DUE RESPECT, ADMIRAL, SIGEL DARE IS NOT THE ENEMY. NOT ANYMORE. TREIS SINDE HAD A POINT -- THE SITH ARE OUR REAL ENEMIES.
WE DON'T NEED TO BE FRIENDS, BUT PERHAPS WE AND ROAN FEL SHOULD BE ALLIES. TREIS SINDE, LIKE MY UNCLE -- LIKE MY PEOPLE! -- WAS WILLING TO SACRIFICE HIMSELF TO THE GREATER GOOD.
MASTER SINDE WAS WILLING TO SACRIFICE HIMSELF --
"-- BUT I BELIEVE HE STILL LIVES. THE FIRST EMPIRE LEARNED TO ITS SORROW THAT THE MON CALAMARI DO NOT SIMPLY LIE DOWN AND DIE. DARTH KRAYT WILL LEARN IT, AS WELL.
"IF I KNOW HIM, MASTER SINDE WILL FIND SOME WAY TO JOIN WHATEVER RESISTANCE GROUP THE MON CALAMARI WILL ALREADY BE CREATING."

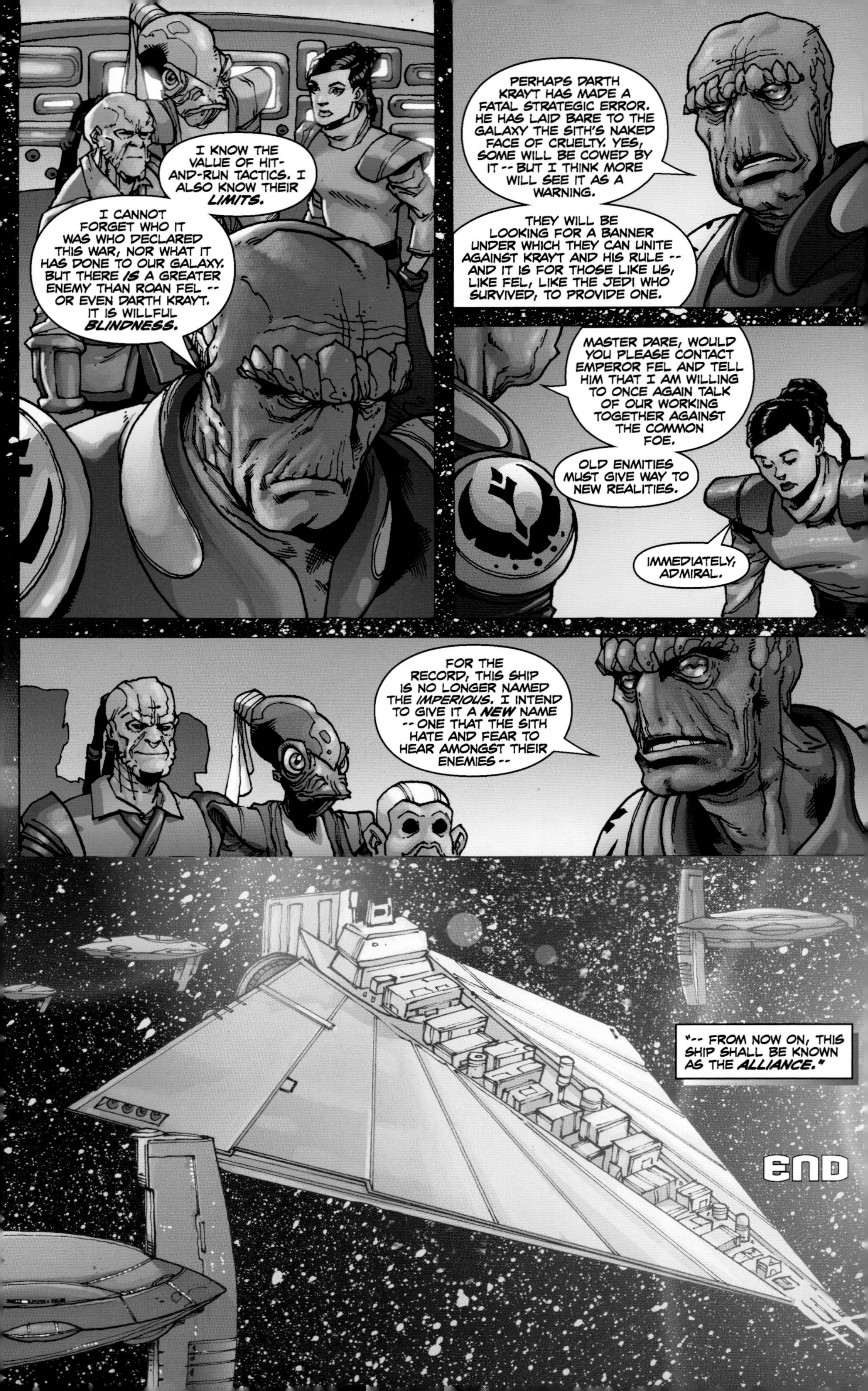
I KNOW THE VALUE OF HIT-AND-RUN TACTICS. I ALSO KNOW THEIR *LIMITS.*
I CANNOT FORGET WHO IT WAS WHO DECLARED THIS WAR, NOR WHAT IT HAS DONE TO OUR GALAXY. BUT THERE *IS* A GREATER ENEMY THAN ROAN FEL -- OR EVEN DARTH KRAYT. IT IS WILLFUL *BLINDNESS.*
PERHAPS DARTH KRAYT HAS MADE A FATAL STRATEGIC ERROR. HE HAS LAID BARE TO THE GALAXY THE SITH'S NAKED FACE OF CRUELTY. YES, SOME WILL BE COWED BY IT -- BUT I THINK MORE WILL SEE IT AS A WARNING.
THEY WILL BE LOOKING FOR A BANNER UNDER WHICH THEY CAN UNITE AGAINST KRAYT AND HIS RULE -- AND IT IS FOR THOSE LIKE US, LIKE FEL, LIKE THE JEDI WHO SURVIVED, TO PROVIDE ONE.
MASTER DARE, WOULD YOU PLEASE CONTACT EMPEROR FEL AND TELL HIM THAT I AM WILLING TO ONCE AGAIN TALK OF OUR WORKING TOGETHER AGAINST THE COMMON FOE.
OLD ENMITIES MUST GIVE WAY TO NEW REALITIES.
IMMEDIATELY, ADMIRAL.
FOR THE RECORD, THIS SHIP IS NO LONGER NAMED THE *IMPERIOUS.* I INTEND TO GIVE IT A *NEW* NAME -- ONE THAT THE SITH HATE AND FEAR TO HEAR AMONGST THEIR ENEMIES --
"-- FROM NOW ON, THIS SHIP SHALL BE KNOWN AS THE *ALLIANCE.*"
END

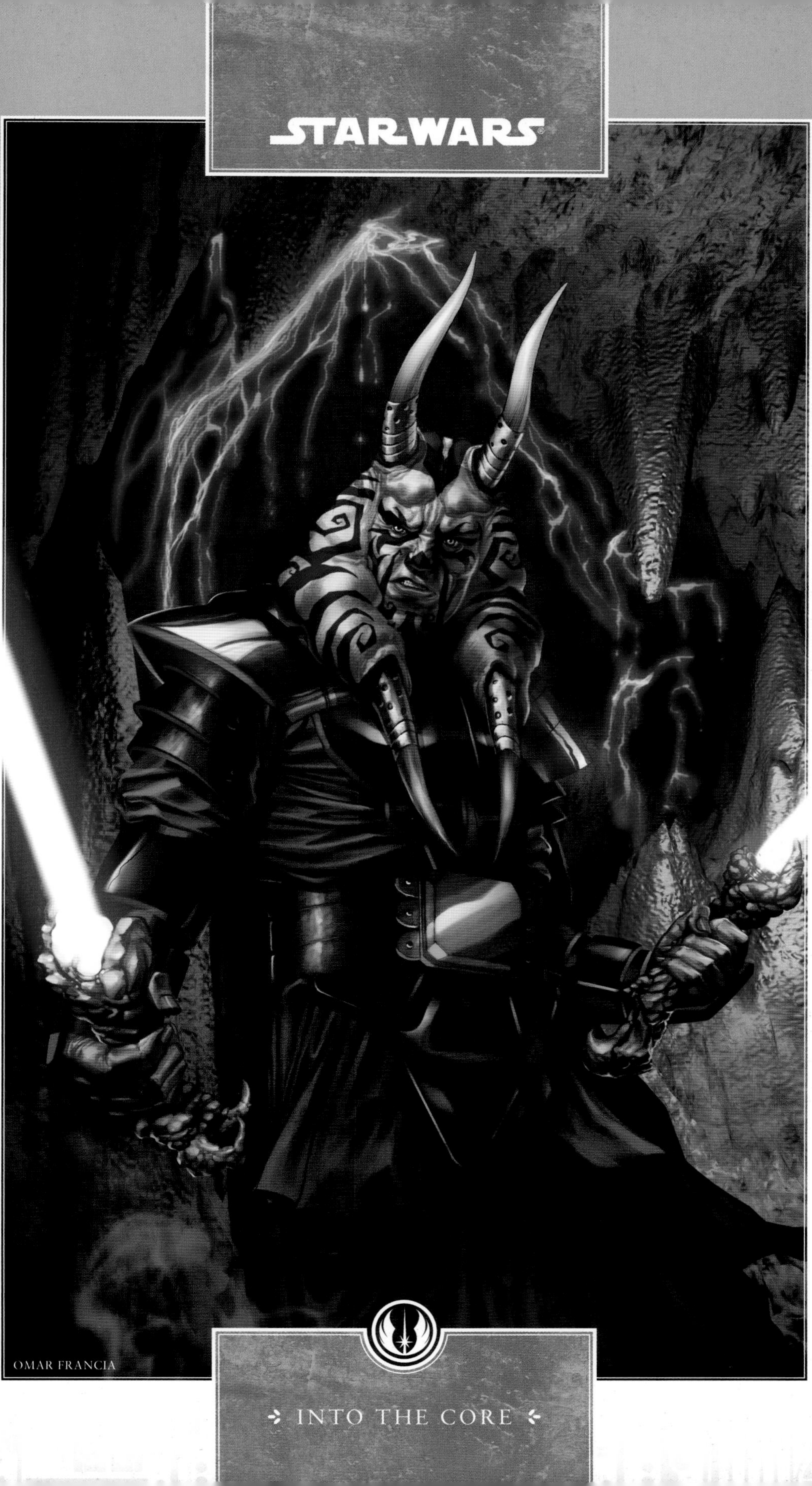
STAR WARS
OMAR FRANCIA
INTO THE CORE

INTO THE CORE

SCRIPT
John Ostrander

ART
Omar Francia

COLORS
Brad Anderson

LETTERS
Michael Heisler

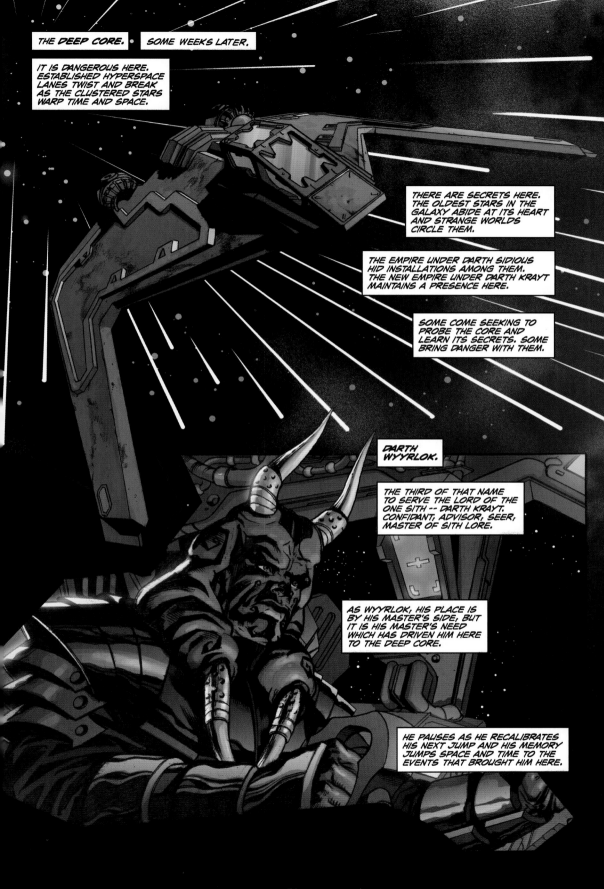

THE *DEEP CORE*.   SOME WEEKS LATER.

IT IS DANGEROUS HERE. ESTABLISHED HYPERSPACE LANES TWIST AND BREAK AS THE CLUSTERED STARS WARP TIME AND SPACE.

THERE ARE SECRETS HERE. THE OLDEST STARS IN THE GALAXY ABIDE AT ITS HEART AND STRANGE WORLDS CIRCLE THEM.

THE EMPIRE UNDER DARTH SIDIOUS HID INSTALLATIONS AMONG THEM. THE NEW EMPIRE UNDER DARTH KRAYT MAINTAINS A PRESENCE HERE.

SOME COME SEEKING TO PROBE THE CORE AND LEARN ITS SECRETS. SOME BRING DANGER WITH THEM.

DARTH WYYRLOK.

THE THIRD OF THAT NAME TO SERVE THE LORD OF THE ONE SITH -- DARTH KRAYT. CONFIDANT, ADVISOR, SEER, MASTER OF SITH LORE.

AS WYYRLOK, HIS PLACE IS BY HIS MASTER'S SIDE, BUT IT IS HIS MASTER'S NEED WHICH HAS DRIVEN HIM HERE TO THE DEEP CORE.

HE PAUSES AS HE RECALIBRATES HIS NEXT JUMP AND HIS MEMORY JUMPS SPACE AND TIME TO THE EVENTS THAT BROUGHT HIM HERE.

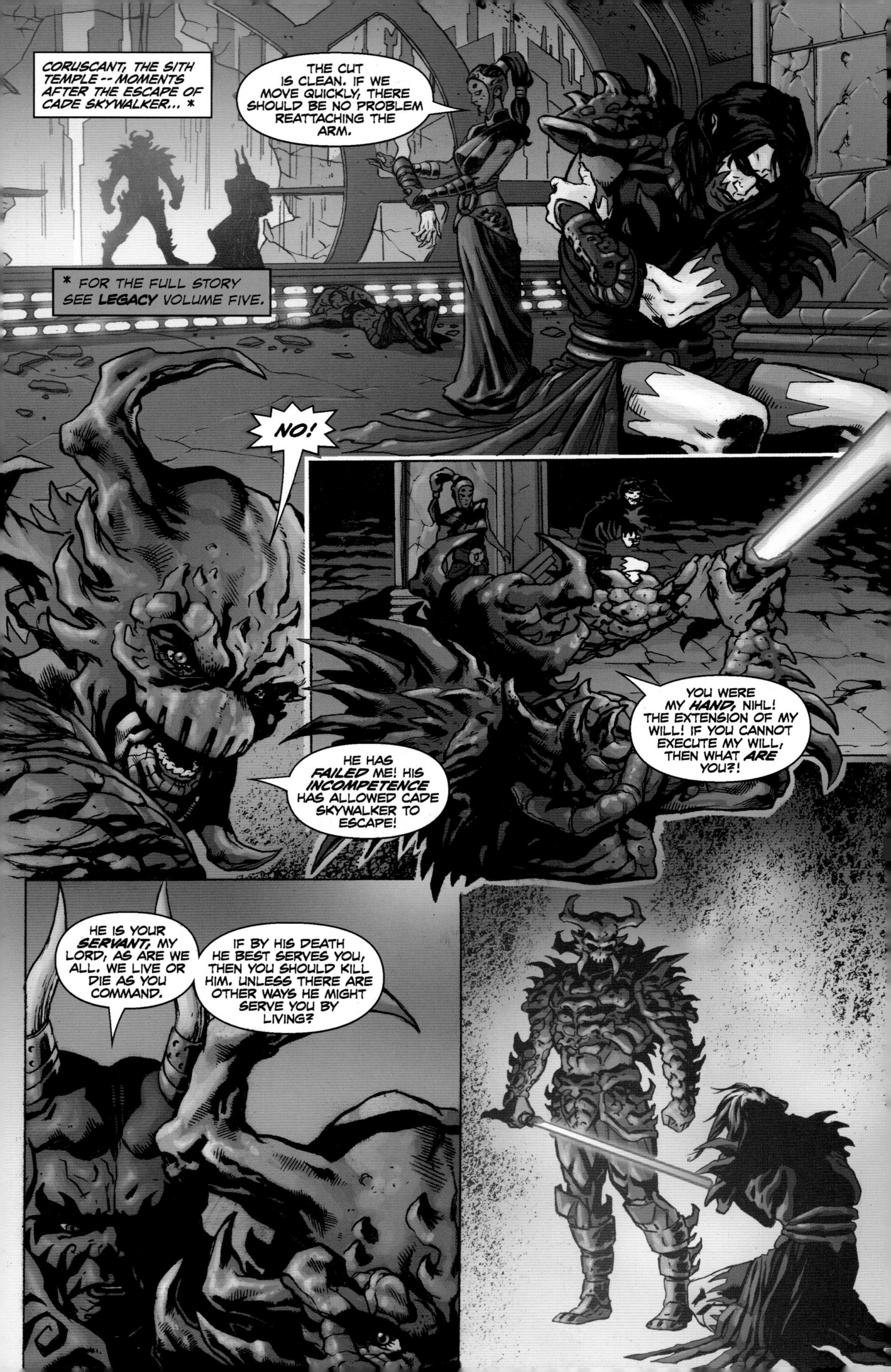
CORUSCANT, THE SITH TEMPLE -- MOMENTS AFTER THE ESCAPE OF CADE SKYWALKER... *
THE CUT IS CLEAN. IF WE MOVE QUICKLY, THERE SHOULD BE NO PROBLEM REATTACHING THE ARM.
* FOR THE FULL STORY SEE LEGACY VOLUME FIVE.
NO!
HE HAS FAILED ME! HIS INCOMPETENCE HAS ALLOWED CADE SKYWALKER TO ESCAPE!
YOU WERE MY HAND, NIHL! THE EXTENSION OF MY WILL! IF YOU CANNOT EXECUTE MY WILL, THEN WHAT ARE YOU?!
HE IS YOUR SERVANT, MY LORD, AS ARE WE ALL. WE LIVE OR DIE AS YOU COMMAND.
IF BY HIS DEATH HE BEST SERVES YOU, THEN YOU SHOULD KILL HIM. UNLESS THERE ARE OTHER WAYS HE MIGHT SERVE YOU BY LIVING?

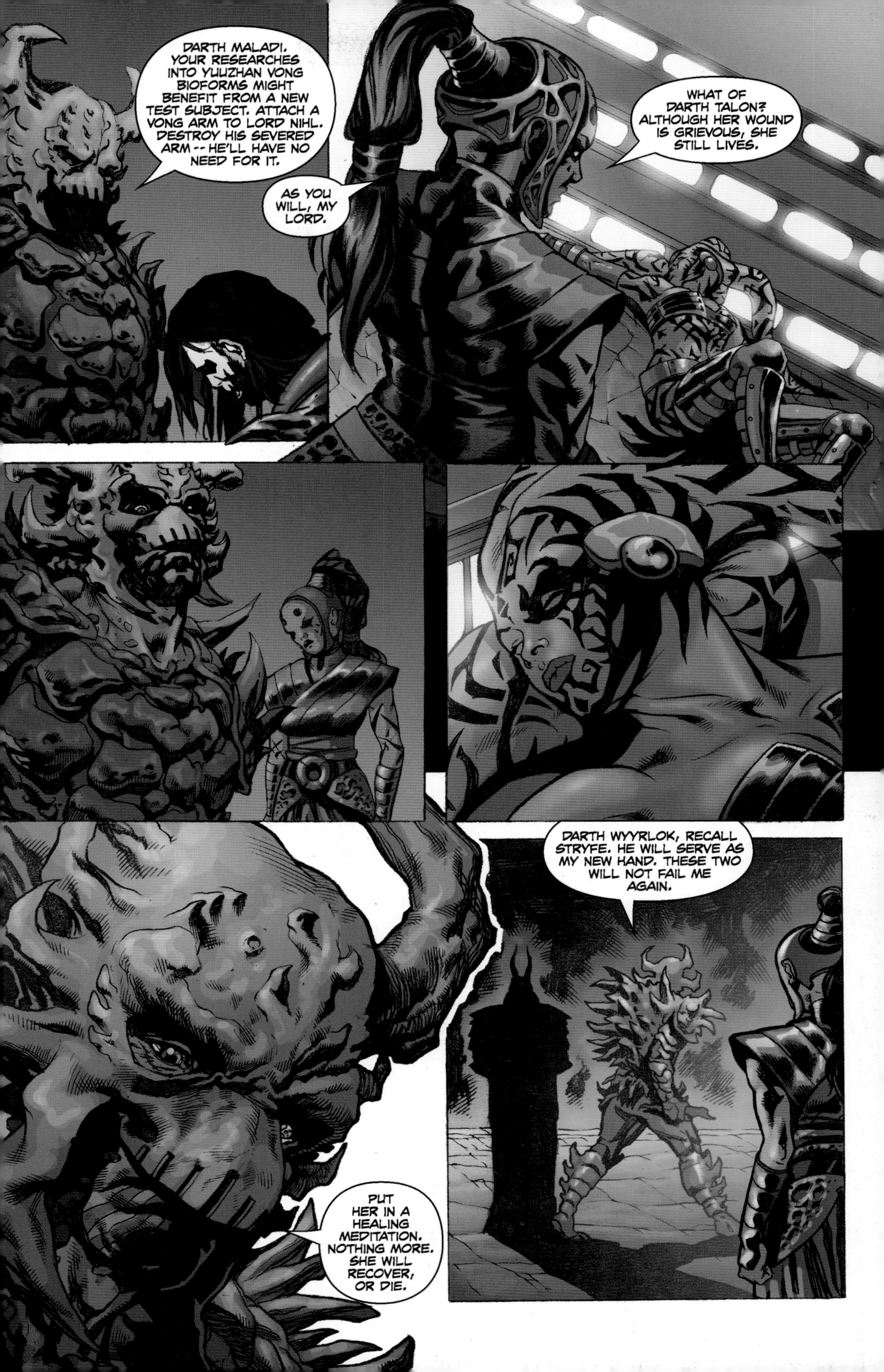
DARTH MALADI. YOUR RESEARCHES INTO YUUZHAN VONG BIOFORMS MIGHT BENEFIT FROM A NEW TEST SUBJECT. ATTACH A VONG ARM TO LORD NIHL. DESTROY HIS SEVERED ARM -- HE'LL HAVE NO NEED FOR IT.
AS YOU WILL, MY LORD.
WHAT OF DARTH TALON? ALTHOUGH HER WOUND IS GRIEVOUS, SHE STILL LIVES.
PUT HER IN A HEALING MEDITATION. NOTHING MORE. SHE WILL RECOVER, OR DIE.
DARTH WYYRLOK, RECALL STRYFE. HE WILL SERVE AS MY NEW HAND. THESE TWO WILL NOT FAIL ME AGAIN.

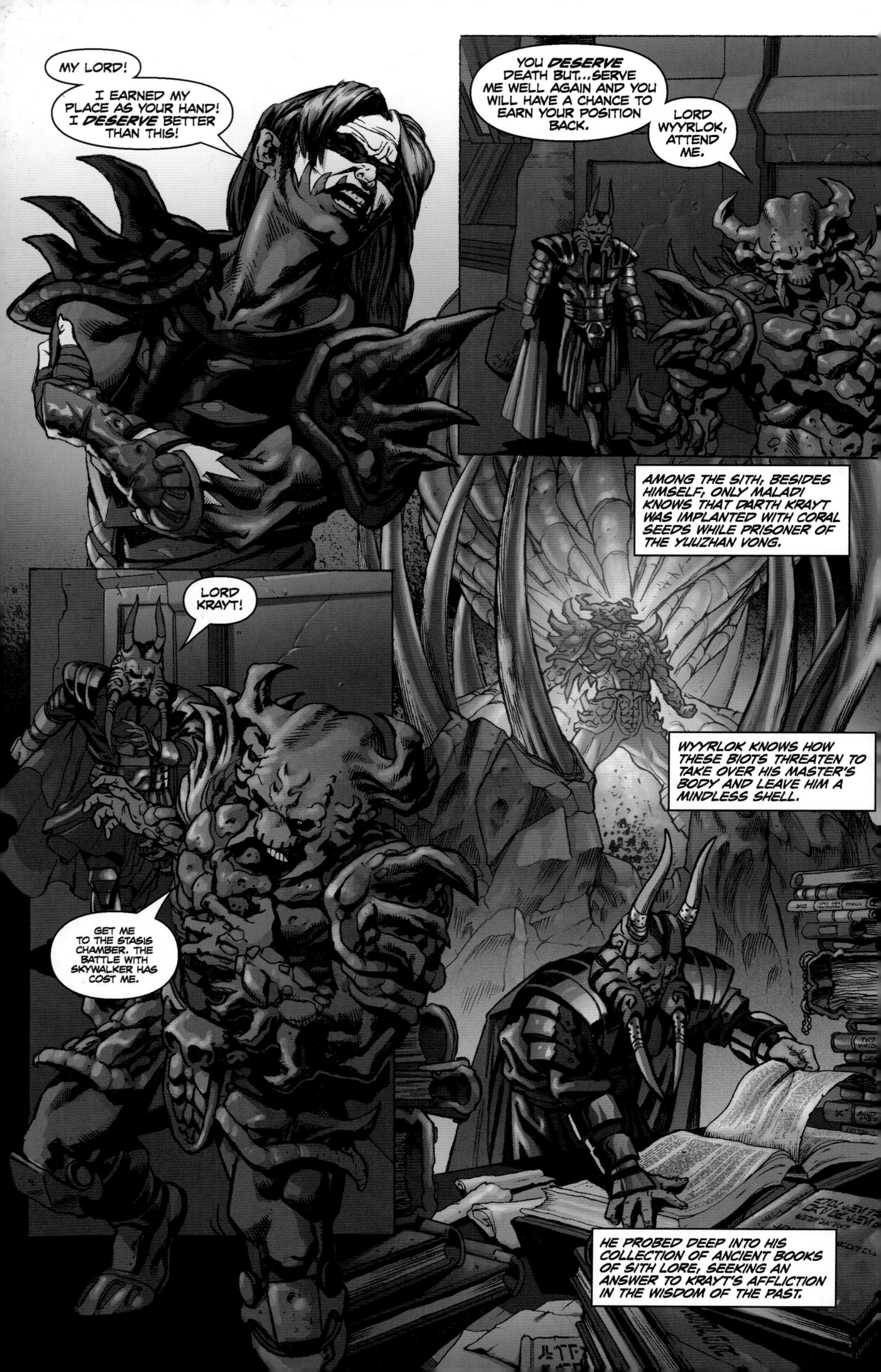

MY LORD!
I EARNED MY PLACE AS YOUR HAND! I DESERVE BETTER THAN THIS!
YOU DESERVE DEATH BUT...SERVE ME WELL AGAIN AND YOU WILL HAVE A CHANCE TO EARN YOUR POSITION BACK.
LORD WYYRLOK, ATTEND ME.
LORD KRAYT!
GET ME TO THE STASIS CHAMBER. THE BATTLE WITH SKYWALKER HAS COST ME.
AMONG THE SITH, BESIDES HIMSELF, ONLY MALADI KNOWS THAT DARTH KRAYT WAS IMPLANTED WITH CORAL SEEDS WHILE PRISONER OF THE YUUZHAN VONG.
WYYRLOK KNOWS HOW THESE BIOTS THREATEN TO TAKE OVER HIS MASTER'S BODY AND LEAVE HIM A MINDLESS SHELL.
HE PROBED DEEP INTO HIS COLLECTION OF ANCIENT BOOKS OF SITH LORE, SEEKING AN ANSWER TO KRAYT'S AFFLICTION IN THE WISDOM OF THE PAST.

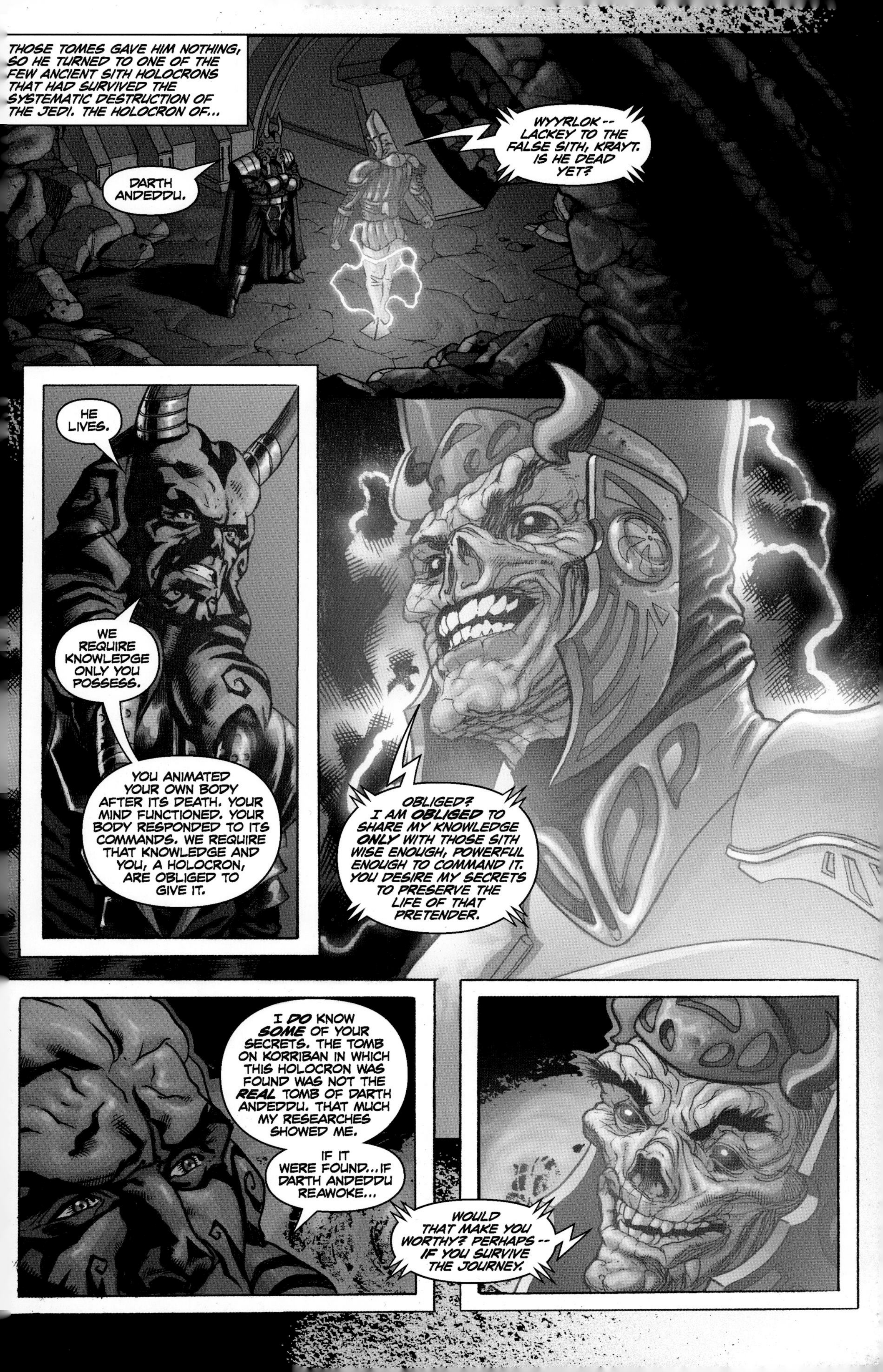
THOSE TOMES GAVE HIM NOTHING, SO HE TURNED TO ONE OF THE FEW ANCIENT SITH HOLOCRONS THAT HAD SURVIVED THE SYSTEMATIC DESTRUCTION OF THE JEDI. THE HOLOCRON OF...
DARTH ANDEDDU.
WYYRLOK -- LACKEY TO THE FALSE SITH, KRAYT. IS HE DEAD YET?
HE LIVES.
WE REQUIRE KNOWLEDGE ONLY YOU POSSESS.
YOU ANIMATED YOUR OWN BODY AFTER ITS DEATH. YOUR MIND FUNCTIONED. YOUR BODY RESPONDED TO ITS COMMANDS. WE REQUIRE THAT KNOWLEDGE AND YOU, A HOLOCRON, ARE OBLIGED TO GIVE IT.
OBLIGED? I AM OBLIGED TO SHARE MY KNOWLEDGE ONLY WITH THOSE SITH WISE ENOUGH, POWERFUL ENOUGH TO COMMAND IT. YOU DESIRE MY SECRETS TO PRESERVE THE LIFE OF THAT PRETENDER.
I DO KNOW SOME OF YOUR SECRETS. THE TOMB ON KORRIBAN IN WHICH THIS HOLOCRON WAS FOUND WAS NOT THE REAL TOMB OF DARTH ANDEDDU. THAT MUCH MY RESEARCHES SHOWED ME.
IF IT WERE FOUND...IF DARTH ANDEDDU REAWOKE...
WOULD THAT MAKE YOU WORTHY? PERHAPS -- IF YOU SURVIVE THE JOURNEY.

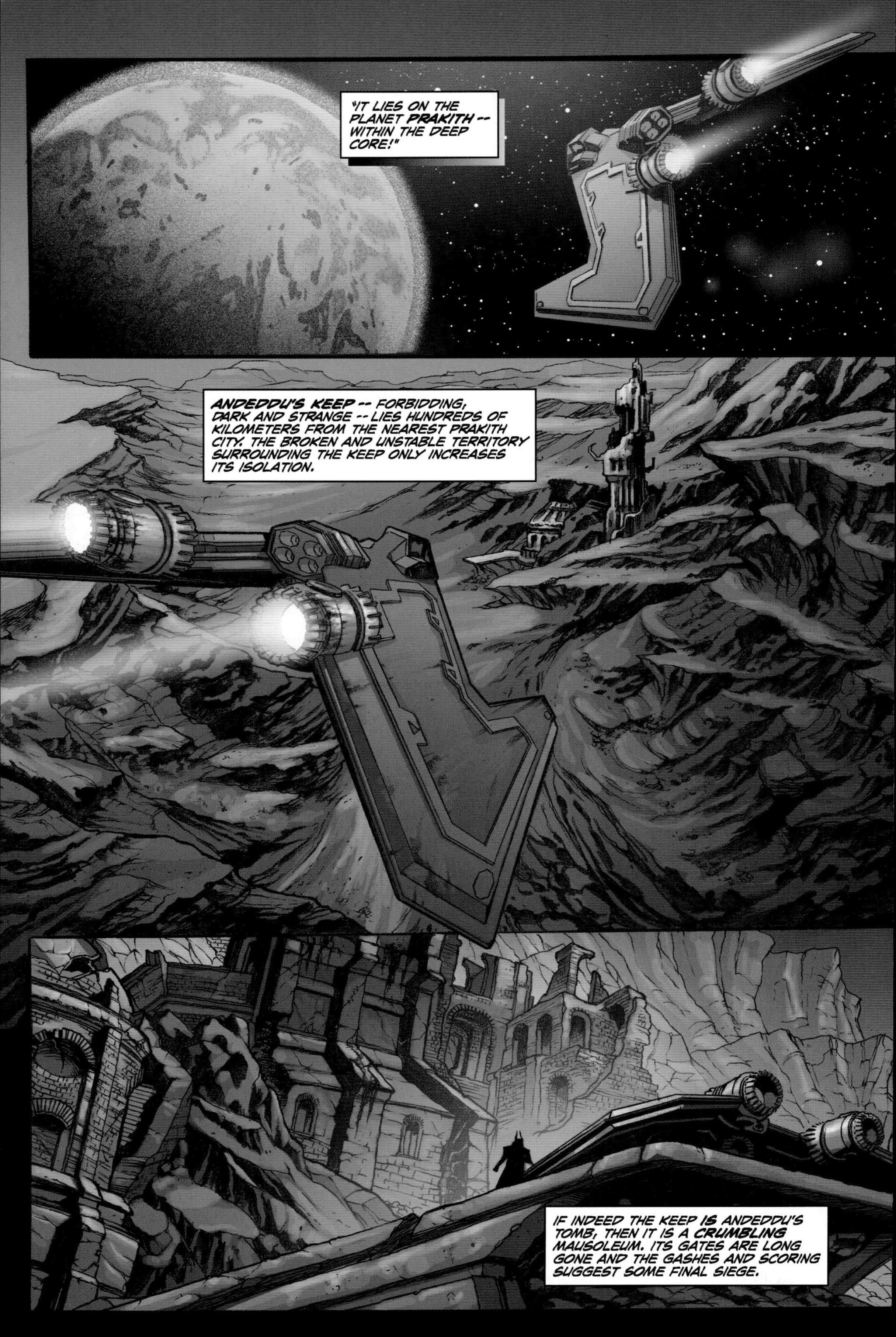
"IT LIES ON THE PLANET PRAKITH -- WITHIN THE DEEP CORE!"
ANDEDDU'S KEEP -- FORBIDDING, DARK AND STRANGE -- LIES HUNDREDS OF KILOMETERS FROM THE NEAREST PRAKITH CITY. THE BROKEN AND UNSTABLE TERRITORY SURROUNDING THE KEEP ONLY INCREASES ITS ISOLATION.
IF INDEED THE KEEP IS ANDEDDU'S TOMB, THEN IT IS A CRUMBLING MAUSOLEUM. ITS GATES ARE LONG GONE AND THE GASHES AND SCORING SUGGEST SOME FINAL SIEGE.

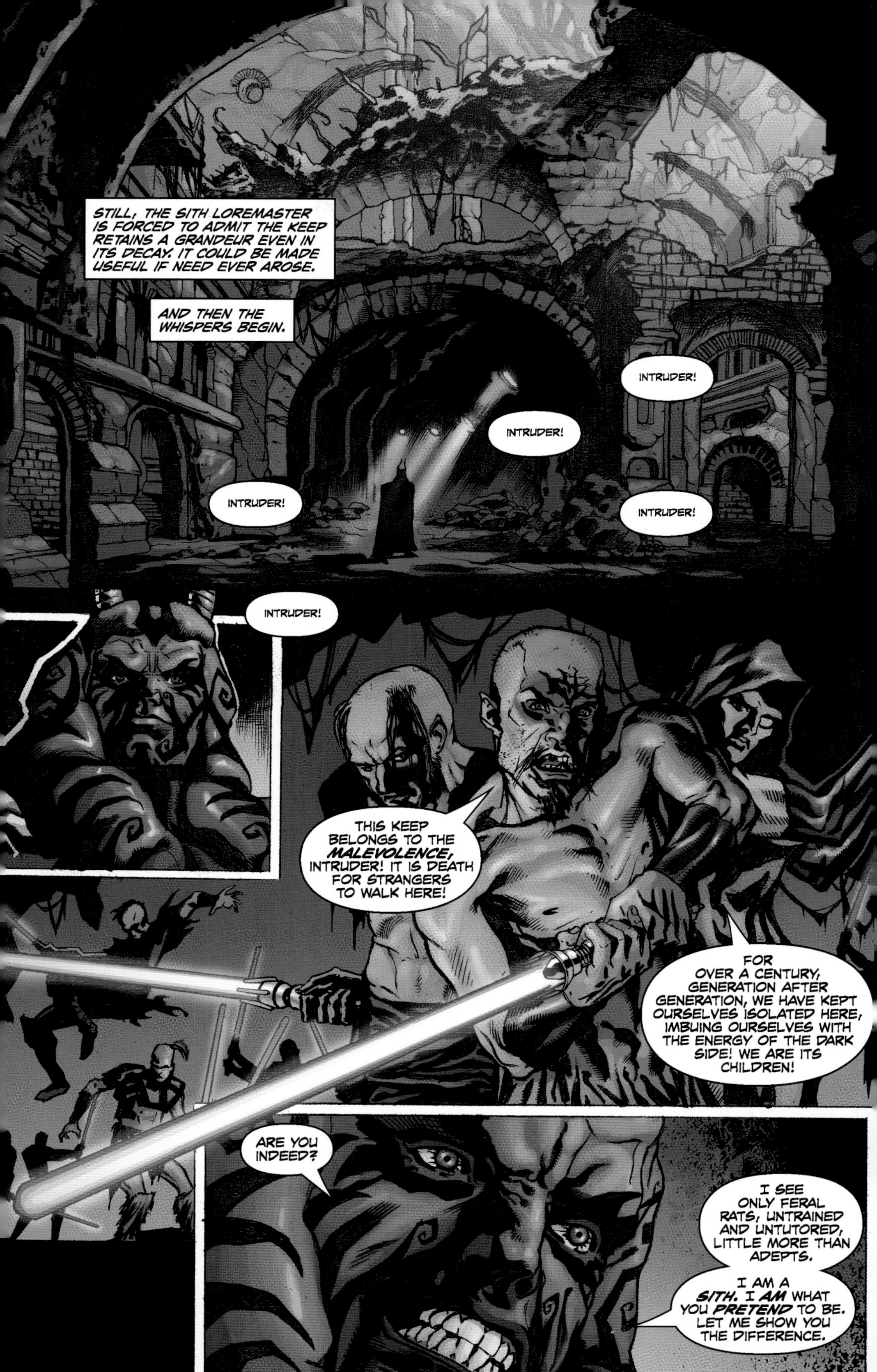
STILL, THE SITH LOREMASTER IS FORCED TO ADMIT THE KEEP RETAINS A GRANDEUR EVEN IN ITS DECAY. IT COULD BE MADE USEFUL IF NEED EVER AROSE.
AND THEN THE WHISPERS BEGIN.
INTRUDER!
INTRUDER!
INTRUDER!
INTRUDER!
INTRUDER!
THIS KEEP BELONGS TO THE *MALEVOLENCE,* INTRUDER! IT IS DEATH FOR STRANGERS TO WALK HERE!
FOR OVER A CENTURY, GENERATION AFTER GENERATION, WE HAVE KEPT OURSELVES ISOLATED HERE, IMBUING OURSELVES WITH THE ENERGY OF THE DARK SIDE! WE ARE ITS CHILDREN!
ARE YOU INDEED?
I SEE ONLY FERAL RATS, UNTRAINED AND UNTUTORED, LITTLE MORE THAN ADEPTS.
I AM A *SITH.* I *AM* WHAT YOU *PRETEND* TO BE. LET ME SHOW YOU THE DIFFERENCE.

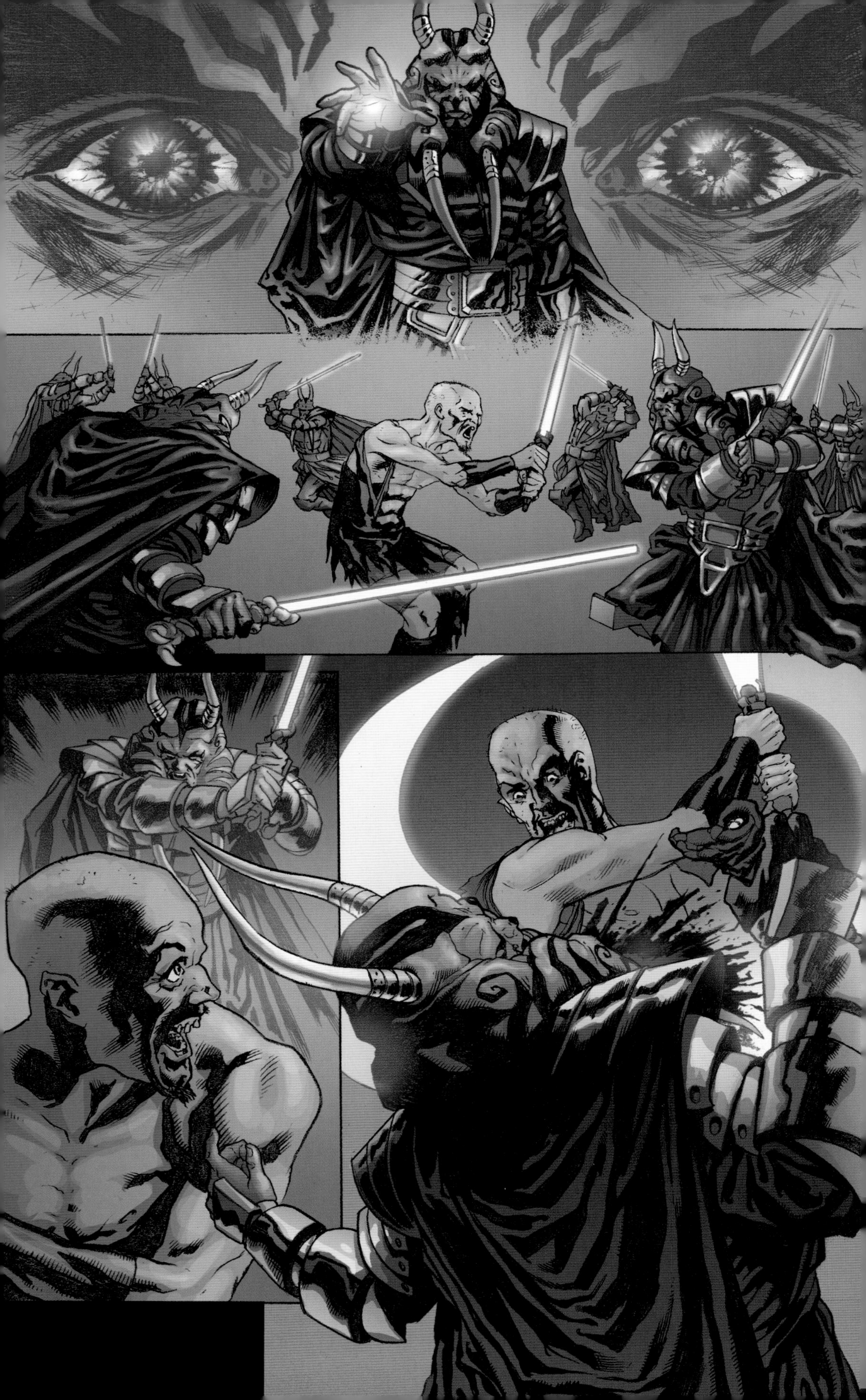

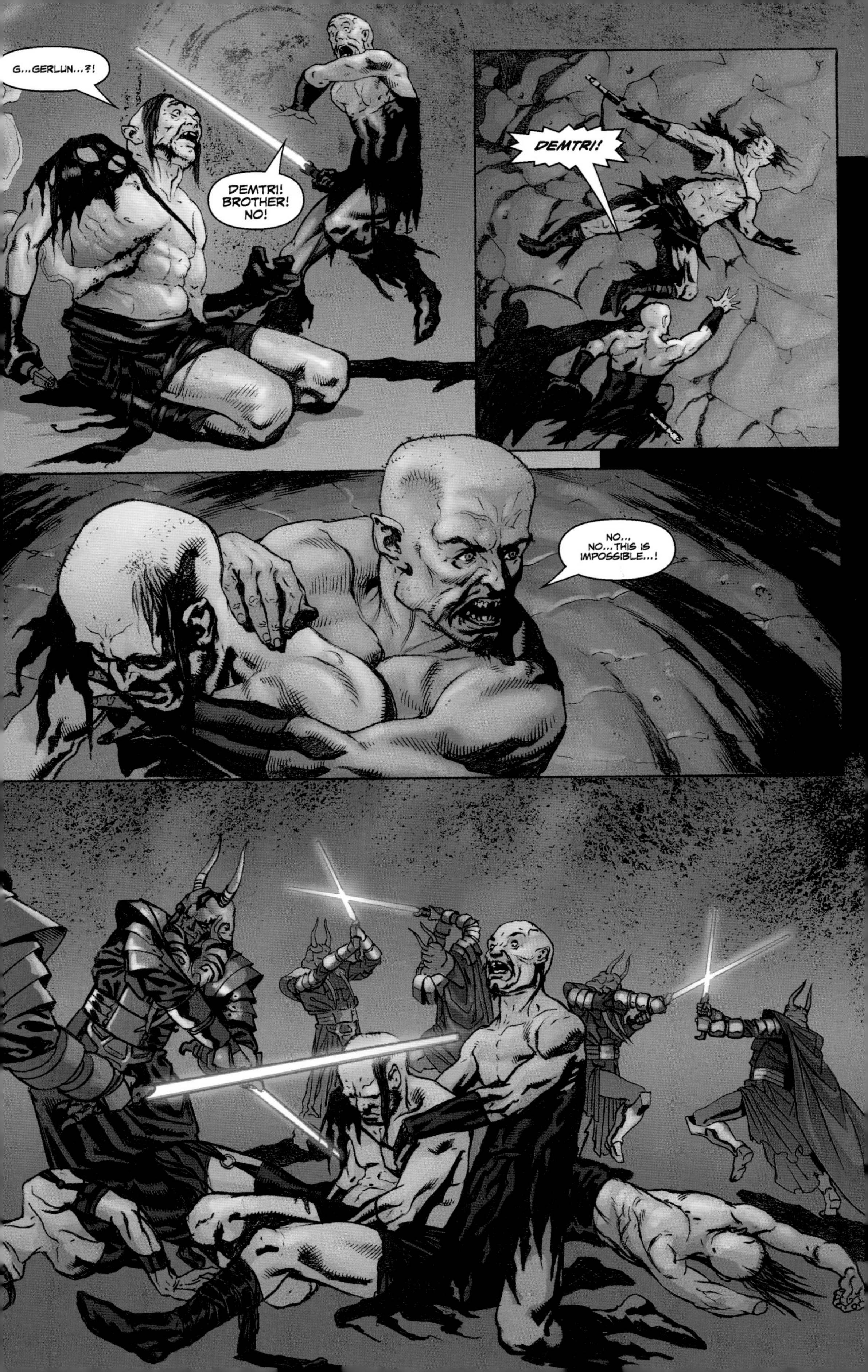
G...GERLUN...?!
DEMTRI! BROTHER! NO!
DEMTRI!
NO... NO...THIS IS IMPOSSIBLE...!

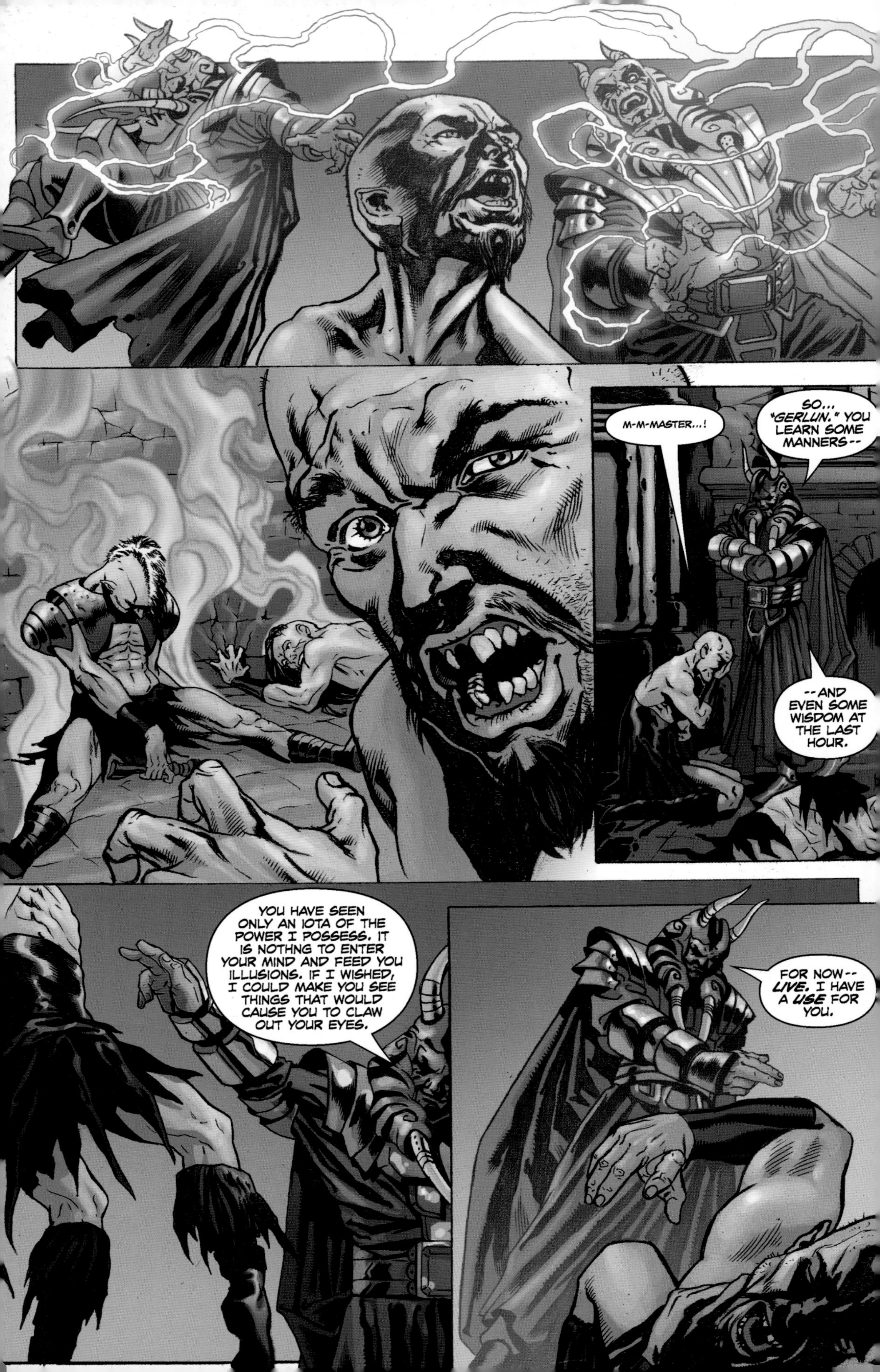

M-M-MASTER...!
SO... "GERLUN." YOU LEARN SOME MANNERS--
--AND EVEN SOME WISDOM AT THE LAST HOUR.
YOU HAVE SEEN ONLY AN IOTA OF THE POWER I POSSESS. IT IS NOTHNG TO ENTER YOUR MIND AND FEED YOU ILLUSIONS. IF I WISHED, I COULD MAKE YOU SEE THINGS THAT WOULD CAUSE YOU TO CLAW OUT YOUR EYES.
FOR NOW-- *LIVE.* I HAVE A *USE* FOR YOU.

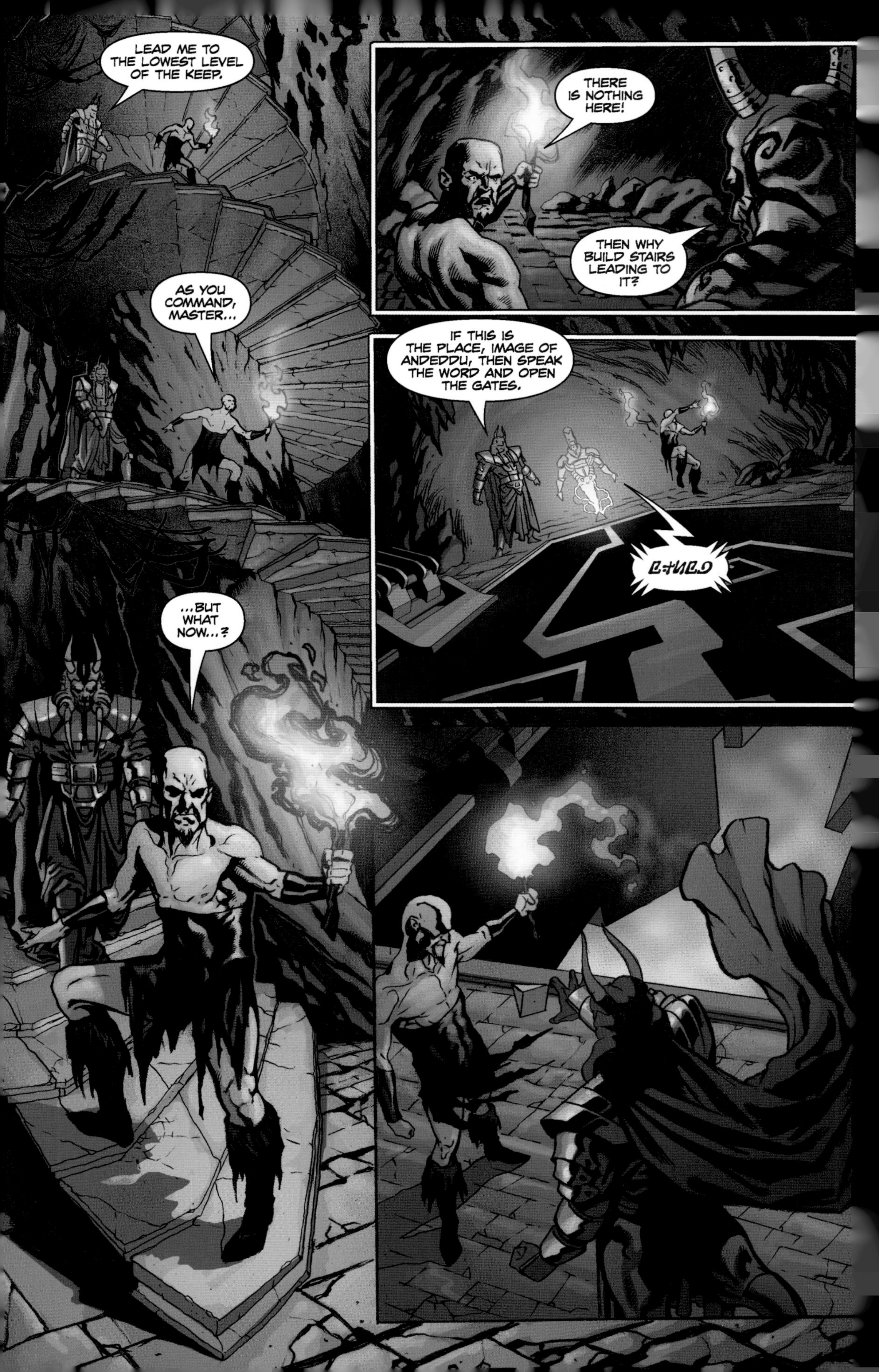
LEAD ME TO THE LOWEST LEVEL OF THE KEEP.
AS YOU COMMAND, MASTER...
...BUT WHAT NOW...?
THERE IS NOTHING HERE!
THEN WHY BUILD STAIRS LEADING TO IT?
IF THIS IS THE PLACE, IMAGE OF ANDEDDU, THEN SPEAK THE WORD AND OPEN THE GATES.

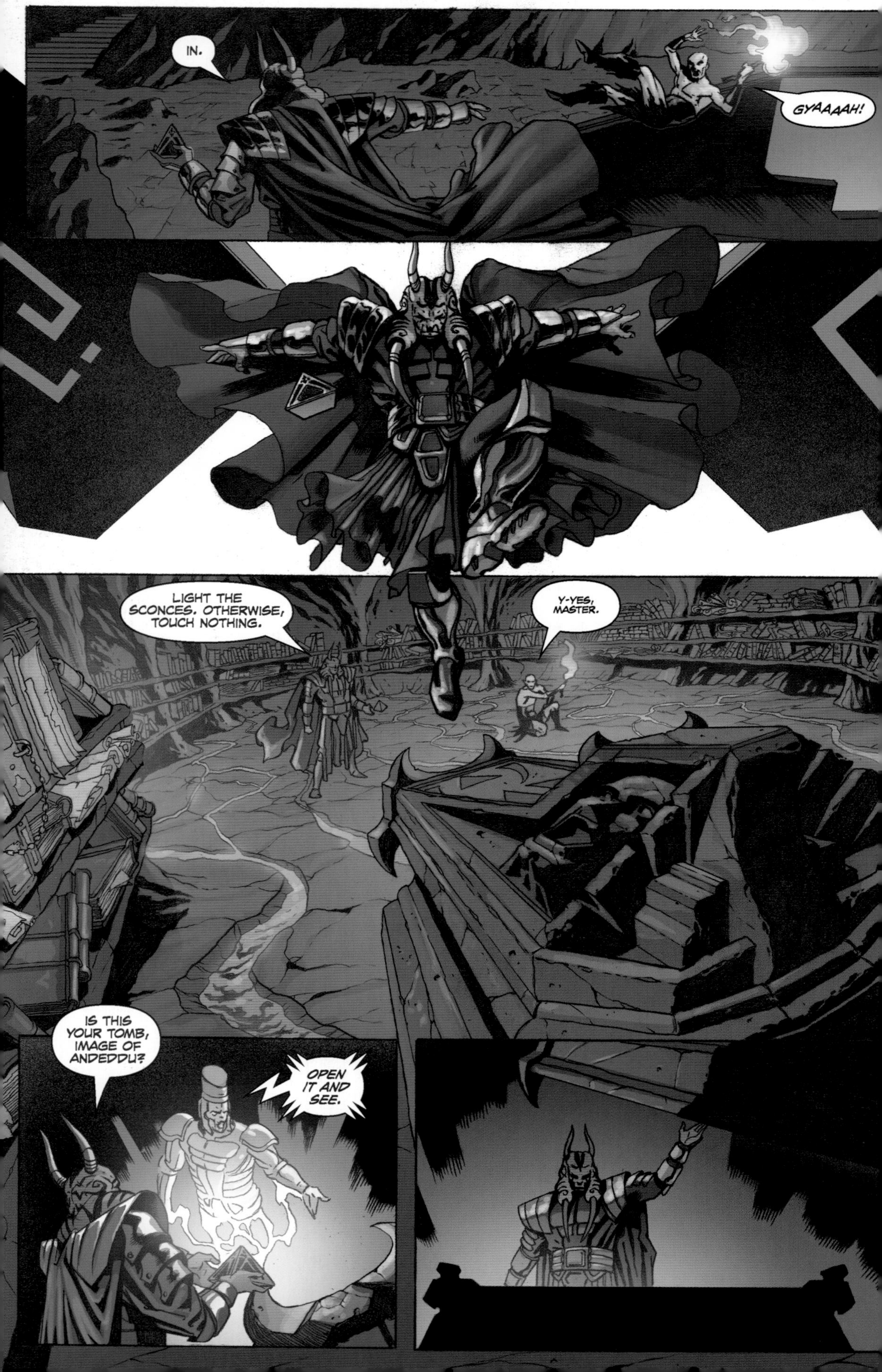
IN.
GYAAAAH!
LIGHT THE SCONCES. OTHERWISE, TOUCH NOTHING.
Y-YES, MASTER.
IS THIS YOUR TOMB, IMAGE OF ANDEDDU?
OPEN IT AND SEE.

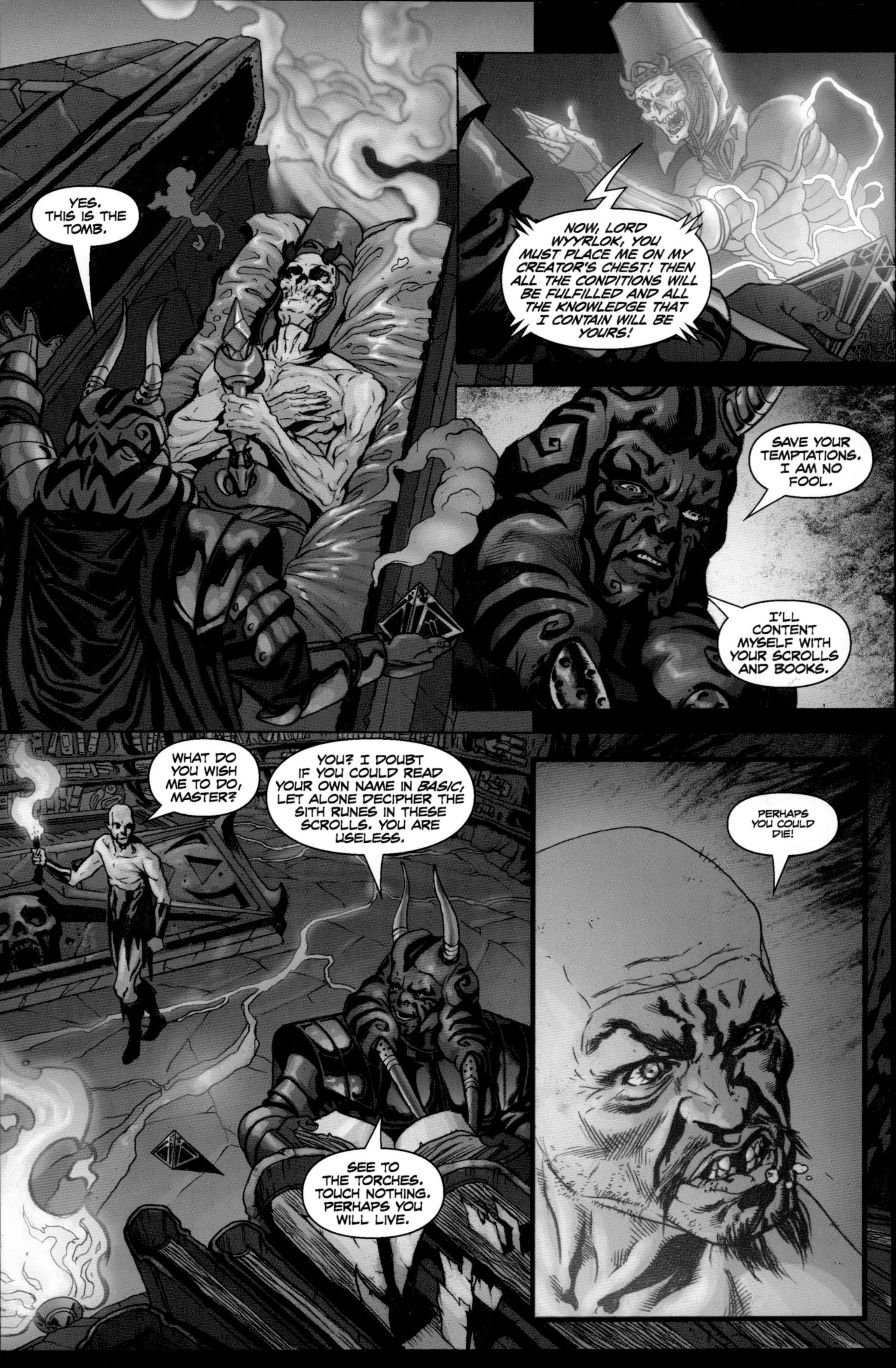
YES. THIS IS THE TOMB.
NOW, LORD WYYRLOK, YOU MUST PLACE ME ON MY CREATOR'S CHEST! THEN ALL THE CONDITIONS WILL BE FULFILLED AND ALL THE KNOWLEDGE THAT I CONTAIN WILL BE YOURS!
SAVE YOUR TEMPTATIONS. I AM NO FOOL.
I'LL CONTENT MYSELF WITH YOUR SCROLLS AND BOOKS.
WHAT DO YOU WISH ME TO DO, MASTER?
YOU? I DOUBT IF YOU COULD READ YOUR OWN NAME IN *BASIC*, LET ALONE DECIPHER THE SITH RUNES IN THESE SCROLLS. YOU ARE USELESS.
SEE TO THE TORCHES. TOUCH NOTHING. PERHAPS YOU WILL LIVE.
PERHAPS YOU COULD DIE!

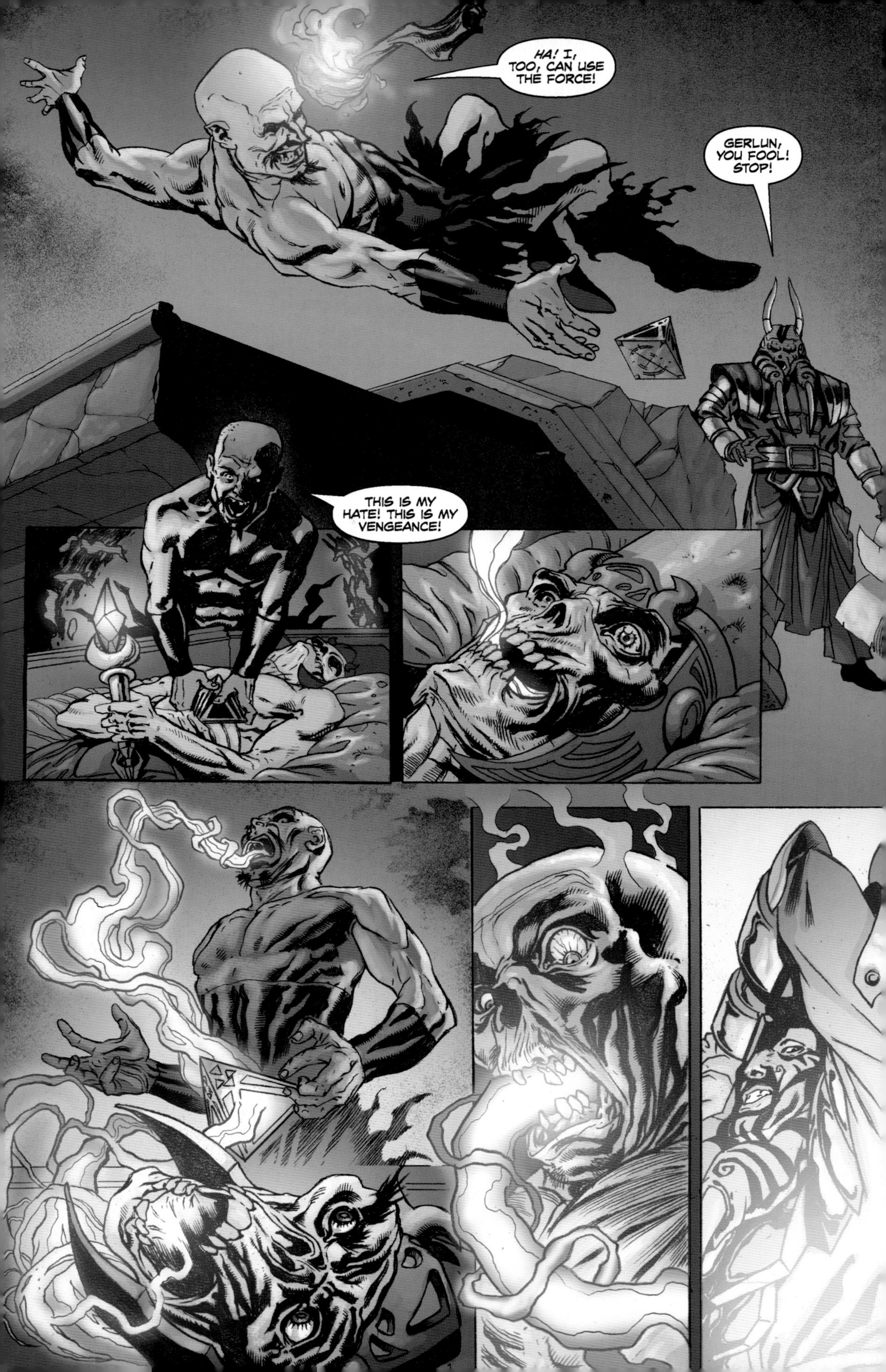
HA! I, TOO, CAN USE THE FORCE!
GERLUN, YOU FOOL! STOP!
THIS IS MY HATE! THIS IS MY VENGEANCE!

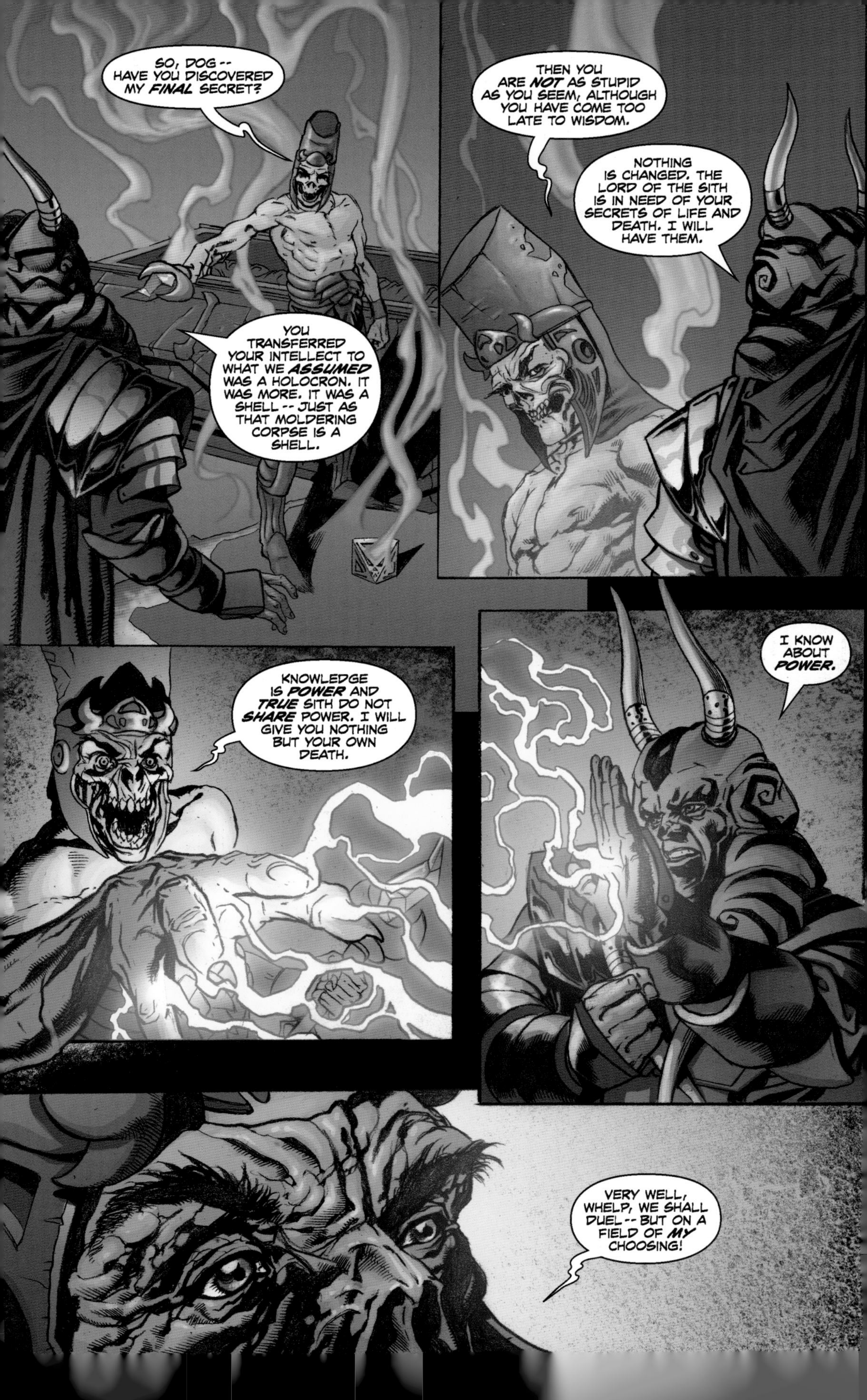
SO, DOG -- HAVE YOU DISCOVERED MY FINAL SECRET?
YOU TRANSFERRED YOUR INTELLECT TO WHAT WE ASSUMED WAS A HOLOCRON. IT WAS MORE. IT WAS A SHELL -- JUST AS THAT MOLDERING CORPSE IS A SHELL.
THEN YOU ARE NOT AS STUPID AS YOU SEEM, ALTHOUGH YOU HAVE COME TOO LATE TO WISDOM.
NOTHING IS CHANGED. THE LORD OF THE SITH IS IN NEED OF YOUR SECRETS OF LIFE AND DEATH. I WILL HAVE THEM.
KNOWLEDGE IS POWER AND TRUE SITH DO NOT SHARE POWER. I WILL GIVE YOU NOTHING BUT YOUR OWN DEATH.
I KNOW ABOUT POWER.
VERY WELL, WHELP, WE SHALL DUEL -- BUT ON A FIELD OF MY CHOOSING!

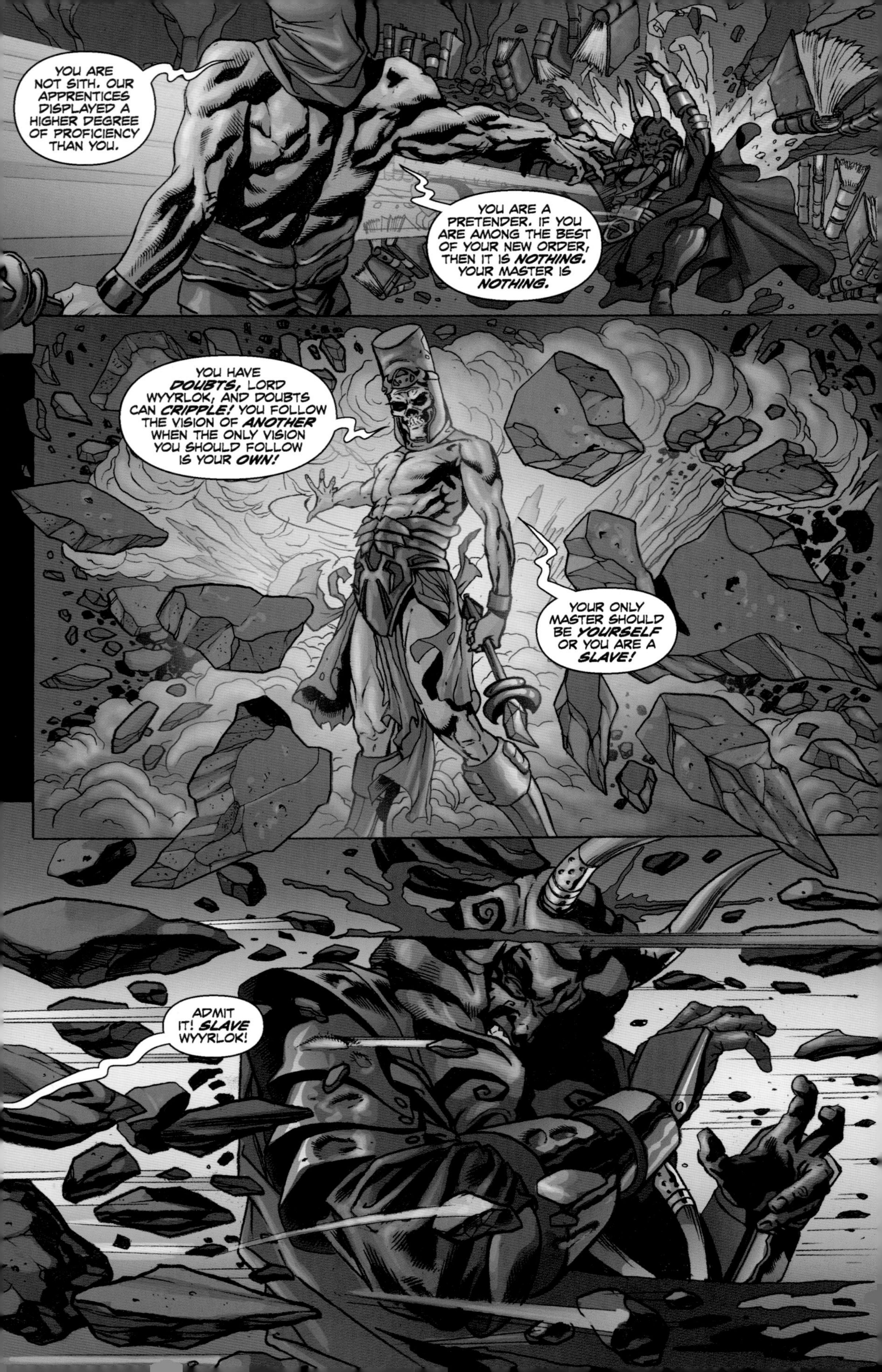
YOU ARE NOT SITH. OUR APPRENTICES DISPLAYED A HIGHER DEGREE OF PROFICIENCY THAN YOU.
YOU ARE A PRETENDER. IF YOU ARE AMONG THE BEST OF YOUR NEW ORDER, THEN IT IS NOTHING. YOUR MASTER IS NOTHING.
YOU HAVE DOUBTS, LORD WYYRLOK, AND DOUBTS CAN CRIPPLE! YOU FOLLOW THE VISION OF ANOTHER WHEN THE ONLY VISION YOU SHOULD FOLLOW IS YOUR OWN!
YOUR ONLY MASTER SHOULD BE YOURSELF OR YOU ARE A SLAVE!
ADMIT IT! SLAVE WYYRLOK!

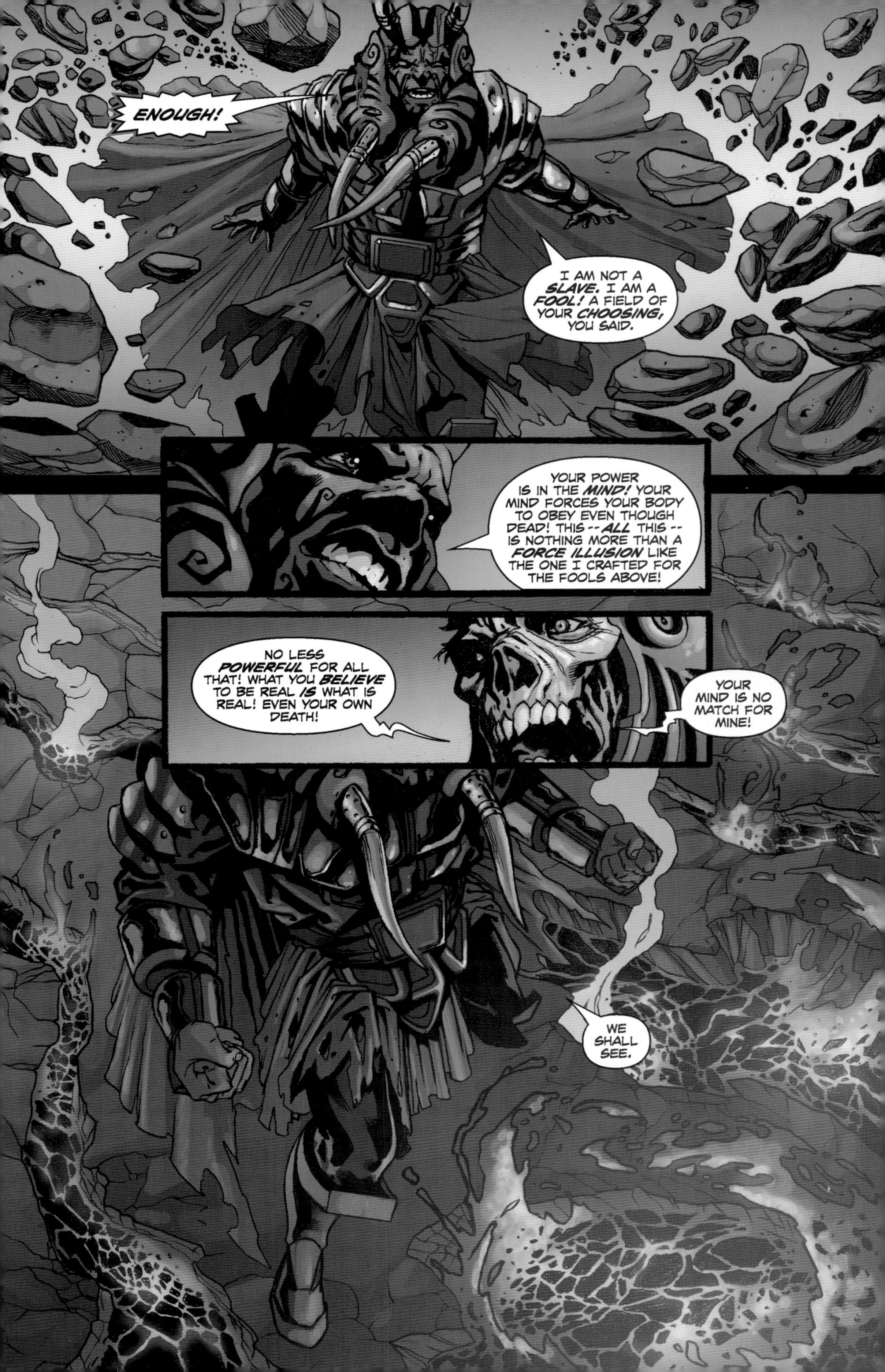
ENOUGH!
I AM NOT A SLAVE. I AM A FOOL! A FIELD OF YOUR CHOOSING, YOU SAID.
YOUR POWER IS IN THE MIND! YOUR MIND FORCES YOUR BODY TO OBEY EVEN THOUGH DEAD! THIS--ALL THIS-- IS NOTHING MORE THAN A FORCE ILLUSION LIKE THE ONE I CRAFTED FOR THE FOOLS ABOVE!
NO LESS POWERFUL FOR ALL THAT! WHAT YOU BELIEVE TO BE REAL IS WHAT IS REAL! EVEN YOUR OWN DEATH!
YOUR MIND IS NO MATCH FOR MINE!
WE SHALL SEE.

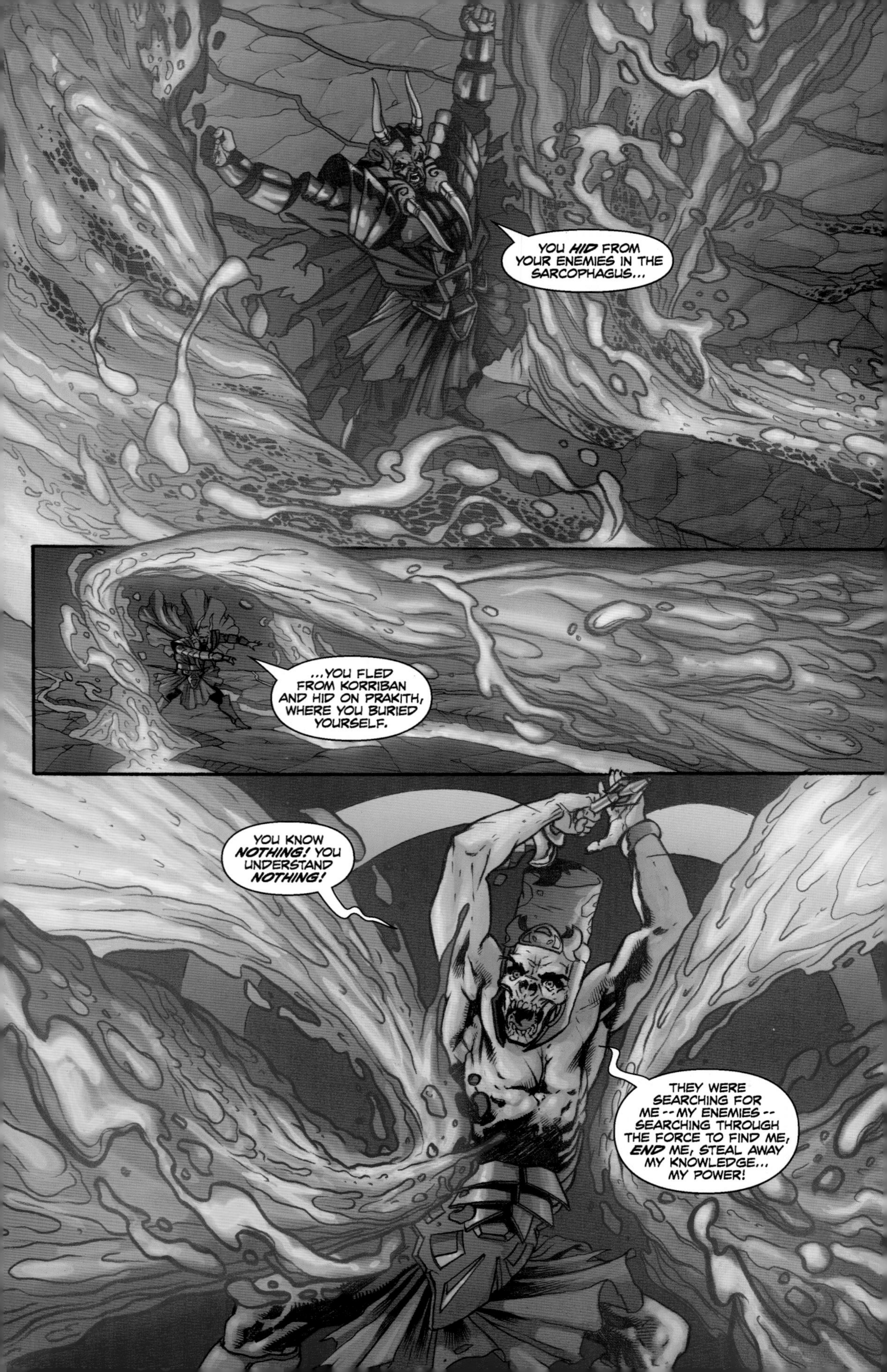
YOU HID FROM YOUR ENEMIES IN THE SARCOPHAGUS...
...YOU FLED FROM KORRIBAN AND HID ON PRAKITH, WHERE YOU BURIED YOURSELF.
YOU KNOW NOTHING! YOU UNDERSTAND NOTHING!
THEY WERE SEARCHING FOR ME -- MY ENEMIES -- SEARCHING THROUGH THE FORCE TO FIND ME, END ME, STEAL AWAY MY KNOWLEDGE... MY POWER!

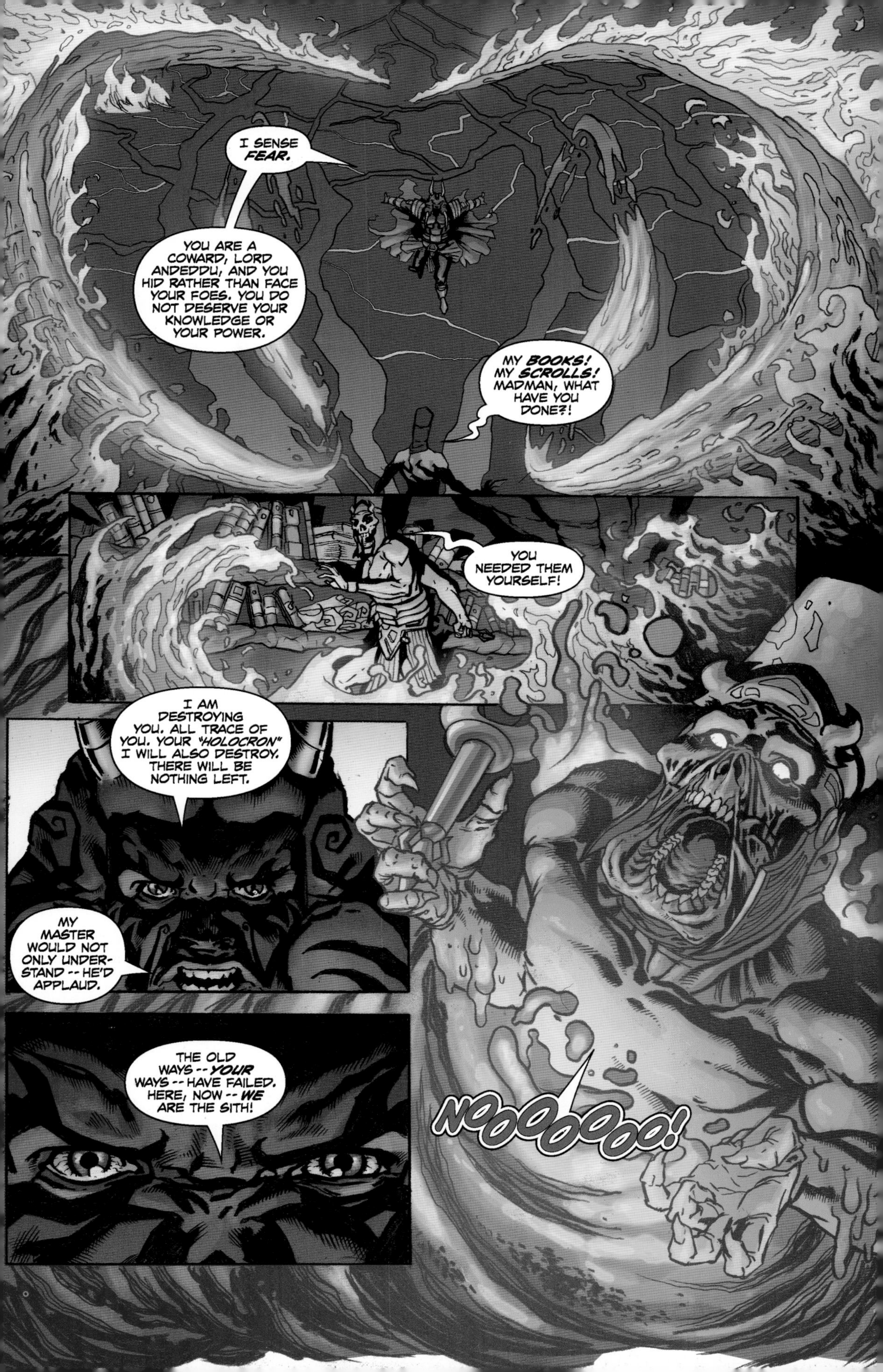
I SENSE *FEAR.*
YOU ARE A COWARD, LORD ANDEDDU, AND YOU HID RATHER THAN FACE YOUR FOES. YOU DO NOT DESERVE YOUR KNOWLEDGE OR YOUR POWER.
MY *BOOKS!* MY *SCROLLS!* MADMAN, WHAT HAVE YOU DONE?!
YOU NEEDED THEM YOURSELF!
I AM DESTROYING YOU. ALL TRACE OF YOU. YOUR "HOLOCRON" I WILL ALSO DESTROY. THERE WILL BE NOTHING LEFT.
MY MASTER WOULD NOT ONLY UNDER-STAND -- HE'D APPLAUD.
THE OLD WAYS -- *YOUR* WAYS -- HAVE FAILED. HERE, NOW -- *WE* ARE THE SITH!
NOOOOOOOO!

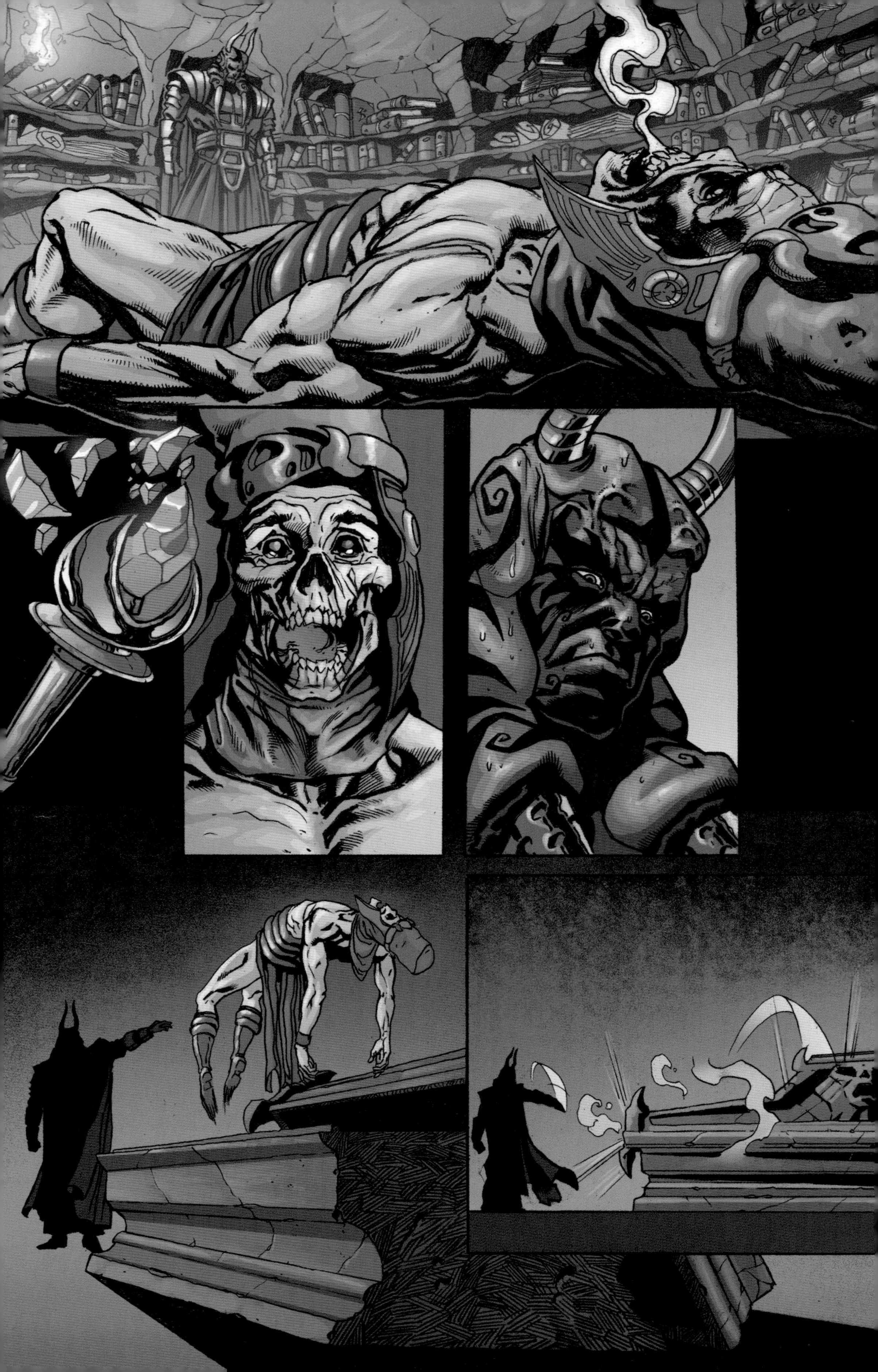

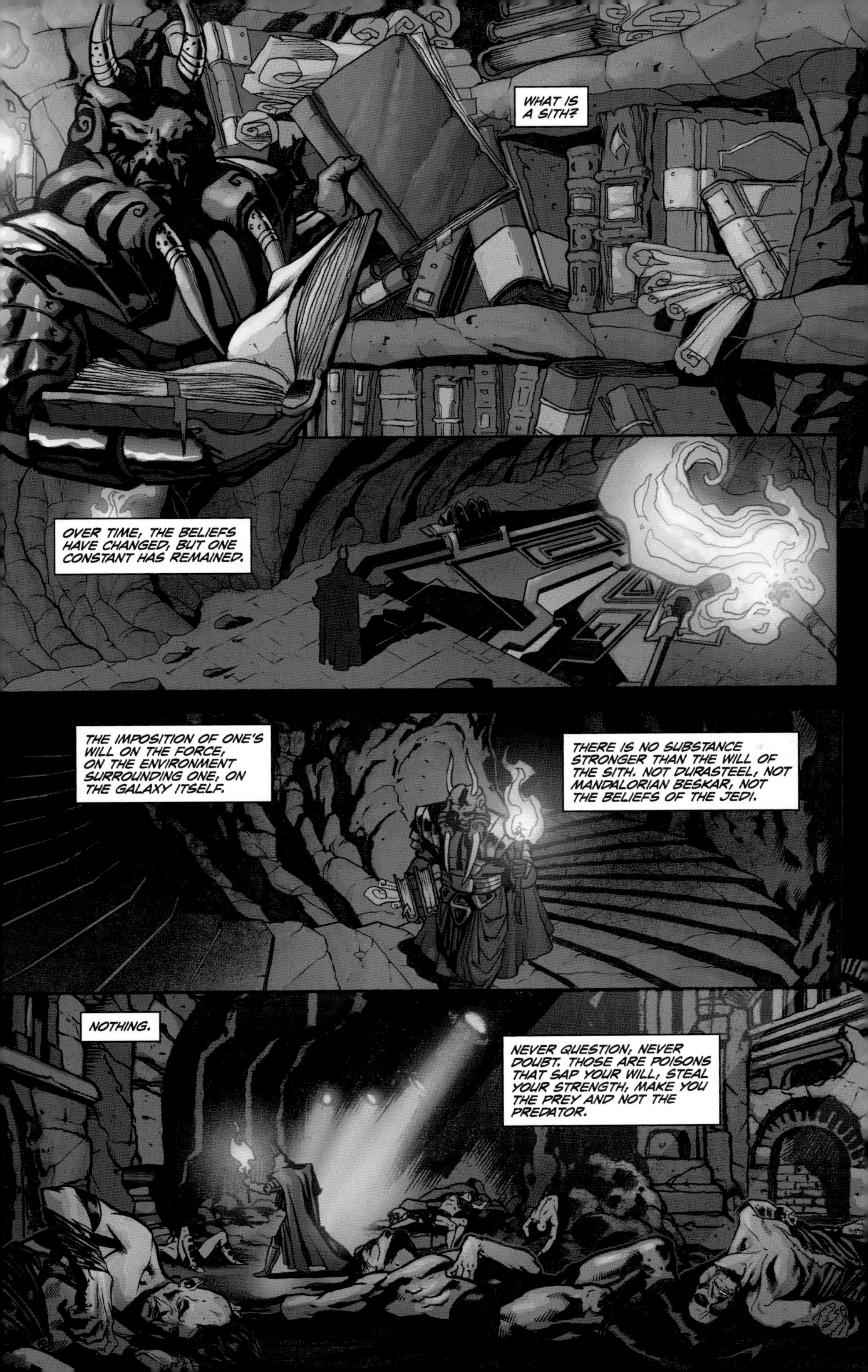
WHAT IS A SITH?
OVER TIME, THE BELIEFS HAVE CHANGED, BUT ONE CONSTANT HAS REMAINED.
THE IMPOSITION OF ONE'S WILL ON THE FORCE, ON THE ENVIRONMENT SURROUNDING ONE, ON THE GALAXY ITSELF.
THERE IS NO SUBSTANCE STRONGER THAN THE WILL OF THE SITH. NOT DURASTEEL, NOT MANDALORIAN BESKAR, NOT THE BELIEFS OF THE JEDI.
NOTHING.
NEVER QUESTION, NEVER DOUBT. THOSE ARE POISONS THAT SAP YOUR WILL, STEAL YOUR STRENGTH, MAKE YOU THE PREY AND NOT THE PREDATOR.

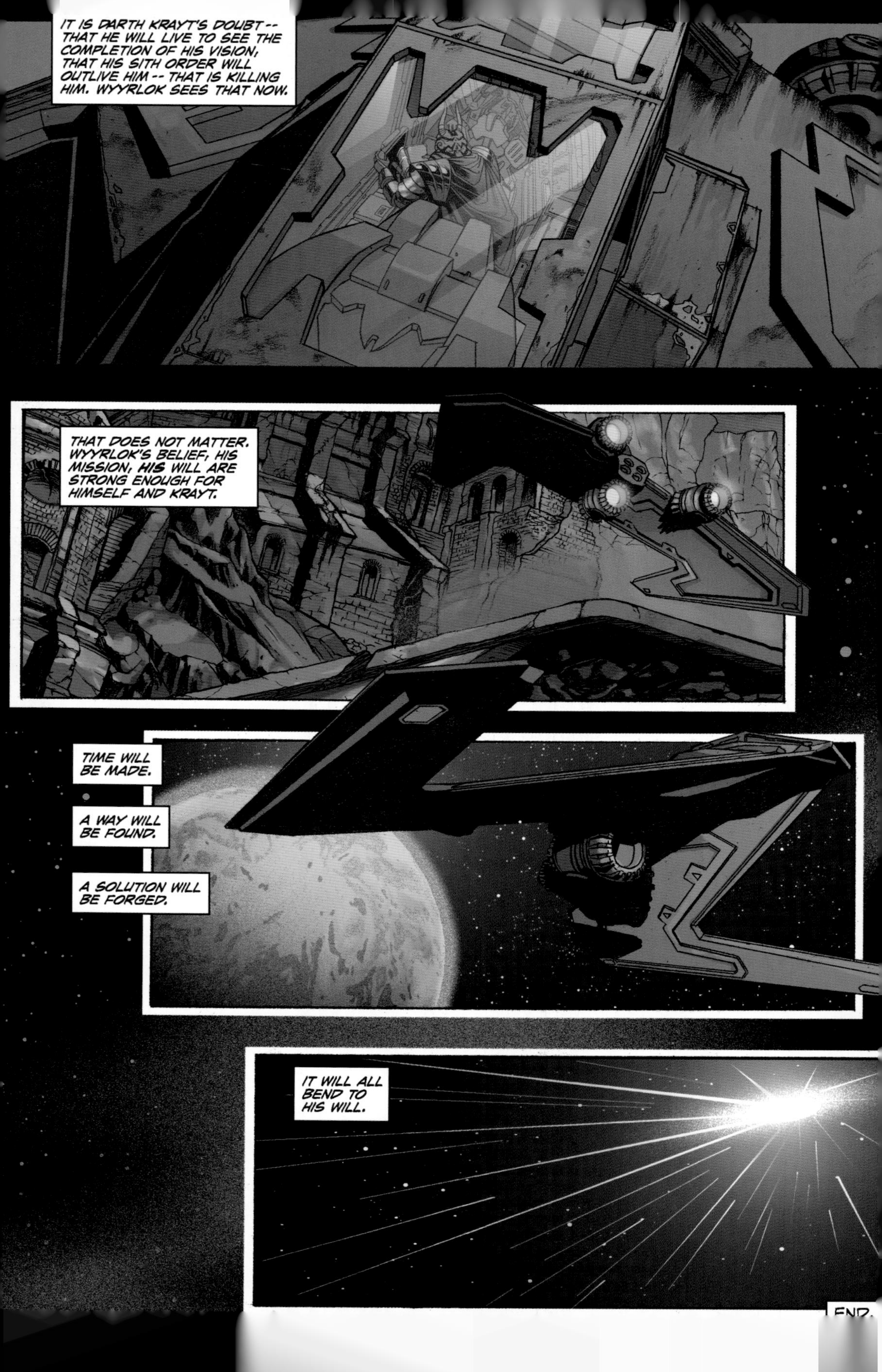
IT IS DARTH KRAYT'S DOUBT -- THAT HE WILL LIVE TO SEE THE COMPLETION OF HIS VISION, THAT HIS SITH ORDER WILL OUTLIVE HIM -- THAT IS KILLING HIM. WYYRLOK SEES THAT NOW.
THAT DOES NOT MATTER. WYYRLOK'S BELIEF, HIS MISSION, HIS WILL ARE STRONG ENOUGH FOR HIMSELF AND KRAYT.
TIME WILL BE MADE.
A WAY WILL BE FOUND.
A SOLUTION WILL BE FORGED.
IT WILL ALL BEND TO HIS WILL.
END.

STAR WARS®

TIMELINE OF GRAPHIC NOVELS FROM DARK HORSE!

OLD REPUBLIC ERA:
25,000—1000 YEARS BEFORE
STAR WARS: A NEW HOPE

Omnibus—Tales of the Jedi Volume 1
ISBN: 1-59307-830-0 $24.95

Omnibus—Tales of the Jedi Volume 2
ISBN: 1-59307-911-6 $24.95

Knights of the Old Republic
Volume 1—Commencement
ISBN: 1-59307-640-1 $18.95

Knights of the Old Republic
Volume 2—Flashpoint
ISBN: 1-59307-761-0 $18.95

Knights of the Old Republic
Volume 3—Days of Fear, Nights of Anger
ISBN: 1-59307-867-6 $18.95

Jedi vs. Sith
ISBN: 1-56971-649-8 $17.95

RISE OF THE EMPIRE ERA:
1000-0 YEARS BEFORE
STAR WARS: A NEW HOPE

The Stark Hyperspace War
ISBN: 1-56971-985-3 $12.95

Jedi Council—Acts of War
ISBN: 1-56971-539-4 $12.95

Prelude to Rebellion
ISBN: 1-56971-448-7 $14.95

Darth Maul
ISBN: 1-56971-542-4 $12.95

Episode I—The Phantom Menace
ISBN: 1-56971-359-6 $12.95

Episode I—
The Phantom Menace Adventures
ISBN: 1-56971-443-6 $12.95

Jango Fett
ISBN: 1-56971-623-4 $5.95

Zam Wesell
ISBN: 1-56971-624-2 $5.95

Jango Fett—Open Seasons
ISBN: 1-56971-671-4 $12.95

Outlander
ISBN: 1-56971-514-9 $14.95

Emissaries to Malastare
ISBN: 1-56971-545-9 $15.95

The Bounty Hunters
ISBN: 1-56971-467-3 $12.95

Twilight
ISBN: 1-56971-558-0 $12.95

The Hunt for Aurra Sing
ISBN: 1-56971-651-X $12.95

Darkness
ISBN: 1-56971-659-5 $12.95

Rite of Passage
ISBN: 1-59307-042-X $12.95

Honor and Duty
ISBN: 1-59307-546-4 $12.95

Episode II—Attack of the Clones
ISBN: 1-56971-609-9 $17.95

Clone Wars Volume 1—
The Defense of Kamino
ISBN: 1-56971-962-4 $14.95

Clone Wars Volume 2—
Victories and Sacrifices
ISBN: 1-56971-969-1 $14.95

Clone Wars Volume 3—
Last Stand on Jabiim
ISBN: 1-59307-006-3 $14.95

Clone Wars Volume 4—
Light and Dark
ISBN: 1-59307-195-7 $16.95

Clone Wars Volume 5—The Best Blades
ISBN: 1-59307-273-2 $17.95

Clone Wars Volume 6—
On the Fields of Battle
ISBN: 1-59307-352-6 $17.95

Clone Wars Volume 7—
When They Were Brothers
ISBN: 1-59307-396-8 $17.95

Clone Wars Volume 8—
The Last Siege, the Final Truth
ISBN: 1-59307-482-4 $17.95

Clone Wars Volume 9—Endgame
ISBN: 1-59307-553-7 $17.95

Clone Wars Adventures Volume 1
ISBN: 1-59307-243-0 $6.95

Clone Wars Adventures Volume 2
ISBN: 1-59307-271-6 $6.95

Clone Wars Adventures Volume 3
ISBN: 1-59307-307-0 $6.95

Clone Wars Adventures Volume 4
ISBN: 1-59307-402-6 $6.95

Clone Wars Adventures Volume 5
ISBN: 1-59307-483-2 $6.95

Clone Wars Adventures Volume 6
ISBN: 1-59307-567-7 $6.95

Clone Wars Adventures Volume 7
ISBN: 1-59307-678-9 $6.95

Clone Wars Adventures Volume 8
ISBN: 1-59307-680-1 $6.95

Clone Wars Adventures Volume 9
ISBN: 1-59307-832-4 $6.95

Clone Wars Adventures Volume 10
ISBN: 1-59307-878-2 $6.95

Episode III—Revenge of the Sith
ISBN: 1-59307-309-7 $12.95

General Grievous
ISBN: 1-59307-442-5 $12.95

Dark Times Volume 1—The Path to
Nowhere
ISBN: 1-59307-792-0 $17.95

Droids—The Kalarba Adventures
ISBN: 1-56971-064-3 $17.95

Droids—Rebellion
ISBN: 1-56971-224-7 $14.95

Classic Star Wars—
Han Solo at Stars' End
ISBN: 1-56971-254-9 $6.95

Boba Fett—Enemy of the Empire
ISBN: 1-56971-407-X $12.95

Underworld—The Yavin Vassilika
ISBN: 1-56971-618-8 $15.95

Dark Forces—Soldier for the Empire
ISBN: 1-56971-348-0 $14.95

Empire Volume 1—Betrayal
ISBN: 1-56971-964-0 $12.95

Empire Volume 2—Darklighter
ISBN: 1-56971-975-6 $17.95

REBELLION ERA:
0-5 YEARS AFTER
STAR WARS: A NEW HOPE

A New Hope—The Special Edition
ISBN: 1-56971-213-1 $9.95

Boba Fett: Man with a Mission
ISBN: 1-59307-707-6 $12.95

Empire Volume 3—
The Imperial Perspective
ISBN: 1-59307-128-0 $17.95

Empire Volume 4—
The Heart of the Rebellion
ISBN: 1-59307-308-9 $17.95

Empire Volume 5—Allies and Adversaries
ISBN: 1-59307-466-2 $14.95

Empire Volume 6—
In the Shadows of Their Fathers
ISBN: 1-59307-627-4 $17.95

Empire Volume 7—
The Wrong side of the War
ISBN: 1-59307-709-2 $17.95

Rebellion Volume 1—
My Brother, My Enemy
ISBN: 1-59307-711-4 $14.95

Rebellion Volume 2—
The Ahakista Gambit
ISBN: 1-59307-890-4 $17.95

A Long Time Ago . . . Volume 1—
Doomworld
ISBN: 1-56971-754-0 $29.95

A Long Time Ago . . . Volume 2—
Dark Encounters
ISBN: 1-56971-785-0 $29.95

Classic Star Wars—
The Early Adventures
ISBN: 1-56971-178-X $19.95

Classic Star Wars Volume 1—
In Deadly Pursuit
ISBN: 1-56971-109-7 $16.95

Classic Star Wars Volume 2—
The Rebel Storm
ISBN: 1-56971-106-2 $16.95

Classic Star Wars Volume 3—
Escape to Hoth
ISBN: 1-56971-093-7 $16.95

Jabba the Hutt—The Art of the Deal
ISBN: 1-56971-310-3 $9.95

Vader's Quest
ISBN: 1-56971-415-0 $11.95

Splinter of the Mind's Eye
ISBN: 1-56971-223-9 $14.95

The Empire Strikes Back—
The Special Edition
ISBN: 1-56971-234-4 $9.95

A Long Time Ago . . . Volume 3—
Resurrection of Evil
ISBN: 1-56971-786-9 $29.95

A Long Time Ago . . . Volume 4—
Screams in the Void
ISBN: 1-56971-787-7 $29.95

A Long Time Ago . . . Volume 5—
Fool's Bounty
ISBN: 1-56971-906-3 $29.95

Battle of the Bounty Hunters
Pop-Up Book
ISBN: 1-56971-129-1 $17.95

Shadows of the Empire
ISBN: 1-56971-183-6 $17.95

Return of the Jedi—The Special Edition
ISBN: 1-56971-235-2 $9.95

A Long Time Ago . . . Volume 6—
Wookiee World
ISBN: 1-56971-907-1 $29.95

A Long Time Ago . . . Volume 7—
Far, Far Away
ISBN: 1-56971-908-X $29.95

Mara Jade—By the Emperor's Hand
ISBN: 1-56971-401-0 $15.95

Shadows of the Empire: Evolution
ISBN: 1-56971-441-X $14.95

NEW REPUBLIC ERA:
5-25 YEARS AFTER
STAR WARS: A NEW HOPE

Omnibus—X-Wing Rogue Squadron
Volume 1
ISBN: 1-59307-572-3 $24.95

Omnibus—X-Wing Rogue Squadron
Volume 2
ISBN: 1-59307-619-3 $24.95

Omnibus—X-Wing Rogue Squadron
Volume 3
ISBN: 1-59307-776-9 $24.95

Dark Forces—Rebel Agent
ISBN: 1-56971-400-2 $14.95

Dark Forces—Jedi Knight
ISBN: 1-56971-433-9 $14.95

Heir to the Empire
ISBN: 1-56971-202-6 $19.95

Dark Force Rising
ISBN: 1-56971-269-7 $17.95

The Last Command
ISBN: 1-56971-378-2 $17.95

Boba Fett—
Death, Lies, and Treachery
ISBN: 1-56971-311-1 $12.95

Dark Empire
ISBN: 1-59307-039-X $16.95

Dark Empire II 2nd ed.
(includes *Empire's End*)
ISBN: 1-59307-526-X $19.95

Crimson Empire
ISBN: 1-56971-355-3 $17.95

Crimson Empire II: Council of Blood
ISBN: 1-56971-410-X $17.95

Jedi Academy: Leviathan
ISBN: 1-56971-456-8 $11.95

Union
ISBN: 1-56971-464-9 $12.95

NEW JEDI ORDER ERA:
25+ YEARS AFTER
STAR WARS: A NEW HOPE

Chewbacca
ISBN: 1-56971-515-7 $12.95

LEGACY ERA:
40+ YEARS AFTER
STAR WARS: A NEW HOPE

Legacy Volume 1—Broken
ISBN: 1-59307-716-5 $17.95

Legacy Volume 2—Shards
ISBN: 1-59307-879-9 $19.95

INFINITIES:
DOES NOT APPLY TO TIMELINE

Infinites: A New Hope
ISBN: 1-56971-648-X $12.95

Infinities: The Empire Strikes Back
ISBN: 1-56971-904-7 $12.95

Infinities: Return of the Jedi
ISBN: 1-59307-206-6 $12.95

Star Wars Tales Volume 1
ISBN: 1-56971-619-6 $19.95

Star Wars Tales Volume 2
ISBN: 1-56971-757-5 $19.95

Star Wars Tales Volume 3
ISBN: 1-56971-836-9 $19.95

Star Wars Tales Volume 4
ISBN: 1-56971-989-6 $19.95

Star Wars Tales Volume 5
ISBN: 1-59307-286-4 $19.95

Star Wars Tales Volume 6
ISBN: 1-59307-447-6 $19.95

Tag & Bink Were Here
ISBN: 1-59307-641-X $14.95

FOR MORE INFORMATION ABOUT THESE BOOKS VISIT DARKHORSE.COM!

AVAILABLE AT YOUR LOCAL COMICS SHOP OR BOOKSTORE
To find a comics shop in your area, call 1-888-266-4226. For more information or to order direct, visit darkhorse.com or call 1-800-862-0052 Mon.–Fri. 9 A.M. to 5 P.M. Pacific Time. *Prices and availability subject to change without notice.

STAR WARS ©2008 Lucasfilm Ltd. & ™. (BL8009)